PATERNOSTER BIBLICAL MONOGRAPHS

Historical Issues in the Book of Daniel

T0385269

Series Preface

One of the major objectives of Paternoster is to serve biblical scholarship by providing a channel for the publication of theses and other monographs of high quality at affordable prices. Paternoster stands within the broad evangelical tradition of Christianity. Our authors would describe themselves as Christians who recognise the authority of the Bible, maintain the centrality of the gospel message and assent to the classical creedal statements of the Christian belief. There is diversity within this constituency; advances in scholarship are possible only if there is freedom for frank debate on controversial issues and for the publication of new and sometimes provocative proposals. What is offered in this series is the best of writing by committed Christians who are concerned to develop well-founded biblical scholarship in a spirit of loyalty to the historic faith.

Series Editors

I. Howard Marshall, Honorary Research Professor of New Testament, University of Aberdeen, Scotland, UK

Richard J. Bauckham, Professor of New Testament Studies and Bishop Wardlaw Professor, University of St Andrews, Scotland, UK

Craig Blomberg, Distinguished Professor of New Testament, Denver Seminary, Colorado, USA

Robert P. Gordon, Regius Professor of Hebrew, University of Cambridge, UK

Tremper Longman III, Robert H. Gundry Professor and Chair of the Department of Biblical Studies, Westmont College, Santa Barbara, California, USA

Stanley E. Porter, President and Professor of New Testament, McMaster Divinity College, Hamilton, Ontario, Canada

PATERNOSTER BIBLICAL MONOGRAPHS

Historical Issues in the Book of Daniel

Thomas E. Gaston

First published 2016 by Paternoster

Paternoster is an imprint of Authentic Media Limited
PO Box 6326, Bletchley, Milton Keynes, MK1 9GG

authenticmedia.co.uk

22 21 20 19 18 17 16   8 7 6 5 4 3 2 1

British Library Cataloguing in Publication Data
A catalogue record for this book is available from the British Library

ISBN 978–1–84227–982-3
978-1-84227-400-7 (ebook)

Printed and bound in Great Britain
for Paternoster
by Lightning Source, Milton Keynes

Andrew Perry, for being older and wiser than me

Contents

Preface to the first edition

My thanks are particularly due to the following scholars for their academic assistance: Dr. William H. Shea, former professor of Old Testament at Andrews University, Berrien Springs; Dr. W. David Pennington, lecturer in Theology at Baptist College of Ministry, Wisconsin; Professor Amélie Kuhrt, Professor of Ancient Near East at University College London; Dr. Jonathan J. Taylor, assistant keeper of the cuneiform collections at the British Museum.

I should also like to thank Robert and Kath Wilkinson for their assistance with translation from French, and Richard Gaston for reading the first draft.

Preface to the second edition

Those familiar with the first edition of *Historical Issues in the Book of Daniel* will notice that the book has been expanded for the second edition. Chapters three, eleven, twelve, thirteen and fourteen have been added. Chapter ten has been expanded. I have also taken the opportunity to revise the text in places to improve the readability. Lastly, I am very pleased to include appendix four, a short satirical essay that just couldn't quite find a home anywhere in the staid world of academic journals.

What has not changed between the two editions is the tenor of the argument nor the general conclusion of the research: that the book of Daniel is based upon real historical events.

Thomas E. Gaston
Oxford, UK
2016

Abbreviations

Journals

AJSLL	The American Journal of Semitic Languages and Literatures
ARTA	Achaemenid Research on Texts and Archaeology (www.achemenet.com)
AUSS	Andrews University Seminary Studies
BA	Biblical Archeologist
BARev	Biblical Archaeology Review
CBQ	Catholic Biblical Quarterly
CJBI	Christadelphian E-Journal of Biblical Interpretation
DJD	Discoveries in the Judean Desert
EQ	Evangelical Quarterly
HUCA	Hebrew Union College Annual
IEJ	Israel Exploration Journal
JANESCU	Journal of the Ancient Near Eastern Society of Columbia University
JAOS	Journal of the American Oriental Society
JATS	Journal of the Adventist Theological Society
JBL	Journal of Biblical Literature
JCS	Journal of Cuneiform Studies
JETS	Journal of the Evangelical Theological Society
JSLBR	Journal of Sacred Literature and Biblical Record
JTS	Journal of Theological Studies
JTVI	Journal of the Transactions of the Victoria Institute
JNES	Journal of Near Eastern Studies
PAAJR	Proceedings of the American Academy for Jewish Research
PSBA	Proceedings of the Society of Biblical Archaeology
TRHS	Transactions of the Royal Historical Society
VT	Vetus Testamentum
WTJ	Westminster Theological Journal
ZAW	Zeitschrift für die alttestamentliche Wissenschaft

Bible Versions

ESV	English Standard Version
HCSB	Holman Christian Standard Bible
KJV	King James Version / Authorized Version
NASB	New American Standard Bible
NETS	A New English Translation of the Septuagint
NIV	New International Version
NKJV	New King James Version
NLT	New Living Translation
NRSV	New Revised Standard Version

NRSVCE	New Revised Standard Version - Catholic Edition
RSV	Revised Standard Version
YLT	Young's Literal Translation

Commentary Series

CE	The Christadelphian Expositor: A Verse-by-Verse Exposition of the Scriptures
OTG	Old Testament Guides (JSOT Press)
OTL	Old Testament Library
TOTC	Tyndale Old Testament Commentaries

Introduction

The book of Daniel is a collection of six narratives and four visions that are centered on an individual named 'Daniel', after whom the book is named. According to the book, Daniel was a member of the Jewish royal household who was taken captive by Nebuchadnezzar to Babylon around 605 BC. He remained in Babylon until the third year of Cyrus the Persian (c.537) and the book strongly implies that he died shortly after (Dan. 12:13). The book records significant incidents from Daniel's experiences in Babylon, excepting one incident that only mentions Daniel's friends: Hananiah, Mishael and Azariah (Dan. 3), and visions in which Daniel is shown in symbol future events regarding his people.

Traditionally the book of Daniel was regarded as an inspired (and thus genuine) account of a real individual and his real experiences (and his authentic prophecies). The narrative chapters had obvious spiritual application for the believer and the visionary chapters provided examples of the foreknowledge of God by successfully predicting future events. The only objections to this view of the book came from critics of Christianity, like Porphyry (3rd century AD), who argued that the book must have been written in the second century BC in an attempt to rebut Christian claims that this was genuine prophecy.

As time moved on, scholars began to analyze the book of Daniel with reference to the historical sources available to them and so doubts emerged about the historicity of the incidents recorded in the book. These scholars could find no record of the kings Belshazzar or Darius the Mede, no substantial reference to the prolonged illness of Nebuchadnezzar, and little or no evidence of a Babylonian campaign against Jerusalem around 605 BC. These conclusions, amongst others, led to the re-emergence of Porphyry's theory of the late-date for the book.

The late-date theory is now accepted by the majority of scholars, though the traditional position is still defended by conservative scholars. These defenders of Daniel argue that the reason that critical scholars posit a late-date for the book is that they, like Porphyry, refuse to accept the possibility of predictive prophecy. If the evidence for a sixth-century date of composition is so certain, why do scholars reject it in favor of an unsupportable Maccabean hypothesis?

The reason is that most scholars embrace a liberal, naturalistic, and rationalistic philosophy.[1]

Appealing as this explanation is to conservatives, it does not do justice to the position taken by many critical commentators. For instance, J.J. Collins disowns the idea that the late-date theory rests on the denial of predictive prophecy, asserting that it is an issue of 'probability':

> There is no apparent reason, however, why a prophet of the sixth century should focus minute attention on the events of the second century. Moreover, the references to Hellenistic history in chapter 11 are essentially accurate, whereas those to the Babylonian and Persian periods in the earlier chapters are notoriously confused.[2]

For Collins, and scholars like him, regardless of whether predictive prophecy is possible, the book of Daniel should be considered late (and fictional) because of the unhistorical details contained therein. This challenge is not new and many conservative scholars – theologians, historians and archaeologists – have attempted to defend the historicity of the book. To his credit, Collins does refer to a number of these studies. Sadly, many critical scholars do not take such an inclusive (dare I say, 'objective') attitude.

Intriguingly, Goldingay has argued that the entire debate regarding the historicity of the Danielic narratives is a red herring as these narratives were intended to be read as fiction:

> To imply that they [ie. The narratives] are at fault if they contain unhistorical features is to judge them on alien criteria; to defend them by seeking to establish that at such points they are factual after all is to collude with such a false starting point.[3]

He reasons that the Danielic narratives are not written as historiography, but contain the features of fictional literary genres such as myth and romance. For Goldingay this proposition is entirely consistent with the inspiration of the book. He draws the comparison with the book of Job and argues that fiction is just another way God uses to teach us about himself:

> One aspect of the genius of narrative in particular is to raise questions and to look at them from several angles, to do justice to their complexity and thereby to give us genuine help in understanding God and in understanding what it means to be

---

[1] B.K. Waltke, 'The Date of the Book of Daniel', *Bibliotheca Sacra* (Oct-Dec 1976), 329. Also, see G.L. Archer Jr, 'Modern Rationalism and the Book of Daniel', *Bibliotheca Sacra* (April-June 1979), 129-47.

[2] J.J. Collins, *Daniel: A Commentary on the Book of Daniel*, with an essay, 'The Influence of Daniel on the New Testament' by Adela Yarbro Collins (Minneapolis: Fortress, 1993), 26.

[3] J.E. Goldingay, *Daniel* (WBC 30; Dallas: Word, 1989), 321.

us. It is especially fictional narrative which does that. I presume this is why God inspired so much fiction within the Bible, not least in Daniel.[4]

The analogy to the book of Job is significant since many conservative scholars readily accept that this book is poetic and not an account of actual events, or else is a dramatic retelling of a story with a historical core. If it was demonstrated that the book of Daniel was similarly written in a fictional genre then the question of historicity could be bypassed and the book of Daniel retained as an inspired work of fiction for the edification of believers. This is a question that needs to be addressed *a priori* and without reference to the disputed historical details.

There are some features of the book of Daniel that might suggest that it is meant to be taken as fiction. Firstly, the book is episodic in nature, rather than being a continuous account. In this sense it feels different from historiographical works like biography or chronicle. Secondly, the episodes in the book have a clear polemic or moral lesson. Take, for example, the narrative in chapter 3. The story opens with a moral dilemma (whether to bow to the golden image), the main characters exhibit their faithfulness to God (they do not bow to the image), and the story resolves with a positive outcome for the faithful (they are saved from the fiery furnace). These stories are clearly not just intended to relay historical information but also to promote and encourage certain behaviours. There is a reason that the book of Daniel is more easily adapted into memorable Sunday School lessons than, say, the book of Chronicles. In this sense the book has a flavor of moral stories, like fable or parable.

Nevertheless there are elements of the book of Daniel that seem more at home in historiography. To begin an account with a dateline – e.g. 'in the third year of the reign of Jehoiakim' (Dan. 1:1, cf. 2:1, 7:1, 8:1, 9:1, 10:1) – would generally indicate that the author is intending to write history, rather than legend. Fables are often purposefully vague as to dates and other details, whereas chroniclers are usually very specific. By positioning his narrative by regnal year of the relevant monarch, the author is trying to position the events he records within historical context and thus seems to be writing history. In addition, the visions within the book are clearly intended to correlate with historical events. Whether or not these visions are truly prophetic, the author intends them to be read as history captured in vision. Either he thinks these are genuine prophecies, or he is trying to pass them off as genuine prophecies, but in either case he does not intend his readers to take these as fictions. After all, what is the purpose of retelling a vision that both author and reader knows to be fiction?

One final problem for the proposal that the book of Daniel is written as fiction is the fact that we have no record that any ancient ever understood the book

---

[4] J.E. Goldingay, 'Daniel in the Context of Old Testament Theology' in *The Book of Daniel: Composition and Reception*, vol.1 (J.J. Collins & P.W. Flint, eds.; Leiden: Brill, 2001), 641.

in this way or regarded Daniel as anything other than a real historical figure until the time of Porphyry. Every ancient writer who commented regarded Daniel as a prophet. This includes the writers of the Dead Sea Scrolls (4Q174 4:3), the writers of the gospels (or Jesus himself; Matt. 24:30, 26:64; Mark 13:26, 14:62; Luke 21:27), early Christian writers (Heb. 11:33; 1 Clement 45:2) and the Jewish historian Josephus (Antiquities 10.10.1-10.11.7). In contrast, we do not have examples of Jewish or Christian writers citing the book of Daniel as though it were a work of fiction. If the book of Daniel was written in a genre recognizable to the ancients as fiction then why was it not recognized as such by ancient Jews or Christians?

The author seems to require us to take his work as a historical account and this seems to be how Jews and Christians from the first century onwards read the book. For the serious student of the book of Daniel the course must be to assess the book primarily as a historical account.

Chapter 1

Daniel in Ezekiel

The events described in the book of Daniel are dated by its author to between 605 and 537 BC, a period of nearly seventy years. If the dates given in the book are accurate then Daniel throughout his long life would have been contemporary with such figures as Jeremiah, in his youth, and Zerubbabel, in his old age. Since Daniel was only a youth when he was taken to Babylon we could hardly expect any reference to him in the books of Jeremiah or Kings. On the other hand, as there is no reference to Daniel returning to Jerusalem, there seems no reason why he should be mentioned in the books of Ezra, Haggai or Zechariah. However, it is recorded that Ezekiel was amongst the captives in the land of Babylon (Ezek. 1:3) and the events recorded in the book of Ezekiel are dated between 593 and 585 BC. Ezekiel, then, is conveniently contemporary with Daniel, both in terms of date and location, so any reference to Daniel in the book of Ezekiel would be both plausible and significant. Ezekiel, in fact, provides us with three.

The first two of these references are in Ezekiel 14, which dates from around 592 BC. (Chapter 8 is dated to September 592 while chapter 20 is dated to August 591, so assuming that the book is written in strict chronological order then it is reasonable to date chapter 14 to some time in the intervening months). This would be around thirteen years after Daniel's original captivity and after Daniel had proved himself by interpreting Nebuchadnezzar's dream. In a prophecy against Jerusalem, which would later be captured (again) and finally destroyed by the Babylonian army (c.585), Ezekiel proclaims that not even the presence of three iconic figures of righteousness would save such a faithless city. He says: 'even if these three men, Noah, Daniel and Job, were in it, they would deliver but their own lives' (Ezek. 14:14, cf. 14:20).

The third reference is found in a long condemnation of Tyre dated to February 585 (Ezek. 26:1). Part of this tirade focuses on the arrogance of the prince of Tyre, who, Ezekiel claims, has claimed divine status, because of his great wealth and his own wisdom. Ezekiel recognizes the prince's great wisdom, ascribing to him the great accolade: 'you are wiser than Daniel; no secret is hidden from you' (Ezek. 28:3). Davies comments that Daniel-E must have been 'known also to the king of Tyre . . . else the jibe loses its effect'.[1] It is, of course, unlikely that the king of Tyre would have known about Daniel-D. However this objection may not be as powerful as it appears since just because Ezekiel's tirade is directed *against* the king of Tyre is no reason to suppose that it was ever addressed *to* the king of Tyre. Ezekiel prophesying amongst the exiles in Babylonia is hardly likely to have traveled to Tyre to deliver his condemnation and probably would have been executed if he had.

From these references it is clear that Ezekiel's Daniel (from now on 'Daniel-E') was both wise and righteous, and was known for these characteristics. This description matches well with the hero of the book of Daniel ('Daniel-D'), who demonstrates both a faithful adherence to his religion in the face of adversity and God-given wisdom to interpret dreams. The Old Testament provides little alternative to this conclusion. Other individuals named Daniel – the second son of David (1 Chr. 3:1; he is named 'Chileab' in 2 Sam. 3:3) and one of the Jews returning from exile (Ezra 8:2, Neh. 10:6) – are too obscure to be linked to Daniel-E. Were it not for the dispute regarding the date of the book of Daniel, I think there could be little hesitation in concluding that Daniel-E = Daniel-D.

Objections

It was previously objected that Ezekiel uses a slightly different spelling for 'Daniel'. The author of Ezekiel uses the spelling דניאל (*Dânîyê'l*) while in the Hebrew sections of the book of Daniel the spelling דנאל (*Dânîê'l*) is used. This might suggest that the author of Ezekiel had a different person in mind. What is interesting is that in the Aramaic sections of Daniel the spelling is exactly the same as that found in Ezekiel, which shows that the spelling of Daniel-D is entirely consistent with that of Daniel-E. In any case, if Ezekiel's acquaintance with Daniel-D's reputation was oral, rather than literary, then any variance in spelling would be insignificant since either spelling is a legitimate vocalization of the name.

More recently there have been three forms of attack against this identification: 1) proof by assertion; 2) imposition of categories; 3) reversal of dependence.

1) **Proof by assertion**. Porteous is an example of the first form, dismissing any connection between Daniel-D and Daniel-E: 'it is *obvious* that this Daniel referred to by Ezekiel cannot be an exilic figure',[2] though he himself cannot find any credible alternative. Day also asserts that Ezekiel 'could *hardly* refer to the young Jewish exile', though he makes no effort to explain why this should be

---

[1] P.R. Davies' *Daniel* (OTG; Sheffield: JSOT, 1985), 40.

[2] N.W. Porteous, *Daniel: A Commentary* (OTL; London: SCM, 1965), 17, my emphasis.

incredible.[3] An impartial observer would judge that proof by assertion is no proof at all and so unlikely to be moved by such rhetoric; he will want to hold out for evidence.

2) **Imposition of categories**. Many scholars, following Montgomery, have argued that Daniel-D would make 'an improbable companion' for Noah and Job.[4] For example, Day reasons that since Daniel-E is conjoined with Noah and Job, he must likewise be 'a figure of hoary antiquity' and a non-Israelite.[5] There is, however, no evidence that Ezekiel would have thought in these categories.

Job is never portrayed as of like antiquity to Noah. In fact many commentators supposed Job to be post-patriarchal. Job's three friends include a Temanite and a Shuhite; Teman was the grandson of Esau (Gen. 36:9-11) and Shuah was the son of Abraham by Keturah (Gen. 25:8). Archer reasons that Ezekiel does not present figures of 'hoary antiquity' but 'paragons of piety' from three different eras of history: Noah from antiquity, Job from the time of patriarchs and Daniel-D from his own age.[6]

Job is assumed to be a non-Israelite, though it is not clear Ezekiel regarded him as such. Job's nationality is not mentioned but some have identified him with the son of Issachar (Gen. 46:13). The book of Genesis does refer to a post-deluvian figure named Jobab, five generations after Noah (Gen. 10:29). Another possibility would be to identify him with Jobab the son of Zerah, one of the kings of Edom (Gen. 36:33-34). It is perhaps significant that this Jobab is succeeded by a 'Husham' of 'the land of Temani'. In any case, to describe Noah as a 'non-Israelite' is a form of category confusion since Noah predates Israel. Dressler says: 'one needs no particularly fertile imagination to view an Israelite Daniel flanked by a pre-Israelite and a non-Israelite to arrive at an equally satisfying theological construction'.[7]

Margalit has responded that it is 'paradigms of non-Israelite righteousness' must be intended, else why not use Abraham and Moses?[8] Yet by the same token, why not use Enoch or Melchizedek? Such arguments show this entire line of reasoning to be fatuous without some conception of how Ezekiel categorized his paradigms; 'it must be noted that the Book of Ezekiel does not attach much

---

[3] J. Day, 'Foreign Semitic Influence on the Wisdom of Israel and its appropriation in the Book of Proverbs' in *Wisdom in Ancient Israel: Essays in Honour of J.A Emerton* (ed. J. Day, R.P. Gordon & H.G.M. Williamson; Cambridge University Press, 1995), 57, my emphasis.
[4] Davies, *Daniel*, 40.
[5] J. Day, 'The Daniel of Ugarit and Ezekiel and the Hero of the Book of Daniel', *VT* 30.2 (1980), 175; cf. Davies, *Daniel*, 40; Day, 'Foreign Semitic Influence', 57.
[6] Archer, 'Modern Rationalism', 133.
[7] H.H.P. Dressler, 'The Identification of the Ugaritic Dnil with the Daniel of Ezekiel', *VT* 29:2 (April 1979), 157.
[8] B. Margalit, 'Interpreting the Story of Aqht: A Reply to H.H.P. Dressler', *VT* 29 (1979), 152-161', *VT* 30 (1980), 363.

importance to exact patterns for enumeration'. [9] The *a priori* imposition of categories upon the text introduces circularity to the argument.[10] Ezekiel does not state that these figures are either non-Israelite or from antiquity; he presents them as paradigms of *righteousness*.

3) **Reversal of dependence**. The third critical attack is by far the most reasonable. It is argued that Ezekiel is not referring to Daniel-D, rather the book of Daniel bases its hero upon Daniel-E.[11] This hypothesis would explain the concurrence of names without requiring critical scholars to accept Daniel-D as a historical figure. Yet the thesis depends on the idea that Ezekiel knew some other Daniel, who was forgotten by the time that the book of Daniel was written. As we shall see, none of the attempts to identify this other Daniel have been particularly convincing.

Other Daniels

Porteous proposes Daniel-E be identified with a Dan'el named in the Book of Jubilees, who is said to be the uncle and father-in-law of Enoch and thereby a forebear of Noah.[12] The text, dating from around second century BC, gives no more detail and Dan'el is only mentioned once in a single verse:

> And in the twelfth jubilee, in the seventh week thereof, he took to himself a wife, and her name was Ednî, the daughter of Dânêl, the daughter of his father's brother, and in the sixth year in this week she bare him a son and he called his name Methuselah (Jubilees 4:20).

There is no mention of him being particularly righteous or particularly wise.

One other Dan'el sometimes put forward as Daniel-E is an angel named in the book of Enoch.[13] Expanding the account of Genesis 6:1-6, the book of Enoch (c.3rd century BC) describes how two hundred angels decide to take for themselves wives from among the sons of men. One of the leaders of these two hundred is named 'Dan'el'.[14] Again, no further detail is given and this angel is not described as being wise or being righteous (given the context, it would seem that this angel was decidedly unrighteous).

Both of these Dan'els are insignificant literary characters, meriting only fleeting reference in their respective texts. This fact, coupled with their late

---

[9] Dressler, 'Identification', 156.
[10] cf. H.H.P. Dressler, 'Reading and Interpreting the Aqhat Text: A Rejoinder to Drs J. Day and B. Margalit', *VT* 34.1 (1984), 79.
[11] Collins, *Daniel*, 1-2. Cf. J.J. Collins, 'Daniel' in *Dictionary of Deities and Demons in the Bible* (ed. K. van der Toorn, B. Becking & P.W. van Horst; Eerdmans, 1999), 220.
[12] Porteous, *Daniel*, 17-18.
[13] Davies, *Daniel*, 41.
[14] 1 Enoch 6:7.

origin, disqualify them from identification with Daniel-E who is, of necessity, a celebrated figure. It has to be said that one cannot help feeling that these feeble candidates were only ever proposed in an effort to avoid the conclusion that Daniel-E = Daniel-D.

Ugaritic Dan'el

Until a discovery of Ugaritic texts made at Ras Shamra, those scholars who refused to identify Daniel-E with Daniel-D had lacked plausible alternatives. An Ugaritic poem, called *Aqhat*, was discovered there which told of a Dan'el. It is previously thought that Dan'el is described as a king. Dressler has argued that the portrayal of Dan'el in the poem is more reminiscent of a village elder than an urban king. He proposes that the single reference to Dan'el as king (*mlk*) is actually a mistranslation.[15] One particular line, saying, '[he] judges the cause of the widow, tries the case of the orphan',[16] is cited as evidence that Dan'el was wise and righteous. The consensus amongst modern scholarship is that Daniel-E = Dan'el. Dressler, who edited one edition of the Ugaritic text, has dissented from this consensus.

The character of Dan'el coheres poorly with the key features of Daniel-E: wisdom and righteousness. Dressler asserts that Dan'el is never called 'wise' (*hkm*) nor is he described as being so, never 'uttering proverbial sayings, riddles, or expressing cleverness'.[17] Most scholars admit this.[18] Day suggests that the judgment of Dan'el might have been considered wisdom (cf. 1 Kings 3) or that Dan'el's 'incantations which result in the killing and remaking of the eagles' might have been considered 'magical-mantic wisdom' (*CTA* 19.iii.107ff).[19] However, neither case is an example of the revealing of secrets that Ezekiel refers to (Ezek. 28:3), while Day admits that this is a 'prominent' feature of Daniel-D.

Likewise Dan'el is never called 'righteous' (*sdq*).[20] Dressler argues that the description of Dan'el judging the cases of widows and orphans may not refer to him singularly, but to his position as one of the village elders.[21] In any case, the favourable judgment of widows and orphans hardly qualifies as *legendary* righteousness, particularly when contrasted with Dan'el's other actions. For

---

[15] Dressler, 'Identification', 153; Margalit agrees.

[16] *CTA* 17.v.7-8.

[17] Dressler, 'Identification', 153.

[18] '[N]ot explicitly referred to as a wise man' (Day, 'Daniel of Ugarit', 180); 'not his most outstanding characteristic' (Margalit, 'Interpreting', 362); 'he is not portrayed as exceptionally wise' (Collins, *Daniel*, 2); 'not explicitly described as wise' (Day, 'Foreign Semitic Influence', 58).

[19] Day, 'Daniel of Ugarit', 180-81.

[20] Dressler, 'Identification', 154.

[21] Dressler, 'Identification', 154; 'the text allows three possibilities: Dnil judges – Dnil only participates in the judging – Dnil is only an observer and does not judge' (Dressler, 'Rejoinder', 82).

instance, after the murder of his son by the vulture, Samal, Dan'el calls a curse from Baal[22] upon all vultures and proceeds to slit open their stomachs till he finds his son's remains. He then puts a curse upon Abelim, the vulture-city, and, after seven years weeping, prompts his daughter, Paghat, to assassinate Yatpan, who conspired in his son's death. Archer concludes, 'nothing could be more unlikely than that a strict and zealous monotheist like Ezekiel would have regarded with appreciation a Baal-worshipper, a polytheistic pagan given to violent rage and unremitting vengefulness, a drunken carouser who need assistance to find his way home to his own bed'. [23] Margalit defends the righteousness of Dan'el, arguing that he contrasts favourably with *Krt*, another Ugaritic figure.[24] He also asserts that Dan'el's piety is demonstrated by his devotion to Baal and El, and that even the drunken incident might have 'a religious complexion'.[25] Yet whatever mitigation is proposed, the fact remains that Dan'el was not worshiper of YHWH – this fact alone precludes any identification with Daniel-E.

In fairness to the critical position, no scholar is proposing that Ezekiel was directly acquainted with the *Aqhat* poem. For instance Day, acknowledging that Dan'el is not a paradigm of Jewish righteousness, proposes that the Dan'el known in 'the Israelite Yahwist tradition' may have developed considerably from his origins in Ugaritic legend, given that eight hundred years separate Ezekiel and the *Aqhat* poem.[26] Grabbe goes one step further, arguing, on the one hand, that the distinction between Canaanite and Israelite culture was purely polemical, not historical, and on the other, that Ugaritic is not Canaanite. Thus, he argues, it is conceivable that a Canaanite figure should differ considerably from the Ugaritic figure on which it was based.[27] Grabbe proposes that the Dan'el of Jubilees 4:20 might represent a transitional stage in the development of the character of Dan'el between the *Aqhat* poem and the reference in Ezekiel.[28] However, the adoption of Dan'el into Israelite discourse remains purely hypothetical and the burden of proof remains on those who would defend this hypothesis; the Dan'el of Jubilees is too late to be considered evidence in the case. Needless to say the 'sanitized' version of Dan'el does not appear in any extant Israelite literature or inscription.

---

22 Day objects that Baal is not referred to in the poem (Day, 'Daniel of Ugarit', 177), though here majority of scholarship is against him (see Dressler, 'Rejoinder', 79-80, for citations).

23 Archer, 'Modern Rationalism', 134.

24 Margalit, 'Interpreting', 362.

25 Margalit, 'Interpreting', 363.

26 Day, 'Daniel of Ugarit', 178.

27 L.L. Grabbe, '"Canaanite": Some Methodological Observations in Relation to Biblical Study' in *Ugarit and the Bible: Proceedings of the International Symposium on Ugarit and the Bible – Manchester, September 1992* (ed. G.J. Brooke, A.H.W. Curtis & J.F. Henley; Münster: Ugarit-Verlag, 1994).

28 Grabbe, 'Canaanite', 120.

Collins, conceding many of the difficulties, still argues that Daniel-E = Dan'el, stating, 'it seems gratuitous to suppose that there were two unrelated legendary figures by the name of Daniel'.[29] Yet such an argument demonstrates sloppy logic – on this basis one would have to conclude that every character named 'Arthur' in every text up to the present day should be identified with King Arthur, regardless of his characteristics. The name 'Daniel' is far too common for Collins' argument to have any weight.[30] There is nothing unusual about the name 'Daniel' ('El is my judge') and any story-teller might select it for a worshipper of El/God, just as any Israelite mother might choose it for her child.

Summary

The facts of the case are these:

1) Ezekiel refers to a man by the name of Daniel;
2) he speaks of him as though he were well known to his audience;
3) he speaks of him as a paradigm of both wisdom and righteousness.

The candidates seem to be, on the one hand, a man named 'Daniel' who interpreted dreams, revealed hidden things and adhered faithfully to the Jewish religion, and on the other, a character otherwise unknown to extant Israelite discourse based upon an Ugaritic poem whose hero is neither especially wise or righteous (particularly to Jewish eyes) but was a Baal worshipper. Once it is concluded that Daniel-D, due to his elevated status, was probably well known to the Jewish exiles of whom Ezekiel was one, then the former alternative must be considered to be the more likely of the two. Given that the latter hypothesis depends upon eight hundred years of evolving narrative-transmission for which there is no evidence, one might suspect that its continuing popularity is motivated by something other than evidence and deduction.

---

[29] Collins, *Daniel*, 2.
[30] For examples see 1 Chr. 3:1; Ezra 8:2; Neh. 10:6; Jubilees 4:20; 1 Enoch 6:7.

Chapter 2

The Exile of Daniel

In the third year of the reign of Jehoiakim king of Judah, Nebuchadnezzar king of Babylon came to Jerusalem and besieged it. And the Lord gave Jehoiakim king of Judah into his hand, with some of the articles of the house of God, which he carried into the land of Shinar to the house of his god; and he brought the articles into the treasure house of his god (Daniel 1:1-2).

The book of Daniel begins by explaining how Nebuchadnezzar besieged Jerusalem and upon capturing it took certain treasures from the Temple. It is later recorded that Nebuchadnezzar instructed the master of the eunuchs, Ashpenaz, to select certain youths, who were both intelligent and good-looking, to be trained for service at the court of Babylon. Among these were Daniel, Hananiah, Mishael and Azariah (Dan. 1:3-7).

Many scholars assert that in these verses the author of Daniel was in error since there is no captivity recorded for the third year of Jehoiakim, either in the book of Kings or in Babylonian texts. Scholars claim these verses are inconsistent with known historical facts as Nebuchadnezzar could not possibly have besieged Jerusalem in 606 BC (generally identified as the third year of Jehoiakim), since he did not defeat Egyptians, who were the dominant power in Palestine, until the following year. Further, it is objected that Nebuchadnezzar was not king until after his defeat of the Egyptian army at Carchemish.[1]

In this section we will examine the evidence to judge the probability of there being a siege in the reign of Jehoiakim and if it can be dated to his third year.

Background

King Josiah (641-609) is the last king of Judah of whom it is recorded 'he did what was right in the sight of the LORD' (II Kgs 22:2). He was succeeded by a series of four kings – Jehoahaz (609), Jehoiakim (609-598), Jehoiachin (598-597) and Zedekiah (597-586) – who are all recorded as being unrighteous and the author of the book of Kings attributes the demise of the kingdom of Judah to their unrighteous behaviour (e.g. II Kgs 24:20).

---

[1]   Davies, *Daniel*, 30; Porteous, *Daniel*, 25-26.

By the end of the reign of Josiah the power of the Assyrian empire was waning. Attacks from the allied Medes and Babylonians had severely diminished the power of Assyria. The Assyrian capital, Nineveh, fell c.612 and for a time Assuruballit, a former Assyrian general, reigned at Harran. Once again, the Babylonians and the Medes came against the Assyrians and, in 609, Pharaoh Necho II, Assuruballit's ally, marched his army towards the Euphrates to aid him. Josiah, presumably in an attempt to hasten Assyria's fall, withstood the Egyptian advance at Megiddo and was slain (II Kgs 23:29).

When news of Josiah's death reached Jerusalem, the people anointed his son, Jehoahaz, as king. Jehoahaz only reigned three months. Pharaoh Necho, on his return from battle, came to Jerusalem and exacted tribute from Judah. He deposed Jehoahaz and selected his elder brother, Eliakim, to reign in his place. Necho changed Eliakim's name to 'Jehoiakim', presumably to assert his authority over his vassal (II Kgs 23:30-34).

Egypt's authority over Palestine and Syria was to be short lived. The Babylonians, having gained supremacy over the Assyrians, set their sights on the western regions. In 605 Nebuchadnezzar, the crown-prince of Babylon, led the army westward and met the Egyptian army in battle at Carchemish (around May-June).[2] Having defeated the Egyptians, Nebuchadnezzar conquered 'the whole area of Hamath'. Later that year, while still on campaign, his father, Nabopolassar, died and so Nebuchadnezzar returned to Babylon to become king. His chronicle records that 'in the accession year Nebuchadnezzar went back again to the Hatti-land and until the month of Šabatu marched unopposed through the Hatti-land; in the month of Šabatu he took the heavy tribute of the Hatti-territory to Babylon'.[3] The Hatti-land is the region of Syria and Palestine, including the kingdom of Judah.

Jehoiakim in Kings

The facts recorded in the book of Kings are entirely consistent with the testimony of the *Babylonian Chronicle* (BM 21946, often known as the *Jerusalem Chronicle*).

> In his days Nebuchadnezzar king of Babylon came up, and Jehoiakim became his vassal for three years. Then he turned and rebelled against him (II Kgs 24:1)

The chronicle records that Nebuchadnezzar received 'heavy tribute' from the kings of the Hatti-land in both his accession and first years (obv.13, 17). It is reasonable to suppose that Jehoiakim was one of these vassal kings. In Kings we are not told when Nebuchadnezzar 'came up'. It is plausible to suppose that

---

[2] For greater detail regarding the battle of Carchemish and surrounding events see D.J. Wiseman, *Chronicles of Chaldaean Kings (626-586 BC) in the British Museum* (London: British Museum, 1956), 25.

[3] BM 21946 obv. 12-13; A.K. Grayson, *Assyrian and Babylonian Chronicles* (Locust Valley, 1975).

following the battle of Carchemish Nebuchadnezzar proceeded to subdue any other resistance in the area since it is recorded that when he returned after his accession he 'march[ed] unopposed through the Hatti-land' (605/604).[4]

Jehoiakim's rebellion is not specifically mentioned in the chronicle. The fourth year of Nebuchadnezzar (601/600) is the last for which it is recorded that his army marched unopposed in Hatti-land (rev.5). This may indicate a rebellion after this point. Kings records that raiding bands of Chaldeans, Syrians, Moabites and Ammonites, came against Judah (II Kgs 24:2). This is not recorded in the chronicle but is consistent with its account as it records that the Babylonian army was committed to the invasion of Egypt and thus was not available to suppress uprisings. It records how in the fourth year the two armies met with no clear victor (rev.6-7). This battle clearly depleted the armies of Nebuchadnezzar, who remained in his own land in his fifth year to gather additional chariots and horses (rev. 8). Before Nebuchadnezzar himself could come to Judah, Jehoiakim had died and his son, Jehoiachin, was reigning.

Alberto Green has shown that Nebuchadnezzar may have been unaware of the death of Jehoiakim and the succession of Jehoiachin. Green asserts that the length of the reign of Jehoiachin was probably less than three months (II Kgs 24:8) rather than three months and ten days as in 2 Chronicles 36:9, which he demonstrates to be a probable scribal error (i.e. the transposition of the word 'ten'). Nebuchadnezzar captured Jehoiachin on 2 Adar (16 March 597), placing the death of Jehoiakim sometime in the month of Tebeth. The Babylonian Chronicle records that Nebuchadnezzar left Babylon with the army in the preceding month (i.e. Kislev). Green writes, 'it is evident from the study of Nebuchadrezzar's Chronicle that the Babylonian king did not conduct a general campaign throughout the West in 598/597, for he did not leave Babylon until late that year, and when he did leave, the Chronicle indicates that he set out directly for Jerusalem to besiege and subdue the rebellious Jehoiakim'. We may, therefore, conclude that Nebuchadnezzar came against Jerusalem in 597 with the intention of deposing Jehoiakim, and perhaps it was for this reason that Jehoiachin was spared death.[5]

The Jerusalem Chronicle records:

> In the seventh year [598/597].the month of Kislîmu, the king of Akkad mustered his troops, marched to the Hatti-land, and besieged the city of Judah and on the second day of the month of Addaru he seized the city and captured the king. He appointed there a king of his own choice, received its heavy tribute and sent to Babylon (rev.11-13).

All these details are entirely consistent with the account given in Kings, which places the three month reign of Jehoiachin in 598/597. Nebuchadnezzar carries treasures both from the Temple and the king's palace and carries many into

---

[4]   Wiseman, *Chronicles*, 26;
[5]   A.R. Green, 'The Fate of Jehoiakim', AUSS 20:2 (Summer 1982), 103-109.

captivity; 'none remained but the poorest people of the land' (II Kgs 24:14). Jehoiachin is replaced by his uncle Zedekiah.

The book of Kings does not record an exile in the reign of Jehoiakim. It is recorded that Nebuchadnezzar 'came up'. If this is linked with the battle of Carchemish then Nebuchadnezzar 'came up' around May/June 605, which would have been the fourth year of Jehoiakim. At this time Jehoiakim became a vassal and Nebuchadnezzar received his tribute. It is likely that this tribute was taken in the form of treasures from the Temple.

Jehoiakim in Jeremiah

The prophet Jeremiah was active during the reign of Jehoiakim and several of his prophecies are directed against him. Jeremiah dates many of his prophecies according to the regnal year of the king so these can be used to provide insight into the historical situation at these times.

Jeremiah confirms that Nebuchadnezzar defeated Pharaoh Necho at Carchemish 'in the fourth year of Jehoiakim' (Jer. 46:2). In the subsequent prophecy Jeremiah predicts the invasion of Egypt by Nebuchadnezzar, which took place 601/600. It is interesting to note that Jeremiah appends this prophecy with comfort for Israel: 'I will save you from far away and your offspring from the land of their captivity' (Jer. 46:27). This may be a reference to the captivity of the northern tribes, but if not then it would require an exile from Judah prior to 601.

It has been objected that in Jeremiah 25:1, a prophecy dated to the fourth year of Jehoiakim, Jeremiah speaks about the captivity of Judah as though it were still future. This would seem odd if there had been an exile that same year. However, Jeremiah prophesies the final end of the kingdom of Judah – 'this whole land shall be a desolation and an astonishment' (Jer. 25:11) – the captivity recorded in Daniel would only be the first rumblings of this great earthquake.

A more substantial objection is that when Jeremiah lists the number of the captives under Nebuchadnezzar, he does not mention an exile during the reign of Jehoiakim. He writes:

> These are the people whom Nebuchadnezzar carried away captive: in the seventh year [597], three thousand and twenty-three Jews; in the eighteenth year [585] of Nebuchadnezzar he carried away captive from Jerusalem eight hundred and thirty-two persons; in the twenty-third year [580] of Nebuchadnezzar, Nebuzaradan the captain of the guard carried away captive of the Jews seven hundred and forty-five persons. All the persons were four thousand six hundred (Jer. 52:28-30).

However, there are some reasons to suppose that the captivity recorded in Daniel wouldn't qualify for this list. Firstly, there is the size of the captivity; Daniel's record gives the impression that only a select few were taken, far less than the hundreds taken in subsequent captivities. Secondly, the three captivities listed by Jeremiah are all listed by regnal years of Nebuchadnezzar. If there was an exile during the aftermath of the battle of Carchemish then it would precede Nebuchadnezzar's accession.

The book of Jeremiah adds to our knowledge of the demise of Jehoiakim. The book of Kings simply records that 'Jehoiakim rested with his fathers' (II Kgs 24:6). Jeremiah prophesies an undignified end:

> They shall not lament for him, saying, 'Ah, my brother!' or 'Ah, my sister!' They shall not lament for him, saying, 'Ah, lord!', or 'Ah, his majesty!' With the burial of a donkey he shall be buried, dragged and dumped beyond the gates of Jerusalem (Jer. 22:18-19).

> His dead body shall be cast out to the heat of the day and the frost of the night (Jer. 36:30).

Assuming the historicity of these prophecies, their description of the desecration of the body of Jehoiakim strongly implies that he was despised and probably murdered. That his body was dumped outside the walls of Jerusalem suggests that his demise was engineered by one of his own people, perhaps a palace coup, though we cannot rule out external intervention. Green comments on the possibility that Jehoiakim was still reigning when the siege of Jerusalem began, writing, 'if the king was still alive when the Babylonians arrived, he could have died in the ensuing coup at the hands of the pro-Babylonian faction in the city as that faction attempted to save Jerusalem from destruction. His body could, in that case, have been thrown out as a sop to appease Nebuchadrezzar and to induce the Babylonian king to change his mind about conquering the city'.[6]

Jehoiakim in Chronicles

The book of Chronicles, though sharing strong affinities with the book of Kings, differs with regard to the reign of Jehoiakim. It does not record the activities of the raiding bands, recorded in Kings,[7] and instead states that Jehoiakim was carried captive to Babylon:

> Nebuchadnezzar king of Babylon came up against him, and bound him in bronze fetters to carry him off to Babylon. Nebuchadnezzar also carried off some of the articles from the house of the LORD to Babylon, and put them in his temple at Babylon (II Chr. 36:6-7)

---

[6] Green, 'Jehoiakim', 108.

[7] The Septuagint does repeat the words of II Kgs 24:1-4 between verses five and six of II Chr. 36. This is, presumably, a scribal addition attempting to reconcile the two texts.

These words are consistent with the account given at the beginning of Daniel and have been taken by some as confirmation of that account. However, there are several reasons to be cautious about the account in Chronicles.

No other Old Testament book, not even Daniel, or any Babylonian texts record that Jehoiakim was made captive. Kings states, 'Jehoiakim rested with his fathers' (II Kgs 24:6), strongly implying that he died in Jerusalem, and Jeremiah is more emphatic stating that his body was dumped outside the walls of Jerusalem. On the other hand, the Chronicles account would seem to imply that Jehoiakim's reign ended with his captivity. On a historical level, it seems implausible that Nebuchadnezzar would take Jehoiakim to Babylon, only to return in three months to carry away his son. Josephus does believe that Nebuchadnezzar came against Jerusalem twice within four months. He accounts for this by asserting that 'a terror seized the king of Babylon', and fearing that Jehoiachin would revolt because of the treatment of his father, Nebuchadnezzar again besieged Jerusalem. However, there is no reason to suppose that this is based on any additional historical information (*Antiquities* 10.7.1).

Also, given the similarity of the accounts in Chronicles and Daniel, P.R. Davies asserts that 'Daniel might be held to be dependent on Chronicles rather than historical fact'.[8]

One possible way to account for these verses in Chronicles is by scribal error. Given that within a few verses Jehoiachin is also recorded as being carried away captive this may be a case of dittography (i.e. the accidental repetition of a phrase by a copyist). The close similarity between the names 'Jehoiakim' and 'Jehoiachin' may, in part, explain such an error. However, comparison between the two sets of verses demonstrates different phraseology so such an error is more likely that of the original author, rather than a copyist.

Perhaps a better explanation is to suppose that the author of Chronicles carelessly copied his information from the book of Daniel, which does not record that Jehoiakim was carried away captive. Supposing some literary dependence between the two accounts, it is difficult to judge which account is the earliest. Since Daniel's account neither records the captivity of Jehoiakim himself nor places the captivity at the end of his reign then, with these issues in doubt, Daniel's account has the greater historicity. The awkwardly repetitive phrase 'to the house of his god; and he brought the articles into the treasure house of his god' in Daniel 1:2 is eased in II Chronicles 36:7 to the smooth 'to Babylon, and put them in his temple', which might imply that Chronicles was later. The use of 'Babylon', instead of 'the land of Shinar', might also support this conclusion. However, the similarities between these two texts should not be overstated; neither is a direct quotation from the other and, despite their parallels, they may actually be independent records.

Several scholars have attempted to explain the Chronicles' account by attempting to reconcile it with known history. For example, Wiseman proposes

---

[8] Davies, *Daniel*, 30.

that Jehoiakim died on the way to captivity, his body being dumped outside Jerusalem.[9] This scenario, though conceivable, rests on the idea that Jehoiakim, though bound, never actually went into captivity. The phrase in Chronicles, 'bound him in bronze fetters *to* carry him off to Babylon', literally only states that Nebuchadnezzar *intended* to make him captive; it does not necessarily entail that he did. Such an interpretation is fragile and one could reasonably expect Chronicles to state that the captivity was aborted if that was the case.

The best way to reconcile the Chronicles account with history is upon the basis of the parallels with the account given in Daniel. If we equate the captivity recorded in Daniel with that in Chronicles, then Jehoiakim was carried captive in his third/fourth year, rather than at the end of his reign. Jehoiakim was taken to Babylon as a captive but later returned to Jerusalem to rule as vassal to Nebuchadnezzar.

The captivity of Jehoiakim at this time is quite plausible given Nebuchadnezzar's claim over the land. For instance, when Pharaoh Necho moved his army into Palestine and Syria to claim these territories he carried away captive a pro-Babylonian king,[10] Jehoahaz, and installed his own man, Jehoiakim, on the throne of Judah. Later, when Nebuchadnezzar again besieged Jerusalem, he carried away captive a king loyal to Egypt, Jehoiachin, and installed Zedekiah to be his vassal. Since Jehoiakim was an Egyptian vassal, we could expect Nebuchadnezzar, after his defeat of Necho at Carchemish, to remove Jehoiakim from the throne. Jehoiakim may have secured his release from captivity by giving assurance to Nebuchadnezzar of his loyalty; we know he then served Nebuchadnezzar as vassal for the next three years. This reconciliation is hypothetical but is certainly plausible.

Berossus

Independent confirmation that there was an exile at this time comes from the historian Berossus (c.3rd century BC). He records how Nebuchadnezzar was sent by his father at the head of the army to quell the Egyptians. Having defeated the Egyptians, Nebuchadnezzar claims dominion over the area of Syria and Palestine. Shortly afterwards his father, Nabopolassar died in Babylon. Berosus continues:

> But as he [Nebuchadnezzar] understood, in a little time, that his father Nabopolassar was dead, he set the affairs of Egypt and the other countries in order, and committed *the captives he had taken from the Jews*, and Phoenicians, and Syrians, and of the nations belonging to Egypt, to some of his friends, that they might conduct that part of the forces that had on heavy armor, with the rest of his bag-

---

[9] Wiseman, *Chronicles*, 20-32.

[10] Since Josiah sought to aid the Babylonians against the Assyrians, it is reasonable to assume that Josiah and his court were decidedly anti-Assyrian and probably pro-Babylonian.

gage, to Babylonia; while he went in haste, having but a few with him, over the
desert to Babylon[11]

While it is true that Berossus does not explicitly mention a raid on Jerusalem,[12]
for Nebuchadnezzar to 'set the affairs of Egypt and the other countries in order'
would require some kind of intervention.

Collins objects that the remarks of Berossus 'must be suspect' because he
states that Nebuchadnezzar was sent against a rebel governor (of Egypt), rather
than an enemy king.[13] Certainly, remarks of this nature demonstrate that Berossus presented an idealized account of Babylon, exaggerating its supremacy over
other nations, but this does not mean that Berossus' account is fictitious.[14]
There is no reason to suppose that Berossus' incidental comment regarding the
Jewish captives was fabricated. Collins prefers to suppose that the Jewish captives were mercenaries who had fought for the Egyptians,[15] though the phrase
'captives . . . taken *from* the Jews' (as opposed to 'Jewish captives') is inconsistent with this supposition. Berossus does not state that these captives were
soldiers.

This account in Berossus only confirms the conclusions we have deduced so
far; that Nebuchadnezzar came to Judah shortly after the battle of Carchemish,
that he attempted to secure the loyalty to Judah and other surrounding nations,
and that he took captives from among the Jews.

The Third or Fourth Year?

From our conclusions so far there is one difficulty arising. Daniel 1:1 attests
that the captivity was in 'the third of the reign of Jehoiakim', while Jeremiah
46:2 states that the battle of Carchemish occurred in 'the fourth year of Jehoiakim'. If Nebuchadnezzar did take captives from Jerusalem following his victory
at Carchemish, as seems likely, then the record in Daniel would seem to be in
error by placing the captivity in the third year of Jehoiakim.

This problem had taxed the minds of commentators for a considerable number of years. E. Young lists in his commentary a selection of solutions proposed
over the years by various writers, including: i) proposing a copyist error
(Aalders), ii) proposing Nebuchadnezzar went to Jerusalem *before* going to
Carchemish (Haevernick, Pusey, *et al*), and iii) proposing that Daniel 1:1 only

---

[11] Berosus, quoted Josephus, *Against Apion*, 1.15.
[12] Collins, *Daniel*, 131.
[13] Collins, *Daniel*, 132.
[14] R. Bichler, 'Some Observations on the Image of the Assyrian and Babylonian Kingdoms within the Greek Tradition' in *Melammu Symposia V: Commerce and Monetary Systems in the Ancient World: Means of Transmission and Cultural Interaction*
(Stuttgart, 2004), 20.
[15] Collins, *Daniel*, 132.

means that Nebuchadnezzar set out from Babylon in the third year of Jehoiakim (Keil).[16]

One solution previously proposed by a number of writers is that Daniel 1:1 was based upon a different calculation of a king's regnal year. The Babylonians did not count a king's regnal years from when he came to the throne but from his first full year, starting from the New Year's Day. A clear example of this is given in Nebuchadnezzar's chronicle, which records that he 'sat on the royal throne' on 1 Ululu (i.e. 7th September; BM 21946, obv.11) but his first year did not begin till the month of Nisannu, when 'he took the hands of Bel and the son of Bel and celebrated the Akitu festival' (obv.14). The intervening months between Ululu and Nisannu are referred to as his 'accession year' (obv.12). It has been asserted that the kings of Judah did not use this system (i.e. they counted their first year from the month they came to the throne). Assuming there was a period of months between Jehoiakim's accession and the next new year's day, it would be consistent for one writer to date an event to the third year while another writer dated the same event to the fourth year.[17]

This solution, while popular, is based upon a simplified view of the way in which the reigns of the kings of Judah were recorded and can now be dispensed with in favour of more subtle explanation.

The careful study of the regnal years of the kings of Israel and Judah made by E. Thiele is widely regarded by scholars as the definitive work on the subject. His seminal work, *The Mysterious Numbers of the Hebrew Kings*, provides the basis on which many of the apparent discrepancies between the OT books have been explained. His thesis has been checked against Assyrian records and has been proved accurate. When his system is applied to Daniel 1:1, the discrepancy disappears.[18]

The kings of Judah did use an accession-year system; they counted the king's first year from the New Year. The complicating factor is that the Hebrews had two calendar years, one commencing in the month of Nisan (spring) and one commencing in the month of Tishri (autumn).[19] Thus, there were two systems for calculating the regnal years of the king; a Nisan-year system and a Tishri-year system. As we have seen the Babylonians used a Nisan-year system (Nisannu is equivalent to the Hebrew Nisan). The book of Jeremiah also appears to have used the Nisan-year system for both Babylonian and Hebrew

---

[16] E.J. Young, *A Commentary on Daniel* (Geneva Series; Eerdmans, 1949; repr., London: The Banner of Truth Trust, 1972), 268-69.

[17] J.G. Baldwin, *Daniel: An Introduction and Commentary* (TOTC; Leicester: Inter-Varsity Press, 1978), 20-21; also, see Young, *Daniel*, 269; A.R. Millard, 'Daniel 1-6 and History', *EQ* 49:2 (April-June 1977), 68-69.

[18] E.R. Thiele, *The Mysterious Numbers of the Hebrew Kings* (Grand Rapids: Zondervan, 1983; new rev. ed., Grand Rapids: Kregel, 1994), 182-86. For an introduction to the various calendars of Israel and Judah see K.A. Kitchen, *On the Reliability of the Old Testament* (Grand Rapids: Eerdmans, 2003), 28.

[19] Thiele, *Mysterious Numbers*, 44.

kings; for instance, it agrees with the Babylonian records, placing the exile of Jehoiachin in the seventh year of Nebuchadnezzar.[20] On the other hand, the book of Kings uses the Tishri-year system (it places the exile of Jehoiachin in the eighth year of Nebuchadnezzar; cf. II Kgs 24:8). Assuming that the author of Daniel also used a Tishri-year system then we can explain the discrepancy with Jeremiah.

---

[20] cf. Jer. 52:28-30; BM 21946, rev.11-12.

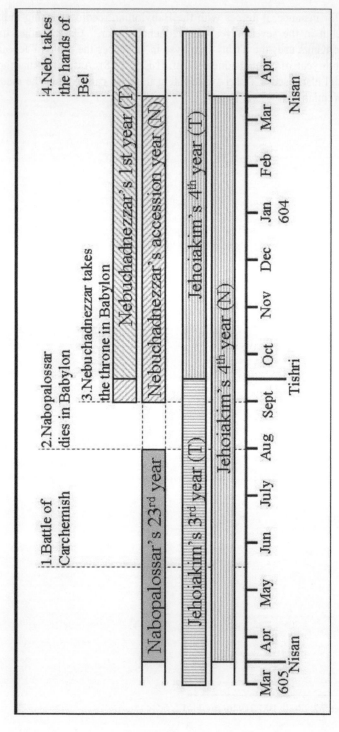

The dates recorded in the Babylonian chronicles allow us to place the death of Nabopolassar in August 605 and the accession of Nebuchadnezzar in September 605. The Battle of Carchemish is not strictly dated, but May/June is a reasonable hypothesis. The captivity of Daniel must have occurred at some point between the Battle of Carchemish and Nebuchadnezzar's return to Babylon, i.e. June-August 605. On a Nisan-year system this would be in the fourth year of Jehoiakim, on a Tishri-year system this would be in the third year.

There is no immediate answer as to the question of why the author of Daniel should use a Tishri-year system, rather than a Nisan-year system as Jeremiah did, except to say that it is entirely plausible that he should have done so. It was the Tishri-year system that was used by the kings of Judah and a captive from the court of Judah would naturally enumerate regnal years using this method. Nehemiah, another exiled Jew, used the Tishri-year system for the regnal years of Artaxerxes, in difference to the customary Persian Nisan-year system.[21]

Summary

The account given in Daniel 1:1-2 is entirely consistent with other historical sources for this period. The Battle of Carchemish (May/June 605) marked the end of Egyptian dominance over the region of Palestine. The crown-prince Nebuchadnezzar, asserting his authority over the region, took the Babylonian army through the Hatti-land and secured the allegiance of its kings. One of these kings was Jehoiakim. At this time Nebuchadnezzar came up against Jehoiakim, and probably took him captive along with others from his court. Upon hearing of the death of his father, Nebuchadnezzar hurried back to Babylon to take up the throne. Jehoiakim, it must be presumed, was able to secure his release in return for his allegiance to Nebuchadnezzar and served him as a vassal for three years.

The names of the captives taken by Nebuchadnezzar from Jerusalem are not recorded outside the book of Daniel but that they were nobles and members of royal family is highly probable (cf. Dan. 1:3), if the chief-captive was Jehoiakim himself.

The remaining objection that Nebuchadnezzar is incorrectly designated 'king' in these verses can only be regarded as pedantry. Though strictly-speaking it is anachronistic, since Nebuchadnezzar's accession did not take place until about three months after the captivity of Daniel, it cannot be sustained as an objection against the historicity of the book of Daniel any more than we could take exception to a modern author referring to the childhood of Queen Elizabeth.

---

[21] Thiele, *Mysterious Numbers*, 53.

Chapter 3

Babylonian Names[1]

According to the book of Daniel, when Daniel and his three friends arrive in Babylon they are each given a Babylonian name; Daniel is named Belteshazzar, Hananiah is named Shadrach, Mishael is named Meshach and Azariah is named Abed-Nego (Dan. 1:7). These four also serve Nebuchadnezzar (1:19) and are each promoted to high office: Daniel is made 'ruler over the whole province of Babylon and chief prefect over all the wise men of Babylon' (2:48) and the other three are also appointed as officials in province of Babylon (2:49; 3:30). Though bureaucratic records for this period are patchy, it is reasonable to suppose that if Daniel and his three friends were high officials in the province of Babylon their names would occur in cuneiform texts for the period. And whilst it is dangerous to conclude too much from silence (particularly given the evidence is far from complete), if Daniel and his three friends are not so named then it might tell against the historicity of their appointments.

In 1982 Professor William H. Shea produced a paper[2] in which he proposed that the names of Daniel's three friends could be identified on a cuneiform text known as the *Istanbul Prism* (VAT 7834). This thesis has been welcomed enthusiastically by evangelicals[3] (not to mention a host of internet apologists), though it is less frequently cited by conservative scholars.[4] Critical scholars have almost entirely overlooked Shea's proposition; the one exception is Collins, who briskly dismisses Shea's identifications.[5] Despite this mixed reception, Shea's proposition remains an intriguing hypothesis and is worthy of some consideration.

---

[1] An earlier version of this essay was published as 'Shadrach, Meshach and Abed-Nego', *CJBI* 2:3 (Jul 2008). Used by permission.

[2] W.H. Shea, 'Daniel 3: Extra-Biblical Texts and the Convocation on the Plain of Dura', *AUSS* 20:1 (Spring 1982).

[3] e.g. C. Missler, *The Book of Daniel: Supplemental Notes* (Koinonia House, 1994), 15; J. Argubright, *Bible Believer's Archeology*, vol.2: The Search for Truth (Xulon, 2003).

[4] S.R. Miller, *New American Commentary: Daniel* (NAC 18; Broadman & Holman, 1994), 108; D.B. Wallace, 'To Bow or Not to Bow: An Essay on Daniel 3', 2005 http://www.bible.org/page.php?page_id=1579

[5] Collins, *Daniel*, 141n, 183n.

The Istanbul Prism

The *Istanbul Prism* contains a list of officials from the reign of Nebuchadnezzar. Wiseman states that the prism seems to have been 'drawn up to record a procession to commemorate a special occasion',[6] though we are currently unaware as to what that occasion might have been. Shea's own thesis places the composition of the *Istanbul Prism* in the events of Daniel 3.

Using the evidence of Nebuchadnezzar's Chronicle Shea establishes that there was a revolt in Nebuchadnezzar's tenth year (c. January 594 BC).

> In the tenth year the king of Akkad was in his own land; from the month of Kislimu to the month of Tebetu there was rebellion in Akkad. With arms he slew many of his own army. His own hand captured his enemy (*Jerusalem Chronicle*, reverse 21-22).

He suggests that references to Zedekiah going to Babylon early 593 BC (Jer. 51:59-64) might imply a large gathering of vassal kings. That Nebuchadnezzar took his army westward (late 594) may have been for the very purpose of gathering these vassal kings, or else *reminding* them that their presence was required.

> In the month of [. . .] he marched to the Hatti-land, where kings and [. . .] officials came before him and he received their heavy tribute and then returned to Babylon (*Jerusalem Chronicle*, reverse 23-24).

Shea connects all these events with Daniel 3, where it is recorded that Nebuchadnezzar erected a large statue on the plain of Dura and sent for 'all the officials of the provinces' to come and attend the dedication (Dan. 3:1-3). Shea reasons that the revolt against Nebuchadnezzar in 594 prompted him to review all his officials (and possibly to replace them) and to reassert his authority over his vassal kings, and this reaffirmation of their loyalty was the purpose of the erection of the statue on the plain of Dura.[7] According to this thesis, the *Istanbul Prism* would be the record of those officials and kings who affirmed their allegiance to Nebuchadnezzar.

The prism is not dated, nor are the events recorded in Daniel 3, so we lack positive confirmation of Shea's thesis but there are some details that make it probable that the *Istanbul Prism* was a loyalty oath following a revolt. First is the comprehensive nature of the list, which is incomparable with any other list of officials from Mesopotamia. Second is the opening statement of the list, which reads: 'I ordered the (following) court officials in exercises of (their) duties to take up position in my (official) suite.' As Shea points out, this implies that all the officials listed were appointed, or at least reappointed, at the

---

[6] D.J. Wiseman, *Nebuchadrezzer and Babylon: The Schweich Lectures* (Oxford: Oxford University Press, 1985; repr., 2004), 75.
[7] Shea, 'Daniel 3', 29-37.

same time.[8] That the text gives 'at least a representative sampling of officials from the major echelons of civil servants and from many of the areas under the control of the government of Babylon'[9] suggests that these appointments represented a major overhaul of the government of Babylon. Thirdly, the fact that the foreign kings are included in the list suggests that this overhaul was far wider than just administrative positions. That Zedekiah did indeed rebel against Nebuchadnezzar a few years later vindicates Nebuchadnezzar's concern regarding the loyalty of his vassals.

Whether or not Shea is correct to link the prism with the events of Daniel 3, he does provide an interesting analysis of some of the names contained on the prism. This includes the possibility that Shadrach, Meshech and Abed-Nego are named on the prism.

Hananiah / Shadrach

One of the court officials (*mašennim*) listed on the prism is 'Hanunu, chief of the royal merchants'. The name 'Hanunu' is not Babylonian in origin, but western Semitic. Oppenheim called it 'a typical Phoenician name'[10] but Shea argues that the name could also be Jewish in origin. 'Hanunu' is philologically the same as the Jewish name 'Hanani' (lit. 'gracious'), which is the same name as 'Hananiah' (lit. 'Yah is gracious') except for the Yahwistic element (i.e. the 'iah' ending).[11]

As well as sharing etymology, the names 'Hanani' and 'Hananiah' are used synonymously. This Shea demonstrates by reference to the *Elephantine Papyi* (nos. 21, 30, 31, 33 and 38) dating from the fifth century BC, which refer to an significant individual in the Jewish community there who designated in the texts both 'Hanani' and 'Hananiah'. Another example of the synonymous use in Nehemiah 7:2, which describes single individual ('*a* faithful man') while seemingly using two names: 'Hanani' and 'Hananiah'.[12] Therefore, the difference between the name recorded on the prism ('Hanunu') and the name recorded in Daniel ('Hananiah') may be accounted for by the fact that the two names were used synonymously. It is, in fact, realistic to suppose that the Babylonian scribes would have sought to suppress the Yahwistic element in Hananiah's name while the author of Daniel would have wished to include it.

Collins objects to the identification of Hanunu with Hananiah, saying, 'it would be anomalous to have the Hebrew name listed, and Shea must further assume that it is modified by dropping the theophoric ending'.[13] However, nei-

---

[8]   Shea, 'Daniel 3', 40.

[9]   Shea, 'Daniel 3', 41.

[10] A.L. Oppenheim, *Ancient Mesopotamia: Portrait of a Dead Civilization* (Chicago, 1964) 94.

[11] Shea, 'Daniel 3', 46.

[12] Shea, 'Daniel 3', 47.

[13] Collins, *Daniel*, 183n.

ther of these objections meets the challenge. Firstly, it is a matter of fact that a Semitic name is listed on the *Istanbul Prism*; whether it was anomalous or not, it is not a matter for dispute. Secondly, since it is clear that Hanani and Hanani-ah were used synonymously, the omission of the theophoric ending would not be unlikely even in a Hebrew document. One would think that it would be *more* likely, not less, that the name Hanani should occur without the Yahwistic element in a Babylonian document. Therefore, neither of Collins' objections tell against the identification of Hananiah with Hanunu.

One curious problem, though not one that tells strongly against the identification of Hananiah with Hanunu, is why Hananiah should be listed on the *Istanbul Prism* by his Hebrew name, instead of his Babylonian name ('Shadrach'). One would naturally assume that the purpose of giving the Jewish captives their Babylonian names was so that they could be used in these contexts. Nevertheless, that a Semitic name occurs on the *Prism* is a matter of record and provides evidence that officials were sometimes listed with a foreign name.

P-R Berger and Alan Millard have proposed that the name Shadrach represents *šādurāku* 'I am fearful (of God)'.[14] An alternative proposal is that Shadrach represents *šudur-aku*, 'the command of Aku'.[15] Either proposal is an attempt to work backwards from Hebrew letters to a presupposed Babylonian original. That the Hebrew renderings in Daniel 1 have plausible Babylonian equivalents lends weight to the credibility of the account.

Azariah / Abed-Nego

On the basis that a Jewish writer would wish to suppress reference to Babylonian gods in the names of the Jewish heroes, it has long been hypothesized that the original form of the name 'Abed-Nego' was 'Abed-Nebo', after Nebo (or Nabu) the Babylonian god (patron of writing and vegetation). Montgomery proposed that Nego was 'an intentional perversion to avoid an idolatrous name'.[16] 'Abed-Nego', then, would literally mean 'servant of Nebo', from *'ābad* meaning 'servant'. On the *Istanbul Prism* we find the entry 'Ardi-Nabu, secretary of the crown prince'. 'Ardi-Nabu' also means 'servant of Nebo'. The Akkadian word for 'servant' at this time was *ardu*, which would be translated in West Semitic languages by *'ābad*. 'Abed-Nebo' would be a translation, rather than a transliteration, of the name 'Ardi-Nabu'.[17] The transition between the names 'Abed-Nabu' (Aramaic) and 'Ardi-Nabu' (Akkadian) is not only

---

[14] P-R. Berger, *Zeitschrift für Assyriologie* 64 (1975), 224-234; Millard, 'Daniel 1-6', 72.

[15] Miller, *Daniel*, 65.

[16] J.A. Montgomery, *The International Critical Commentary: A Critical and Exegetical Commentary on the Book of Daniel* (Edinburgh: T&T Clark, 1927), 130.

[17] Shea, 'Daniel 3', 49.

theoretically possible, but is known to have occurred in other occurrences of the name in contract tablets.[18]

There is little room for criticism of this proposal. Millard provides an alternative explanation for Abed-Nego based upon Babylonian onomastics, stating that the name is 'an Aramaic form meaning "servant of the shining one"',[19] but he notes a possible play on words with Nabu. However, known occurrences of the name Abed-Nebo / Ardi-Nabu make this a preferable explanation. If it is granted that a Jewish writer would suppress an idolatrous name, and this does not seem particularly controversial, then it is a matter of semantics to match the name Abed-Nego with Ardi-Nabu on the prism. Collins assents to the correspondence between these two names, though only allows that this is witness to the name, not the individual.[20] On this point we must agree with Collins. The name Abed-Nebo / Ardi-Nabu is too common amongst extant texts to guarantee identification. Therefore, we cannot say for certain that Ardi-Nabu of the prism is Abed-Nego of Daniel.

It is interesting to note that the crown prince at the time, to whom Ardi-Nabu was secretary, would have been Amêl-Marduk (Evil-Merodach) who is recorded as treating favourably Jehoiachin, the former king of Judah (2 Kgs 25:27-28). Could it have been the influence of a Jewish secretary that prompted this favourable treatment?

Mishael / Meshach

Shea admits that his identification for Mishael is more tentative. The identification he proposes is with Mušallim-Marduk, one of the overseers of the slave girls.

The name 'Meshach' (*Mešak*) is similar to 'Mishael' (*Mišael*) with the exception of the final element. The '-el' stands for 'God' in Mishael's name (lit. 'who is like God') and it is reasonable to suppose that when Mishael's name was changed the intention was to suppress or replace this element. One proposed explanation for Meshach is *misha-aku* ('who is like Aku'),[21] which replaces the Jewish theophoric element 'el' with a Babylonian theophoric element. Along similar lines, Shea proposes that the theophoric element could have been replaced by a reference to the Babylonian god Marduk, as is implied by the final element of Meshach ('k'). Mishael's Babylonian name would thus be Miša-Marduk, perhaps shortened to Meshach (Miša[-Mardu]k) by the Jewish author to avoid reference to the Babylonian god. However, Shea writes, 'better sense can be made out of this name if the whole Hebrew name Mišael is

---

[18] J.H. Stevenson, *Assyrian and Babylonian Contracts with Aramaic Notes* (America Book Company, 1902), 51.

[19] Millard, 'Daniel 1-6', 72.

[20] Collins, *Daniel*, 141n, 183n.

[21] Miller, *Daniel*, 65. In contrast, Millard proposes Meshech should be explained as *mēšāku*, 'I am of little account' (Millard, 'Daniel 1-6', 72).

adapted into the participial form of *mušallim*.[22] Thus, he argues, Mišael's Hebrew name might have been adapted by his Babylonian captors to Mušallim-Marduk, which in turn was adapted by the Jewish author of Daniel to Mešak.

Collins' accusation that this identification is 'farfetched'[23] is perhaps too harsh. The names are, at least, etymologically related, 'Mishael' meaning 'who is like El' and 'Mušallim-Marduk' meaning 'who is like Marduk'. Shea relates these two names on the assumption that the Babylonian captors would wish to transpose 'Marduk' for 'El', which, while not implausible, is without positive evidence. Even granting this assumption, we still require a leap of imagination to account for the fact that the Jewish writer transliterated 'Mušallim-Marduk' in the abbreviated form 'Meshach'. In any case, the name 'Mušallim-Marduk' is too common for this individual to be definitively identified with the Mishael of Daniel.

Daniel / Belteshazzar (omitted)

In Daniel 4, Nebuchadnezzar explains that Daniel is named Belteshazzar 'according to the name of my god'.[24] It has previously been assumed that the intended god in this instance was Bel and since the name was understood as a transliteration of *balatšu-usur* (lit. 'may he protect his life'), the explanation of Daniel 4 has been described as 'false etymology'.[25] However, Millard provides an alternative suggestion, proposing that Belteshazzar is a transliteration of *bēlēt-šar-usur*, literally 'Lady, protect the king'. He explains that Bēlēt was 'a title for the wife of Marduk or Bel, the patron of Babylon'.[26]

Elsewhere Shea has proposed that Daniel was originally given the name 'Belshazzar', which was adapted by the Jewish writer to Belteshazzar to distinguish him from the blasphemous king who features in Daniel 5. On this basis, Shea identifies Daniel with a Belshazzar mentioned in two texts as 'the chief officer' (*šaqu šarri*) of Neriglissar and Amel-Marduk respectively. These identifications remain hypothetical as we lack positive evidence for the shift from Belshazzar to Belteshazzar.[27]

There is no reference to either Daniel or Belteshazzar on the *Istanbul Prism*, nor can these names be plausibly linked with any other name on the prism. It is possible that Daniel's entry has been lost since the prism is damaged.[28] The office that Daniel held of 'chief over the wise men' is not included on the prism. Yet the omission of Daniel from the prism is consistent with Shea's the-

---

[50] Shea, 'Daniel 3', 50.
[23] Collins, *Daniel*, 141n.
[24] Daniel 4:8.
[25] Porteous, *Daniel*, 28.
[26] Millard, 'Daniel 1-6', 72.
[27] W.H. Shea, 'Bel(te)shazzar meets Belshazzar', *AUSS* 26:1, (Spring 1988), 67-81.
[28] There is a break at the top of column four and another at the bottom of column five (Shea, 'Daniel 3', 39).

ory that the *Istanbul Prism* relates to the events of Daniel 3 since Daniel is conspicuously absent from the events recorded in that chapter, though there is no indication in the chapter as to why he should have been absent.

Conclusion

Seeking to identify biblical characters in non-Semitic texts is not straightforward as it is not always clear how the foreign scribe would have rendered Semitic names. The Semitic names Hananiah, Mishael and Azariah are quite common, which would make us rightly cautious of any proposed identification. In the case of Daniel and his three friends the problem is compounded by the fact the double names of the characters and the real possibility that the Jewish renderings of their Babylonian names is imperfect or intentionally corrupted (to disguise references to foreign gods). Assuming that these names have been intentionally corrupted, we can only make reasonable speculations about the way the names may have been corrupted and thus any proposals for the original forms of the names will be equally speculative.

The thesis Shea proposes is intriguing and plausible. Though the identification between Mušallim-Marduk and Mishael requires significant assumptions and is thus problematic, the other two identifications are reasonable. However, as Collins notes, the identification cannot be conclusive beyond equating the names; the critical scholar can legitimately respond that this is just some other Hanunu and Ardi-Nabu. It is significant that these two names are found on the same tablet but further than this we cannot go.

Whether or not Shea is correct, our foregoing discussion still provides some useful conclusions. Firstly, the presence of a Western Semitic name on the prism indicates that foreigners were engaged as high officials in the Babylonian administration and corroborates the idea of Daniel's appointment at the court of Nebuchadnezzar. Secondly, that the Babylonian names recorded in the book of Daniel have credible etymologies and, in the case of Ardi-Nabu, are known from extant texts indicates that the author did not haphazardly create these names. Such conclusions as these add to the historical quality of the book of Daniel.

Chapter 4

Amongst the Exiles

A recurring theme amongst the book of Daniel's detractors is a questioning, and sometimes a ridiculing, of the book's depiction of the general character of the Babylonian exile. On the one hand, the favorable treatment of Daniel and his three friends is called into question, particularly their acceleration to positions of authority.[1] On the other, the cruel persecution of Daniel and his friends for their religious observance is considered a-historical and a product of Jewish reaction to later Hellenistic persecution.[2] Yet any assessment of the depiction of life amongst the exiles is severely hampered by our lack of evidence, archeological or literary. The OT remains our most substantial insight into the thoughts and feelings of the Jewish exiles. Babylonian records are limited and we are often dependent on analogies to other ancient near eastern societies to reconstruct the situation of the exiles at court. Nevertheless, there are sources available for historical assessment and this assessment should be made before we decide upon what is conceivable.

The Nature of the Exile

Modern studies of the exile have tended to approach it as a literary phenomenon, while the extent of the actual deportation and its impact upon the Jewish nation is questioned. It has become popular to talk of the 'myth of the exile'.[3] Such approaches draw upon the hyperbole of the Chronicler[4] but give little attention to archaeological and sociological approaches. Yet that Jews were deported by the Babylonians is a matter of historical fact. Cuneiform rations tablets for Jehoiachin and other Jewish officials confirm the captivity of the Jewish court. Archeological excavations indicate that around this time cities such as

---

[1] For example, S.R. Driver, *An Introduction to the Literature of the Old Testament* (1st ed., 1891; 7th ed., Edinburgh: T&T Clark, 1898), 500.

[2] For example, Davies, *Daniel*, 31.

[3] R.P. Carroll, 'Exile, Restoration, and Colony: Judah in the Persian Empire' in *The Blackwell Companion to the Hebrew Bible* (L.G. Perdue ed.; Oxford: Blackwell, 2001), 102-16.

[4] cf. II Chronicles 36:21. The Chronicler speaks of the land lying 'desolate' yet both archaeology and other OT books indicate that many Jews remained in the land and were not taken into exile.

Jerusalem, Lachish and Beth-Shemesh were left desolate,[5] while the Murashu texts confirm that large Jewish communities were established around Nippur.[6] As we have seen, there is good reason to suppose that Nebuchadnezzar took some Jewish captives back to Babylon after the battle of Carchemish, the first of several captivities. While the proportion of the population taken into captivity might be open to debate[7] that the captivity occurred cannot be seriously doubted.

It has been common amongst biblical historians to portray the Babylonian captivity as a fairly comfortable experience for the Jews.[8] This portrayal has been based upon the relative prosperity of those Jews named in the Murashu texts and the fact that a significant proportion of the exiles did not return to the land after the fall of Babylon. Recently this portrayal has been questioned by D.L. Smith-Christopher, who argues that much of the language of the prophets is only explicable if understood against a background of difficult circumstances.[9] In addition, he cites several inscriptions that indicate that captives were pressed into forced labor. The Murashu texts date from the reigns of Artaxerxes I and Darius II (464-404) and probably reflect the easier conditions of Persian governance.

If parallels with the Assyrian deportation of the Israelites are legitimate then we may expect the majority of the captives to have endured subsistence rations and forced labor. The exceptions would be the literate elite, who were employed in the Assyrian administration. Cuneiform texts reveal that under the Assyrians Israelites became court officials, scribes, advisors, and even priests.[10] Ration texts demonstrate that foreigners also served in the Babylonian administration and were employed as skilled craftsman.[11] It is difficult to judge the exact number of foreigners, and specifically Jews, employed in this way since the cuneiform scribes infrequently mention the nationality of the persons

---

[5]   D.L. Smith-Christopher, 'Reassessing the Historical and Sociological Impact of the Babylonian Exile (597/587-539 BCE)' in *Exile: Old Testament, Jewish, and Christian Conceptions* (J.M. Scott ed.; Leiden: Brill, 1997), 16-17, citing the excavations of Kenyon.

[6]   J.D. Purvis & E.M. Meyers, 'Exile and Return: From the Babylonian Destruction to the Reconstruction of the Jewish State', *Ancient Israel* (1999).

[7]   A common estimate is that 90-95% of the population of Judah remained in the land (see Purvis & Meyers, 'Exile and Return'). Archaeologists note that towns such as Bethel and Gibeon continued to flourish during this period (Smith-Christopher, 'Babylonian Exile', 17).

[8]   cf. Purvis & Meyers, 'Exile and Return'. Also, see L.J. Wood, *A Survey of Israel's History* (rev. D. O'Brien; Grand Rapids: Zondervan, 1986), 328f.

[9]   Smith-Christopher, 'Babylonian Exile', 24f. For example, the image of the 'chains' of the captives is only pertinent if they actually experienced some form of restriction (cf. Jer. 40:4, Ezek. 19:9, etc.).

[10]   K.L. Younger Jr., 'Israelites in Exile', *BAR* 29:6 (Nov/Dec 2003).

[11]   Wiseman, *Nebuchadrezzer*, 83-84.

named.[12] Daniel, and his friends, would have been part of this privileged exception to the fate of the majority, being selected for their abilities to serve at the court of Babylon and given a daily ration (Dan. 1:3-5).

Scholars at Court

The tales of Daniel, and his three friends, as scholars in the court of Nebuchadnezzar are consistent with the realities of the courts at Asshur and Babylon. K. van der Toorn argues persuasively that 'though clearly exceptional, his [i.e. Daniel's] career follows the model of a successful Mesopotamian scholar at the king's court'.[13]

Daniel and his friends are given into the care of the 'master of the eunuchs', the *rab saris* – a term known from a bilingual docket dating from the mid-seventh century.[14] The *rab saris* of Daniel is named 'Ashpenaz'. Naturally, some skeptics have denied the existence of this individual since, as yet, he is not known from any Babylonian text. However, there is nothing implausible in the name and no particular reason to doubt his existence. It has been suggested that 'Ashpenaz' is not a name but refers to the role of innkeeper (Old Persian).[15] This idea should be briskly dismissed; it reflects neither the usage in Daniel nor the etymology of the word.[16] In the early twentieth century various, rather dubious, attempts were made to interpret 'Ashpenaz' as a Babylonian name: R.D. Wilson proposed *Ashipu-Anu-Izzu* ('the Aship-priest of Anu is mighty'); G.R. Tabouis proposed *Ashpenazar* ('the Lady formed the Seed').[17] Many commentaries follow the explanation that 'Ashpenaz' means 'horse-nose', deriving from the Old Persian *as* ('horse') and the Sanskrit *nâsâ*

---

[12] See W.D. Davies & L. Finkelstein, *The Cambridge History of Judaism*, vol.1: Introduction; The Persian Period (Cambridge: Cambridge University Press, 1984), 344. This problem is compounded if, as in the case of Daniel and his friends, these foreigners are given Babylonian names.

[13] K. van der Toorn, 'Scholars at the Oriental Court: The Figure of Daniel against its Mesopotamian Background' in *The Book of Daniel: Composition and Reception* (vol.1; ed. J.J. Collins & P.W. Flint; Leiden: Brill, 2001), 37-54. However, van der Toorn does not believe that the author of Daniel obtained his knowledge of the Babylonian court from first-hand acquaintance but through the medium of court tales such as those found in Ludlul and Ahiqar (52).

[14] Aramaic: *rbsrs*; Akkadian: *rab ša-rēši* (LU.GAL.SAG); cf. רב סרים (Dan 1:3); cf. H. Tadmor, '*Rab-sārîs* or *Rab-shakeh* in 2 Kings 18' in *The Word of the Lord Shall Go Forth: Essays in Honor of David Noel Freedman in Celebration of His Sixtieth Birthday* (ed. C.L. Meyers & M. O'Connor; Eisenbrauns, 1983), 279-85. The docket is now in the British Museum. Also, see the *Nebo-Sarsekim Tablet* (BM 114789), which also refers to a *rab ša-rēši* (LU.GAL.SAG; line 2; cf. Jer. 39:3).

[15] e.g. Collins, *Daniel*, 127n

[16] Cf. Z. Stefanovic, *Daniel: Wisdom to the Wise: Commentary on the Book of Daniel* (Pacific, 2007), 51.

[17] G.R. Tabouis, *Nebuchadnezzar* (1931; repr. Kessinger, 2003), 302.

('nose').[18] T.C. Mitchell has argued that the name is more likely Median, rather than Old Persian, in origin, from *asp* ('horse').[19] We must also make reference to the proposal of S.H. Horn, who claims the name occurs as '*SPNZ* in an Aramaic text from Nippur and again in cuneiform records as *Ashpazdnda*.[20] There is an odd claim repeated in many minor commentaries and internet apologists that a monument/brick now in the British Museum (occasionally, the Berlin Museum) bears the phrase "Ashpenaz, master of eunuchs in the time of Nebuchadnezzar". It is possible that this is based upon a misunderstanding of Siegfried Horn's proposal.[21]

The Mesopotamian kings frequently made inquiries from groups of experts – sages (*enqūtu*) and scholars (*ummânū*) – whom they kept in service for this purpose. These experts included astrologers (*tupšarrū Enūma Anu Enlil*), exorcists (*āšipū*), lamentation priests (*kalû*), physicians (*asû*) and diviners (*bārû*) (cf. Dan. 1:20, 2:2, 10, 4:7) and each of these groups was led by a *rab* ('chief') (cf. Dan. 2:48, 5:11).[22] Van der Toorn suggests that Daniel's role at court is unhistorical as there was no oneiromancer (interpreter of dreams) at the Babylonian court.[23] Yet Daniel was not employed as an oneiromancer (cf. Dan. 1:19) and the incident of Nebuchadnezzar's dream is described as being exceptional (cf. Dan. 2:1).

The court scholars depended upon the king's favour for their livelihood; those closer to the king reaped the rewards. This naturally led to competition as is evidenced from letters in which court scholars denigrate one another.[24] Kings also became suspicious of their scholars and their purposes, and thus often gave credence to allegations made against them.[25] In this atmosphere, the situation described in Daniel 6 of a group of scholars conspiring against Daniel is entirely plausible.

The description of Daniel's induction into the court of Babylon is also consistent with other Mesopotamian examples. S.M. Paul has noted the similarities

[18] Cf. e.g. Gesenius' lexicon.
[19] T.C. Mitchell, 'Achaemenid History and the Book of Daniel' in *Mesopotamia and Iran in the Persian Period: Conquest and Imperialism 539-331 BC: Proceedings of a seminar in memory of Vladimir G. Lukonin* (ed. J. Curtis; London: British Museum, 1993), 77.
[20] S.H. Horn, *Seventh-Day Adventist Bible Dictionary* (Washington: Review & Herald, 1960) 83. This is probably the basis of Stefanovic's assertion that 'the name is attested outside the Bible' (*Daniel*, 51).
[21] E. Watke Jr., *A Study of the Book of Daniel* (Augusta: Revival in the Home Ministries, 1992); T.Y. Malalty, *The Book of Daniel*, (trans. F. Moawad); http://www.truthnet.org/Daniel/Introduction/ [cited 01 Oct 08]; http://forum.bib-arch.info/index.php?action=printpage;topic=67.0 [cited 01 Oct 08]; http://www.grovebaptist.freeserve.co.uk/800by600/dl039.htm [cited 01 Oct 08].
[22] van der Toorn, 'Mesopotamian Background', 40.
[23] van der Toorn, 'Mesopotamian Background', 41.
[24] van der Toorn, 'Mesopotamian Background', 40.
[25] van der Toorn, 'Mesopotamian Background', 41.

between the narrative in Daniel 1 and the induction of a group of weavers into the service of a Mesopotamian court, as described in a letter between Mari and Šibtu, the wife of King Zimrilim.[26] These similarities include: a) that candidates were taken as booty, b) they already possessed unique skills and c) unblemished appearance, d) they were supervised by officials and e) were taught a new profession. There is also explicit mention of food rations during the training period to maintain their healthy appearance.

The Chaldeans

It was previously thought that the use of the term 'Chaldean' (*kasdiy* כשדימה) to refer to a class of wise men (Dan. 2:2, 4, 5, 10; 4:7; 5:7, 11) was an anachronism. The term 'Chaldean' comes from the Akkadian term *Kasdu*. In late Akkadian there was phonetic shift such that in certain words the sibilant *s* became *l* before *t* and *d*, so *Kasdu* became *Kaldu*.[27] This term, *Kaldu*, appears in Greek writers as Χαλδαιος, hence 'Chaldean'. The *Kasdu* were a people from the region around Ur; Nebuchadnezzar and his father, Nabopolassar, were *Kasdu*. Since the ruling dynasty during the Neo-Babylonian period was *Kasdu*, it is objected that the author is in error to use *Kasdiy* as a class of wise man, rather than as an ethnic term. In the fifth century Herodotus refers to the Χαλδαιος as priests of Bel (Marduk).[28] It is conjectured that the term would not have become a technical term for these priests until the end of Chaldean dynasty.

In fact, the author does use *kasdiy* in the ethnic sense (Dan. 5:30; 9:1; pos. 3:8) so his other use of the term cannot be due to ignorance of its ethnic origins. The designation of certain wise men as 'Chaldeans' cannot be explained by dependence on late sources, such as Herodotus, since the term *kasdiy* almost certainly derives from the earlier Akkadian form of the term. Therefore, we must look for an alternative explanation for the dual-use of *kasdiy* in the book of Daniel.

One suggestion proposed by R.D. Wilson, and defended by Archer, is that the two meanings of *Kaldu* have separate etymologies. Wilson hypothesized that while *Kaldu* (ethnic) was derived from *Kasdu*, *Kaldu* (priestly) was derived from the Sumerian *gal-du* meaning 'master builder'. While *Kaldu* (ethnic) referred to the race, *Kaldu* (priestly) referred to a group of high-ranking officials.[29] However, even if the link between *gal-du* and *Kaldu* could be substantiated, there would be no link with the Hebrew *kasdiy*.

---

[26] See S.M. Paul, 'The Mesopotamian Background of Daniel 1-6' in *The Book of Daniel: Composition and Reception* (vol.1; ed. J.J. Collins & P.W. Flint; Leiden: Brill, 2001) 55-68; S.M Paul, 'From Mari to Daniel: Instructions for the Acceptance of Servants into the Royal Court', *Eretz Israel* 24 (1993), 161-3.

[27] Miller, *Daniel*, 79; Millard, 'Daniel 1-6', 69-71.

[28] *Histories* I.181, 183.

[29] G.L. Archer Jr., *The Expositor's Bible Commentary: Daniel – Minor Prophets* (vol.7; Grand Rapids: Zondervan, 1985), 14n.

An alternative suggestion is that both meanings could have been used concurrently. Despite the early application of 'Chaldean' to the priests of Bel, the term continued to be used in an ethnic sense at least till the first century BC when it is used by the historian Strabo. Baldwin reasons:

> There is nothing incongruous about the use of the term in both   meanings,   nor
> need it cause confusion, any more than our use in English of the word "Morocco"
> to designate both the country and the leather for which it is famous.[30]

Millard finds a possible analogy with the Magi, who performed a religious function in the Persian Empire and were probably a tribe of the Medes.[31] Given that the Chaldean dynasty was instrumental in the elevation of Marduk to supreme god, it is possible that the priests of Marduk were ethnically Chaldean. It is certainly conceivable that the theological shift towards Marduk would have been characterized as a Chaldean innovation, even if all the priests were not ethnically Chaldean.

It is interesting to note that there is no extant use of the term *Kaldu* in cuneiform texts from the Neo-Babylonian period. This may be due to our lack of information but it is likely that the term was not used by Chaldeans of themselves during this period.

Religious Persecution

There is no evidence that the Babylonians made any attempt to persecute the Jewish exiles because of their religion but there is also no reference in the book of Daniel to any attempt to persecute the Jewish exiles because of their religion. In Daniel 1 the exiles are never in danger, only the prince of the eunuchs feels threatened (Dan. 1:10) and he does not resist the trial of their chosen diet. In Daniel 6 the plot against Daniel is motivated by jealousy of his position; for the other satraps his religious practice is only a means of entrapment (Dan. 6:5). Darius is actually favorably disposed towards Daniel and immediately regrets his brash decree (Dan. 6:14). In Daniel 3 the threat of the fiery furnace is made against all gathered officials, not just Hananiah, Mishael and Azariah (Dan. 3:3-6). At no point in the book does a king or official launch an attack against the Jewish religion.

Though there is no evidence of anti-Jewish persecution during the Babylonian exile, there is strong reason to suppose that the Jewish community felt threatened, particularly with regard to their faith. Smith-Christopher gives the following sociological analysis: 'It is clear that the exilic, and particularly post-exilic community, reveals the typical behavior patterns of a minority community that has closed ranks tightly to maintain identity and faith.'[32]

---

[30] Baldwin, *Daniel*, 28.
[31] Millard, 'Daniel 1-6', 70.
[32] Smith-Christopher, 'Babylonian Exile', 35.

He bases this conclusion upon the prophetic polemics against idolatry, which are only pertinent if there is a perceived danger of syncretism and assimilation with the Gentile religions. Historical texts demonstrate that such assimilation actually took place as they record that Jews adopted Babylonian names. For instance, a sixth century seal, published by N. Avigad, bears the impression 'belonging to Yehoyishama, daughter of Sawas-sar-usur'.[33] The names Sheshbazzar and Zerubbabel, mentioned in the book of Ezra, are also a sign of Babylonian influence.[34]

The book of Daniel also reflects the pressure on the exiles to assimilate into Babylonian culture, though Daniel and his friends never succumb to these pressures. In Daniel 1 they are expected to eat the rations appointed for the other eunuchs but have to refuse because these rations are inconsistent with their religion. In Daniel 3 they are expected to bow before the golden statue like the other officials but refuse because their religion will not allow any syncretism with the Babylonian religions.

While it is likely that some Jewish exiles did adopt Babylonian cultural and religious practices, it is not clear to what extent they were pressured to do so by the Babylonians. Davies, presumably in reference to Daniel 3, has asserted: 'There is no evidence of successive attempts by any of the kings mentioned in the stories of Daniel to enforce observance of a particular cult.'[35]

To be correct, the book of Daniel does not refer to 'successive attempts' to enforce any form of worship. The incident in Daniel 3 reads as a unique event and, given that only officials were present, a political event.[36] Wiseman notes several examples of images being used as symbols of political authority, on which a subject might have to swear an oath of loyalty.[37] We are not told in Daniel 3 who was represented by the golden image, whether Nebuchadnezzar himself or a god, such as Marduk patron-god of Babylon, yet in either case the image would have been a symbol of Nebuchadnezzar's authority. Marduk was connected with Nebuchadnezzar's dynasty. Nebuchadnezzar was instrumental in bringing Marduk and his son Nabu into prominence in Babylonia, undertaking the restoration of temples and cults throughout the region. In the Neo-Babylonian period Marduk became chief god in the Babylonian pantheon and his temple and ziggurat the centre of the universe.[38] Whoever was represented,

---

[33] N. Avigad, 'Seals of Exiles', *Israel Exploration Journal* 15:4.
[34] Purvis & Meyers, 'Exile and Return'; Wiseman, *Nebuchadnezzar*, 81.
[35] Davies, *Daniel*, 31.
[36] Shea has suggested that the incident in Daniel 3 is an attempt by Nebuchadnezzar to reaffirm the loyalty of his officials after a revolt which occurred in his tenth year (Shea, 'Daniel 3').
[37] Wiseman, *Nebuchadnezzar*, 110. Wiseman's own thesis is that the image represented Nebuchadnezzar himself.
[38] See J.A. Black, A. Green & T. Rickard, *Gods, Demons and Symbols in Ancient Mesopotamia* (University of Texas Press, 1992), 128-29; G. Leick, *A Dictionary of An-*

obeisance to the image would have had political connotations and to refuse to bow would have been interpreted as an act of defiance to Nebuchadnezzar's authority.

Punishment

Though Babylon is famed for the laws of Hammurabi, the punishments of the Babylonian kings were often cruel. Executions, even for minor offences, were not unusual and the kings of the ancient near east were often inventive regarding their methods.[39] The book of Daniel records two seemingly unusual punishments, though neither is particularly improbable.

Jeremiah writes that Zedekiah and Ahab were 'roasted in the fire' by the king of Babylon (Jer. 29:22). There are other stories in other ancient texts of individuals being burnt alive.[40] An eighteenth century BC letter from Rim-Sin, king of Larsa, may record a case of the furnace being used as a judicious punishment.[41]

There is no evidence that this was a common punishment for malefactors – it is, after all, rather inefficient – but Daniel 3 implies that this was a special penalty for a special occasion. It is usually noted that there would have been massive kilns around Babylon to complete the substantial construction work conducted by Nebuchadnezzar;[42] it is certainly plausible that one of these was pressed into service as special 'inducement' to bow before the image.

The use of lions as a method of execution is unknown in texts from this period – it certainly was not a regular form of punishment. This being said, we know that the kings kept lions and so it is probable that king Darius would have had animals available to use for this purpose. Van der Toorn has pointed out that these lions were kept in specially made 'zoological gardens'; pits were used to catch lions, not to house them.[43] This observation, though valid, disregards the practicalities of using lions for execution. It is hardly likely that the king would have allowed condemned criminals to run around his personal gardens – if lions were ever used for executions then it is probably that an enclosed space, such as a pit, would have been used to contain them.

---

cient Near Eastern Mythology (Routledge, 1991), 116; S.I. Johnston, *Religions of the Ancient World: A Guide* (Harvard University Press, 2004), 171.

[39] Miller, *Daniel*, 181.

[40] 2 Macc 13:4-8; Ctesias, *Persae*, 48, 51, 58; van der Toorn, 'Mesopotamian Background', 41; Collins notes a story about a Persian sage named 'Sijawusch', 'who was vindicated through an ordeal by fire' (J.J. Collins, *Daniel: with an Introduction to Apocalyptic Literature* (Eerdmans, 1984), 57).

[41] J.B. Alexander, 'Critical Notes: New Light on the Fiery Furnace', *JBL* 69.4 (1950), 375-76. The Aramaic *'attûnâ* ('furnace') in Dan. 3 is equivalent to the Akkadian *utûnum* ('furnace') in the letter of Rim-Sin. Alexander suggests that the former is either a loan-word or shares a root with the latter.

[42] Wiseman, *Nebuchadnezzar*, 112.

[43] Van der Toorn, 'Mesopotamian Background', 50-51.

It is interesting to note van der Toorn's explanation of the source of the tradition of the lion's den. She proposes that this tradition is based upon a metaphor used in an ancient text, *Ludlul bēl nēmeqi*, in which a courtier describes his experiences at the hands of adversaries as like being in a pit of lions.[44] Her assumption is that somehow the second-century author of the book of Daniel knew of this text and composed the story of the lion's den based upon his misunderstanding of the metaphor. Whether or not a second-century Jew would have had access to such a text is debatable but the more significant issue is the source of the metaphor. Figurative language is generally born out of real (and usually well-known) occurrences; would we talk figuratively of a 'trial by fire' if no one had ever been physically tortured in this way? We cannot say whether the author of *Ludlul* was acquainted with a penal use of a pit of lions but it is likely that he was aware of some circumstance when a man had died in this way.

Summary

The stories recorded in the book of Daniel characterize well the period of the Babylonian exile. While the majority of the captives probably faced hardship, a very different fate awaited a chosen few as Daniel 1 describes. The career of Daniel and his friends parallels the careers of scholars in the ancient near east. Contrary to some commentaries, the book does not describe a period of intense persecution against the Jewish religion but rightly highlights the pressures of syncretism with Babylonian religion and customs.

It is not enough for skeptics to state (correctly) that consumption by lions does not feature in any extant Babylonian or Persian penal code; this is not evidence that it did not occur. Since we know that the kings of the near east kept lions, the burden of proof is upon the skeptic to prove conclusively that it is inconceivable that a despot should, upon a whim, use such a punishment. Nor, in the absence of any contemporary usage in cuneiform, can the term 'Chaldean' be explained as an anachronism, especially given the probability that the author's knowledge of the term comes from the earlier form.

In sum, the narrative chapters of the book of Daniel are consistent with the milieu in which they are set. This increases the likelihood that the author was familiar with this environment.

---

[44] Van der Toorn, 'Mesopotamian Background', 43, 50-52.

Chapter 5

The Insanity of Nebuchadnezzar

One of the objections to the historicity of the book of Daniel made by its critics is the account of the insanity of Nebuchadnezzar.[1] The event is not recorded in any extant cuneiform text and there is speculation amongst critical scholars that the biblical narrative may, in fact, be based upon a story about Nabonidus.

In response, conservative scholars have pointed out that our knowledge of the reign of Nebuchadnezzar is not expansive. For instance, the Babylonian Chronicle for the reign of Nebuchadnezzar is damaged and only records the first eleven of his forty-three years. It is also questionable whether such an event would have been recorded at all; which chronicler would be brave enough to record the humiliation of the despot?[2]

While the historical record remained silent the speculations of either viewpoint might be considered of equal merit. However, there are several texts that shed light upon this question and should be given critical examination.

4QPrayer of Nabonidus ar (=4Q242)[3]

frags. 1-3

Words of the prayer which Nabonidus, king of the la[nd of Babylon,[4] [a great] king, prayed [when he was afflicted]

by a malignant inflammation,[5] by decree of the G[od Most] High, in Teiman. [I, Nabonidus] was afflicted [by a malignant inflammation]

for seven years, and was banished far [from men,[6] until I prayed to the God Most High]

---

[1] Driver, *Introduction*, 500.
[2] Baldwin, *Daniel*, 108.
[3] A useful review of critical scholarship on the Prayer of Nabonidus is provided by P.W. Flint, 'The Daniel Traditions of Qumran' in *The Book of Daniel: Composition and Reception* (ed. J.J. Collins & P.W. Flint; Leiden: Brill, 2001), 329-67.
[4] Milik: 'king of [Assyria and of Ba]bylon'; Cross: 'king of [Ba]bylon'; Collins: 'King Nabonidus of [Baby]lon'.
[5] Milik: 'malignant disease'; Vermes: 'evil ulcer'; Cross: 'evil disease'; Collins: 'serious skin disease'.

and an exorcist[7] forgave my sin. He was a Je[w] from [the exiles, who said to me:]

Make a proclamation in writing, so that glory, exal[tation and honour] be given to the name of G[od Most High. And I wrote as follows: When]

[I was afflicted by a malign[nant] inflammation, [and remained] in Teiman, [by decree of God Most High, I]

prayed for seven years [to all] the gods of silver and gold, [of bronze and iron],

of wood, of stone and of clay, because [I thought] that they were gods […]

frag. 4

[…] … I had a dream[8]

[…] has gone far off, the peace of[9] [...]

[…] my friends. I could not […]

[…] as you were like […]

translated by F.G. Martínez (variant translations noted) [10]

Prior to the discovery of the Prayer of Nabonidus text at Qumran it was proposed by some commentators that Nabonidus was the original subject of the Daniel 4 narrative. The discovery of 4QPrNab has been seen as vindication of this thesis. This proposition was made upon the dubious premise that the period of the king's incapacity could more easily be reconciled with the reign of Nabonidus, who was absent from Babylon for ten years, than the reign of Nebuchadnezzar. The Babylonian accounts of Nabonidus' reign, particularly the *Verse Account* and the Harran Inscription, preclude the idea that Nabonidus was absent from Babylon due to illness or insanity indicating, rather, that he removed to Tema of his own volition. The widely held view is that Nabonidus'

---

6   Milik: 'and became unlike [men]'; Vermes: 'I was afflicted [with an evil ulcer]'; Eshel: 'sin[ce G]od set his face on me]'; Cross: 'and from [that] I was like [unto a beast]'; Collins: 'and wh[en] G[od turned his face to me'.
7   Milik: 'magician'; Eshel, Cross: 'diviner'.
8   Collins: 'you gave me a dream'.
9   Collins: 'the peace of [my] restfulness [he took from me]'.
10 The words in square brackets are hypothesized reconstructions where the text is damaged. F.G. Martínez, *The Dead Sea Scrolls Translated: The Qumran Texts in English* (Leiden: Brill, 1994), 289; J.T. Milik, *Ten Years of Discovery in the Wilderness of Judea*, 36-37; G. Vermes (trans.), *The Complete Dead Sea Scrolls in English* (London: Penguin Books, 2004), 614; E. Eshel, 'Possible Sources of Daniel' in Collins & Wright, *Composition and Reception*, 388; F.M. Cross, 'Fragments of the Prayer of Nabonidus', *IEJ* 34 (1984) 260-64; J.J. Collins, '4QPrayer of Nabonidus ar' in *Qumran Cave 4. XVII: Parabiblical Texts, Parts 3* (ed. J.C. Vanderkam; DJD XXII; Oxford: Clarendon Press, 1996).

devotion to the moon-god Sin brought him into conflict with the priests of Marduk and for this reason that he removed to Tema. Some historians have thrown doubt upon this conclusion and suggested that Nabonidus sought to establish a second capital at Tema to gain economic advantage from the Arabian trade routes. The story of Nabonidus' illness, as preserved in 4QPrNab, is likely to be late origin, even spelling his name erroneously.[11]

The extant form of Daniel 4 shows little vestige of Nabonidus; there is not even reference to things intimately connected to Nabonidus, like Tema and the god Sin. Rather the narrative as we have it reflects far better the character of Nebuchadnezzar, particularly his boast, 'Is not this great Babylon, which I have built . . .?' which would be a remarkable reminiscence for a second-century author. Taken on its own merits, the proposition that Nabonidus was the original subject of the Daniel 4 narrative has little to recommend it.

There are several parallels between 4QPrNab and Daniel 4 which indicate some relation, namely, (a) a king is struck with an illness, (b) by decree of God, (c) for a period of seven times/years and (d) later recovers. Also, the key theme of both texts is the recognition of the supremacy of the Jewish God by a heathen king, though in 4QPrNab this is in response to the king's idolatry whereas in Daniel 4 it is the problem of the king's pride. However, there are also some substantial differences between the texts leading some scholars to suggest that they are independent lines of tradition.[12] Apart from the name and location of the king, the differences include:

- the nature of the king's affliction – Nebuchadnezzar appears to have been afflicted by some form of mental illness, whereas Nabonidus has a 'malignant inflammation', probably a skin disease.
- the means of revival – Nebuchadnezzar is restored at the end of the period decreed. Nabonidus appears to have been required to write some form of confession or testimony to bring about his cure.
- the function of the Jewish exile in the narrative – Daniel interprets Nebuchadnezzar's dream and warns him to repent of his pride. The Jewish 'exorcist' in 4QPrNab seems to have either healed Nabonidus directly or acted as mediator, receiving his confession and forgiving his sin.

Cross attempted to strengthen the parallels between the two texts reconstructing line 3 as 'and from [that] I was like [unto a beast]'. However this reconstruction has been generally rejected by commentators.[13] Perhaps the most obvious paral-

---

[11] The Qumran text spells Nabonidus נבני *nbny* as opposed to the expected spelling נבנד *nbnd*.

[12] Baldwin, *Daniel*, 118; D.N. Freedman, 'The Prayer of Nabonidus', BASOR 145 (1957), 31f.

[13] For example, '4QPrNab has no place for the transformation of the king into a beast, and there is no mention of a beast in the extant fragments' (Flint, 'Daniel Traditions of Qumran', 336).

lel – 'seven years' – is also the most insignificant given that 'seven' is stock-symbolism in Jewish texts.

The parallels between 4QPrNab and Daniel 4 make some form of dependence likely, despite the differences. Though 4QPrNab (c.75-50 BC) is of later date than the earliest extant manuscript of Daniel (c.125 BC), the majority of scholars suppose the Nabonidus-form is the earlier form of the story. The priority of the Nabonidus-form is based on three observations: 1) the Jewish exorcist is unnamed, 2) the text is a standalone rather than part of a collection, and 3) Nabonidus was less well-known than Nebuchadnezzar. None of these observations carry much weight since 1) a large part of the text is missing so the absence of the name is of questionable significance, 2) there are several standalone texts from Qumran based upon larger works and 3) Nabonidus was known to Berossus, Ptolemy and Josephus; the idea that Nabonidus was unknown to Jewish tradition is a shaky assumption. Since the case for the priority of 4QPrNab is not substantial, we should consider the possibility that 4QPrNab is based on Daniel 4.

Steinmann has argued persuasively that the dependence of 4QPrNab upon the book of Daniel can be demonstrated on literary grounds.[14] Steinmann identifies several words and phrases that seem to be based Daniel 4 and other chapters (implying that the author of 4QPrNab was aware of the whole book, not just Daniel 4). These phrases included 'diviner' (cf. 2:27; 4:4; 5:7, 11), 'Judean' (cf. 3:8, 12), and 'honor and exalt[ation and glory]' (cf. 4:33; 5:18).[15] He also argues that several phrases in 4QPrNab are more likely to be later than their parallel in Daniel 4, for instance he proposes 'by a decree of God' (line 2) is a 'theological hypercorrection' of 'the decree of the Watchers' (4:14) to remove any appearance of polytheism.[16] Since 'times' in Daniel 4 is ambiguous as to its length, 'seven years' (lines 3 & 5) is better understood as an interpretation of 'seven times', than *vice versa*. Perhaps the most significant phrase is 'gods of silver and gold, [of bronze and iron], of wood, of stone and of clay' (lines 7-8), which does not occur in Daniel 4 but occurs in Daniel 5:4, 24. Steinmann writes: 'a striking feature of this formula is that in ancient Jewish writings in Aramaic or Hebrew up to the Herodian period this formula occurs in no other texts of which I am aware'.[17]

Given these indications of literary dependence upon the book of Daniel, 4QPrNab should be categorized as one of the para-Danielic writings. Steinmann proposes that 4QPrNab was composed as part of a supplementation pro-

---

[14] A. Steinmann, 'The Chicken and the Egg: A New Proposal for the Relationship between the "Prayer of Nabonidus" and the "Book of Daniel"', *Revue de Qumran* 20:4 (December 2002), 557-70.

[15] Steinmann, 'Chicken and Egg', 563-67.

[16] Steinmann, 'Chicken and Egg', 563.

[17] Steinmann, 'Chicken and Egg', 566. Steinmann proposes that the addition of 'clay' is based upon Daniel 2 and the desire to show God's supremacy over all the elements of Nebuchadnezzar's dream-image.

cess that occurred during the second and first centuries BC, as witnessed by additions to the book of Daniel found in the Greek versions.[18] Since 4QPrNab does not name the Jew as Daniel, it may be better explained as part of a wider supplementation of the OT. The books of Daniel, Esther and Nehemiah include several court tales about various Babylonian and Persian kings. It is conceivable that a Jewish writer might have sought to supplement this material with other court tales for other heathen kings.

The Legend of Megasthenes (Eusebius, *Praeparatio Evangelica* IX.41)

I found also the following statements concerning Nebuchadnezzar in the work of Abydenus, *Concerning the Assyrians:*

'Now Megasthenes says that Nebuchadnezzar was braver than Hercules, and made an expedition against Libya and Iberia, and, having subdued them, settled a part of their inhabitants on the right shore of Pontus. And afterwards, the Chaldeans say, he went up to his palace, and being possessed by some god or other uttered the following speech:

'"O men of Babylon, I Nebuchadnezzar here foretell to you the coming calamity, which neither Bel my ancestor, nor Queen Belet are able to persuade the Fates to avert. There will come a Persian mule, aided by the alliance of your own deities, and will bring you into slavery. And the joint author of this will be a Mede, in whom the Assyrians glory. O would that before he gave up my citizens some Charybdis or sea might swallow him up utterly out of sight; or that, turning in other directions, he might be carried across the desert, where there are neither cities nor foot of man, but where wild beasts have pasture and birds their haunts, that he might wander alone among rocks and ravines; and that, before he took such thoughts into his mind, I myself had found a better end."

He after uttering this prediction had immediately disappeared, and his son Amel-Marduk became king.'

translated by E.H. Gifford (adapted)[19]

The (so-called) *Legend of Megasthenes* has been widely quoted by conservative scholars as corroboration of biblical account of Nebuchadnezzar's madness, though almost all acknowledge its limitations as evidence.[20] The historian Megasthenes (c third century BC) was not a contemporary witness and his ac-

---

[18] Steinmann, 'Chicken and Egg', 562-63.

[19] E.H. Gifford (trans.), *Eusebius of Caesarea: Praeparatio Evangelica (Preparation for the Gospel)* vol.3 (1903), 456.

[20] C.H.H. Wright, *Daniel and his Prophecies* (London: Williams & Norgate, 1906; repr., Kessinger), 118-21; C. Boutflower, *In and Around the Book of Daniel* (London: SPCK, 1923; repr., Grand Rapids: Kregel, 1977), 105-13; Young, *Daniel*, 110-11; Baldwin, *Daniel*, 108-109.

count is preserved through Abydenus (c. second century BC) through Eusebius of Caesarea (c. 265-339 AD).

On the other hand, the extant form of the *Legend* shows no sign of literary dependence on the biblical text (or *vice versa*)[21] and there is no indication that Eusebius has been free in his quotation of the text. Thus, despite the nature of the textual transmission, at the core of the *Legend* we have preserved an independent tradition which bears some similarity to the narrative of Daniel 4.

Henze identifies four key parallels, or 'reverberations', with Daniel 4:[22]

- Nebuchadnezzar receives the divine message upon the roof of his palace (cf. 4:28-32)
- the emphasis upon Nebuchadnezzar's power (cf. 4:30)
- the divine origin of the decree (cf. 4:31)
- the condemnation on a king to wander amongst the rocks and ravines with the wild beasts and birds (cf. 32-33)

Despite these similarities, the two texts are substantially different in both detail and purpose. The focus of the *Legend* is upon Nebuchadnezzar's prediction of the conquest of Babylon by the Medes and Persians; the concept of a king's banishment amongst the animals is subsidiary. Also, in the *Legend* Nebuchadnezzar is not afflicted by madness, but rather he desires that the 'Mede' would be carried away to live amongst the beasts.

In the text, the 'Persian mule' refers to Cyrus, who conquered Babylon, but the identity of the 'Mede, in whom the Assyrians glory' is not so clear. He is usually identified with Nabonidus, on the basis that his mother, Adad-Guppi, may have had Median ancestry.[23] It is conceivable that the usurper Nabonidus should be characterized as the co-author of Babylon's downfall by those who regarded Nebuchadnezzar as archetypal king. On the other hand, the 'Mede' may be one of Cyrus' generals, for instance Ugbaru who led the Persian army into Babylon. (It is interesting to note that Xenophon depicts Ugbaru (=Gobyras) as an 'Assyrian' (=Babylonian) turncoat).[24] The reference to the Babylonian deities aiding the 'Persian mule' is reminiscent of Cyrus' own propaganda (e.g. *Cyrus Cylinder*), which asserts that Marduk commanded Cyrus to 'liberate' Babylon from Nabonidus.

The 'prophecy' of Nebuchadnezzar may be regarded as a form of lament for the Neo-Babylonian Empire placed in the mouth of its greatest king. How

---

[21] Collins suggests the *Legend* as a 'possible non-biblical source' for Daniel 4 (Collins, *Daniel: with an Introduction to Apocalyptic*, 64).

[22] M. Henze, *The Madness of King Nebuchadnezzar: The Ancient Near Eastern Origins and Early History of Interpretation of Daniel 4* (Leiden: Brill, 1999), 43.

[23] Collins, *Daniel: with an Introduction to Apocalyptic*, 64. Adad-Guppi' was born in Harran, which was captured by the Medes upon the fall of the Assyrian empire. However Adad-Guppi' was born while the Assyrians still reigned over Harran.

[24] We will discuss the figure of Ugbaru in greater detail later, including his role in the fall of Babylon and the likelihood that he was a Median.

Megasthenes came by this story is unclear, but we may speculate that it was composed some time during the Persian period by a Babylonian dissatisfied with foreign rule. Assuming the polemical origins of the tradition then the historical reminiscences must be judged vague at best. Yet they cannot be considered worthless while there are parallels in an independent source (i.e. Dan. 4).

One intriguing element of the *Legend* is the way Nebuchadnezzar contrasts the fate of the 'Mede' with his own (e.g. 'and that, before he took such thoughts into his mind, I myself had found a better end'). If this contrast is intended then Nebuchadnezzar's stated desire for 'a better end' carries with it the implication that he suffered in a similar fate to that he wishes upon the 'Mede', which in turn may imply that Nebuchadnezzar himself was banished to dwell among the beasts. Such a reading is extremely tentative and cannot be pressed, except to allow the possibility that the imagery found in this narrative may derive from a historical tradition about Nebuchadnezzar.

Berossus (Josephus, *Contra Apion* I.20)

Nebuchadnezzar, after he had begun to build the forementioned wall, fell sick, and departed this life, when he had reigned forty-three years
translated by W. Whiston (adapted)[25]

Additional support is sometimes sought from Josephus, who also refers to Megasthenes.[26] Josephus alludes to Megasthenes' attempt to prove that Nebuchadezzar was superior to Hercules, which probably indicates that he was aware of the same text as Eusebius though he does not quote it. After mentioning the passage in Megasthenes, Josephus quotes the above lines from Berossus regarding the end of Nebuchadnezzar's reign. Baldwin cites the reference to the king's sickness as support of the account in Daniel,[27] though Berossus does not describe the nature of the illness except that it was terminal (contrary to Dan. 4). Josephus himself does not appear to cite either Megasthenes or Berossus as evidence for the madness of Nebuchadnezzar recorded in the book of Daniel.

The East India House Inscription (BM 129397; column VIII, lines 19-41)

Four years (?), the seat of my kingdom in the city . . . which . . . did not rejoice (my) heart. In all my dominions I did not build a high-place of power; the precious treasures of my kingdom I did not lay up. In Babylon, buildings for myself and the honor of my kingdom I did not lay out. In the worship of Merodach my lord, the joy of my heart (?), in Babylon, the city of his sovereignty and the seat of my empire, I did not sing his praises (?), and I did not furnish his altars (i.e. with victims), nor did I clear out the canals.

---

[25] W. Whiston (trans.), *The Works of Josephus: Complete and Unabridged* (Peabody: Hendrickson, 2004).
[26] Baldwin, *Daniel*, 108-109.
[27] Baldwin, *Daniel*, 109.

translation by H. Rawlinson[28]

In the mid-nineteenth century Sir Henry Rawlinson published a translation of the *East India House Inscription* (also known as the *Standard Inscription*), which included the passage quoted above. The main theme of the inscription is the architectural achievements of Nebuchadnezzar, while this passage seems to present us with a four year period of inactivity. The text offers no explanation for this abrupt cessation of construction. Reverend George Rawlinson saw the possible implications for the book of Daniel and, in his Bampton Lectures, proposed that the illness of Nebuchadnezzar provided the best available explanation for this inactivity.[29]

Many Christians enthusiastically welcomed Rawlinson's defense of the Scriptures; in *Bibliotheca Sacra* his Bampton Lectures were hailed as the beginning of a great movement of research that had already 'put to shame the anti-scriptural myth-makers of the generation which is now passing away'.[30] Rawlinson's explanation of the *Inscription* was quickly accepted and was repeated by many Bible commentators[31] and even printed in popular encyclopedias.[32] There were some critics of the proposition. P. Smith considered it 'very doubtful'[33] and S. Davidson called it 'far-fetched indeed',[34] though neither attempts an alternative explanation for the *Inscription.* Yet the popularity of Rawlinson's proposition was not to last and it was rarely repeated in the twentieth century except in a few apologetic works.[35]

---

[28] G. Rawlinson, *The Seven Great Monarchies* (vol. II); also, see G. Rawlinson, *History of Herodotus* (vol. II) (London: John Murray, 1858), 486-87; G. Rawlinson, *The Historical Evidences of the Truth of the Scriptural Records* (Boston: Gould & Lincoln, 1860), 352-53.

[29] 'The reader may judge for himself to what event in his life it is likely that the monarch alludes' (Rawlinson, *Historical Evidences*, 353); 'it really seemed to allude to the temporary insanity of the monarch' ('Colonel Rawlinson's Assyrian Discoveries', *The Edinburgh Christian Magazine* 7 (November 1865), 253.

[30] E.A. Park & S.H. Taylor (eds.), *Bibliotheca Sacra and Biblical Repository* (vol.17), (Andover: Warren F. Draper, 1860), 440.

[31] R. Jamieson & A.R. Fauset, *A Commentary, Critical and Explanatory, of the Old and New Testaments* (vol.1) (Glasgow: William Collins, 1863), 655; W. Smith (ed.), *A Dictionary of the Bible* (London: John Murray, 1863), 483; *Illustrations of Scriptural History from the Monuments of Egypt, Chaldee, Assyria and Babylonia* (London: Lothian, 1866), 42; J. Brown, *A Dictionary of the Bible* (Edinburgh: William Oliphant, 1866), 402.

[32] G. Ripley & C.A. Dana (eds.), *The New American Cyclopaedia: A Popular Dictionary of General Knowledge* (vol.12) (New York: D. Appleton, 1861), 157.

[33] P. Smith, *A History of the World from the Earliest Records to the Present Time* (vol.1) (New York: D. Appleton, 1865), 285.

[34] S. Davidson, *An Introduction to the Old Testament* (vol.3) (London: William & Norgate, 1863), 186.

[35] A.R. Short, *Modern Discovery and the Bible* London: Inter-Varsity Fellowship, (1942, repr., 1954), 193; Argubright, *The Search for Truth*, 62; also, see H.P. Mans-

The reassessment of Rawlinson's thesis was due to the publication of new translations of the *East India House Inscription*, by C.J. Ball[36] and R.F. Harper.[37] Rawlinson had admitted that some of the translation might be doubtful[38] and that much of the passage was 'extremely obscure'.[39] His explanation rested upon his translation of line 19 (*aš-šum ni-me-du šar-ri-ti-ia*) which he rendered as 'for four years the seat of my kingdom'. This translation seemed to differentiate the section from the rest of the inscription as an exception to the general theme. This implied that for a set period Nebuchadnezzar ceased his construction. On this basis Rawlinson interpreted the other negative clauses as descriptions of this inactive period.

The translations of Ball and Harper demonstrated that line 19 did not refer to a period of time and so the idea that this section refers to a period of inactivity should be rejected. Harper renders the section as follows:

> Because my heart did not love the abode of my royalty in another city, in no human habitation did I build a residence for my lordship. Property, insignia of royalty, I did not establish anywhere else. In Babylon a chamber for my dwelling-place, as befitted my royalty, was not to be found. Because the fear of Marduk, my lord, was in my heart, in Babylon, his treasure city, in order to enlarge my royal residence, his street I did not change, his shrine I did not impair, his canal I did not dam up[40]

The implication of Harper's translation is that these negative clauses do not indicate cessation of construction but the especial selection of Babylon for the construction of Nebuchadnezzar's royal residence.

BM 34113 (=SP 213)

[. . .] . . . [. . . . . .]

[Nebu]chadnezzar considered [. . . . . .]

His life appeared of no value to [him . . . . . .]

[H]e stood and [took] the good road to [. . .]

And (the) Babylon(ian) speaks bad counsel to Evil-Merodach [. . .]

Then he gives an entirely different order but [. . .]

---

field & G.E. Mansfield, *The Book of Daniel* (CE; Findon: Logos, 1992), 110; H.A. Whittaker, *Visions in Daniel*, (Wigan: Biblia, 1991), 6.

36 C.J. Ball, 'Inscriptions of Nebuchadnezzar II: 1. The India House Inscription', *PSBA* 10 (December 1887), 87-129.

37 R.F. Harper, *Assyrian and Babylonian Literature: Selected Translations* (New York: D. Appleton, 1901), 141.

38 Rawlinson, *Historical Evidences*, 353.

39 'Rawlinson's Assyrian Discoveries', 253.

40 Harper, *Assyrian and Babylonian Literature*, 141.

He does not heed the word from his lips, the cour[tier(s) . . .]

He changed but did not block [. . .]

Concerning the treasures of Esagil an Babylon and securing [their foundations]

The cult-centre of the great gods they/he considered . . . [. . .]

He does not show love to son and daughter [. . .]

. . . family and clan do not exist [. . .]

In his heart, towards everything that was abundant [. . .]

His attention was not directed towards promoting the welfare of Esagil [and Babylon]

with his ears alert he went into the Holy Gate [. . .]

He prays to the lords of lords, he raised [his hands (in supplication) (. . .)]

He weeps bitterly to Marduk,[41] the g[reat] gods [. . .]

His prayers go forth, to [. . . . . .]

translated by A. K. Grayson[42]

The lines above come from a small piece of tablet (6x8cm) of what was once a long historical epic. Though this fragment only mentions Nebuchadnezzar and Evil-Merodach, Grayson calculates, by comparison with other texts, that the original may have continued its account to the reign of Cyrus.[43]

The relationship between this cuneiform text and the account of Daniel 4 was first proposed by the archeologist Siegfried Horn, a few years after its publication.[44] The proposal has remained popular amongst Adventists.[45] It has not been entirely overlooked by wider scholarship. D.J. Wiseman also examines the parallels with the biblical account.[46]

Grayson comments on the difficulty of interpreting this fragment, stating he can do little more than describe its contents. Assuming that Evil-Merodach is the subject of these lines, he describes the main theme these lines as 'the im-

---

[41] Grayson supplies 'Marduk' for the word *ilišu* ('god'). Wiseman notes from other texts that 'the name of a specific deity is not needed in confession' (Wiseman, *Nebuchadrezzer*, 102n).

[42] A.K. Grayson, *Babylonian Historical-Literary Texts* (Toronto: University of Toronto Press, 1975), 88-91.

[43] Grayson, *Babylonian Historical-Literary Texts*, 87.

[44] S.H. Horn, 'New Light on Nebuchadnezzar's Madness', *Ministry* (April 1978), 38-40.

[45] K.K. Down, *Daniel: Hostage in Babylon* (Grantham: Stanborough, 1991), 30-31; U. Unruh, *The Great Tree and Nebuchadnezzar's Insanity* [cited May 2008]. Online: http://dedication.www3.50megs.com/dan/daniel_4.html.

[46] Wiseman, *Nebuchadnezzar*, 102-103.

proper behaviour of Evil-Merodach, particularly with regard to Esagil, followed by a sudden and unexplained change of heart and prayers of Marduk'.[47] This may be consistent with Berossus' statement that Evil-Merodach 'governed public affairs in an illegal and improper manner', a fact that led to his downfall.[48] Against this interpretation it may be noted that there is no record that Evil-Merodach had a son or daughter, and Berossus makes no mention of his repentance prior to his assassination.[49] Given that lines 2-3 refer to Nebuchadnezzar, it is possible that he is the subject and that Evil-Merodach is an incidental character in this section.

Horn proposed that the text refers to Nebuchadnezzar during a period when he exhibited particularly strange behaviour, including the neglect of his children (lines 11), of the temple of Marduk (line 14) and even of his own life (line 2). Horn proposes that sense can be made of this behavior if it is understood in the light of Daniel 4.[50] Wiseman also notes the parallels between the text and Daniel 4, drawing attention to the end of the text which may mirror the contrition of Nebuchadnezzar after his restoration.[51] The role of Evil-Merodach in the text, though unclear, may also be explicable in the light of Daniel 4. The biblical narrative notes that after his restoration, Nebuchadnezzar's officials sought him and reinstated him as king (4:36). Therefore, Horn proposed that the 'counsel' (line 5) was that of the king's officials who advised Evil-Merodach to assume the throne; this counsel may have been considered 'bad' given the king's recovery.[52] Wiseman notes a later tradition recorded by Jerome that the king's officials refused to make Amel-Marduk king for fear of Nebuchadnezzar's restoration.[53]

It is unfortunate that so little of the text has survived; as Grayson notes, there is not sufficient material for a confident interpretation. As such, the text has limited application as confirmation of the biblical account. Even if we could be sure that Nebuchadnezzar was the subject of these lines, there are not sufficient parallels to sugggest that the account of Daniel 4 is the only explanation. At most, BM 34113 would show that there was a period during Nebuchadnezzar's reign when he acted in a way contrary to his usual behavior – the explanation for this is left a mystery. On the other hand, if we allow that Daniel 4 may be, at very least, rooted in some historical tradition then we have in that account the only explanation available for Nebuchadnezzar's behavior.

---

[47] Grayson, *Babylonian Historical-Literary Texts*, 87.
[48] Josephus, *Contra Apion*, I.20.
[49] Wiseman, *Nebuchadnezzar*, 102.
[50] Horn, 'Nebuchadnezzar's Madness', 40.
[51] Wiseman, *Nebuchadnezzar*, 103.
[52] Horn, 'Nebuchadnezzar's Madness', 40.
[53] Wiseman, *Nebuchadnezzar*, 102.

Summary

At present, the historicity of Daniel 4 still hangs in the balance. On the one hand, we still lack any definitive confirmation from any source, cuneiform or otherwise, for the insanity of Nebuchadnezzar. On the other, we do not have sufficient information about Nebuchadnezzar's reign to rule out such an illness. The evidence we do have is intriguing and tantalizing but not conclusive. BM 34113 seems to record a period of inactivity during his reign that is otherwise inexplicable and the *Legend of Megasthenes* preserves a narrative tradition associated with Nebuchadnezzar that parallels Daniel 4 in some respects. If the historicity of Nebuchadnezzar's insanity is assumed then both phenomena become explicable. Yet we must allow that there may be others explanations.

This handful of evidence is admittedly meager, but contrasts favourably with the evidence for the illness of Nabonidus (for which there is none). The *Prayer of Nabonidus* should be understood as a product, rather than a source, of the Danielic narratives. Once this critical imposition is removed then the scales tip in favour of the book of Daniel.

Chapter 6

Belshazzar

The case of Belshazzar is often trumpeted by conservative commentators, and not without reason, as it is one instance (of many) where the Bible has turned out to be historical, contrary to the accusations of some of its critics.

With the rise of Bible criticism in the early nineteenth century the historicity of Belshazzar began to be called into question. The Canon of Ptolemy recorded the last king of Babylon as Nabonidus; the name 'Belshazzar' was unknown to the Greek historians and did not feature in any extant text other than *Baruch* (1:11) and Josephus, both of which were based upon the book of Daniel. While some conservative scholars endeavored to reconcile Belshazzar with known history, some critics dismissed the figure as entirely fictitious.[1]

In 1854 J.E. Taylor, a British vice-consul in southern Iraq, conducted some explorations of the ancient ruins at Tell Muquyyar on behalf of the British Museum. He began digging an ancient mud-brick tower. Unbeknown to Taylor this tower was the Temple of Sin, the moon god, and the site was the ancient city of Ur. Whilst digging, Taylor discovered several clay cylinders buried in the brickwork of the tower, each bearing a Babylonian inscription. Taylor passed these cylinders to a colleague in Baghdad, Sir Henry Rawlinson, who was able to read the cuneiform script and saw that each bore the name *Bēl-šarra-usur*.[2]

The significance of this discovery as validation of Daniel's record was quickly noted.[3] However, though the existence of Belshazzar was now beyond doubt, many critics objected that Belshazzar was not king of Babylon, only the king's son.[4] Once again, these objections proved to be premature.

In 1924 Sidney Smith published a previously unknown text, now known as the *Verse Account*, in which it was recorded that Nabonidus 'entrusted the kingship [*šarrutam*]' to his eldest son.[5] The discovery was received by con-

---

[1]   For example, F. Hitzig, *Das Buch Daniel* (Leipzig: Weidman, 1850), 75.
[2]   See A. Millard, *Discoveries from Bible Times* (Oxford: Lion, 1985; repr. 1997), 139-40; A.R. Millard, 'Daniel and Belshazzar in History', *BARev* 11 (May-June 1985), 73-79; Collins, *Daniel*, 32.
[3]   'Correspondence', JAOS 5 (1855-56), 269.
[4]   For example, Driver, *An Introduction to the Literature of the Old Testament*, 498-99; A. Farrer, *The Expositor's Bible* (1895), 54-55.
[5]   S. Smith, *Babylonian Historical Texts* (1924).

servative scholars as validation of Daniel's description of Belshazzar as 'king'.[6] It was these considerations that led R.P. Dougherty to publish his seminal work *Nabonidus and Belshazzar*,[7] in which he proposed that Belshazzar reigned as co-regent with Nabonidus while the latter resided in Tema. Dougherty drew attention to Belshazzar's promised reward to Daniel – 'you shall be third in the kingdom' – as evidence that the author of Daniel was aware of this co-regency.[8]

A few years after the publication of Dougherty's book, H.H. Rowley responded with an assault on the historicity of Daniel 5.[9] He presents five challenges to the chapter's historicity, the last of which we will consider elsewhere:

- Daniel 5 depicts Belshazzar as king – 'this must still be pronounced a grave historical error'.[10]
- The meaning of the phrase 'third ruler' is uncertain and may not mean that there would be two rulers above Daniel.[11]
- 'The book of Daniel represents Belshazzar as the son of Nebuchadnezzar.'[12]
- 'The circumstances of the death of Belshazzar, as we have them in book of Daniel, cannot be fitted into the events of the time, as we learn them from indisputable records.'[13]
- 'The book of Daniel represents Belshazzar as being succeeded by Darius the Mede.'[14]

More recent critical commentators have reiterated these objections, though added little.[15] There has, however, been much research added by conservative scholars that must be brought to bear upon this question.

King Belshazzar

Belshazzar the king made a great feast for a thousand of his lords, and drank wine in the presence of the thousand (Daniel 5:1).

---

[6] H.A. Thompson, 'British Museum Gossip', *The Testimony* 1:1 (Jan 1931), 20; 'Notes and News', *The Testimony* 1:11 (Nov 1931), 341.
[7] R.P. Dougherty, *Nabonidus and Belshazzar* (New Haven: Yale University Press, 1929).
[8] Dougherty, *Nabonidus*, 196.
[9] H.H. Rowley, 'The Historicity of the Fifth Chapter of Daniel', *JTS* 32 (1931), 12-31.
[10] Rowley, 'Historicity', 12.
[11] Rowley, 'Historicity', 18.
[12] Rowley, 'Historicity', 20.
[13] Rowley, 'Historicity', 26.
[14] Rowley, 'Historicity', 30.
[15] cf. L.L. Grabbe, 'The Belshazzar of Daniel and the Belshazzar of History', *AUSS* 26:1 (1988), 59-66; also, see Porteous, *Daniel*, 76-77; Collins, *Daniel*, 32-33.

Belshazzar is named 'king' (מלך *melek*) seventeen times in Daniel 5, and described as 'king of the Chaldeans' (5:30). Also, two visions of Daniel are dated to the first and third years of Belshazzar respectively (7:1, 8:1).

In Nabonidus' sixth year (550/549)[16] he removed to Tema in Arabia. The Harran Stele records that Nabonidus remained in Tema for ten years after which, on 25 October 540, he returned to Babylon, one year before the city fell to Cyrus. Before leaving for Tema, Nabonidus appointed his son to rule in his absence. The *Verse Account* reads:

> He entrusted the army [?] to his oldest son, his first born, the troops in the country he ordered under his command. He let everything go, entrusted the kingship [*šarrutam*] to him, and, himself, he started out for a long journey.

This situation is also confirmed by the *Nabonidus Chronicle*,[17] the entries of the seventh, ninth through to eleventh years[18] each commence with the statement:

> The king stayed in Tema; the crown prince, his officials and his army were in Akkad

Thus, whilst Nabonidus remained (in name) king of Babylon it was his son, Belshazzar, who ran the day-to-day affairs of state. Dougherty expands this evidence noting that Belshazzar is mentioned alongside his father in prayers, oaths and other documents – strong indicators of co-regency.[19]

Rowley concurs that the work of government was left to Belshazzar but objects that this would not justify the title 'king'. He notes Dougherty's admission that 'no cuneiform text applies the term *šarru* ["king"] to Belshazzar'[20] and adds that there is no evidence Belshazzar occupied the throne.[21] Many would argue that the term *šarrutam* in the *Verse Account*, as a derivative of *šarru*, is evidence that Belshazzar was king,[22] but Rowley judges that *šarrutam* is 'merely a poetic expression' which cannot be pressed in face of other evidence.[23]

There are two factors, noted by Rowley, which mean that Belshazzar could not have been *šarru* during the ten years sojourn of Nabonidus. Firstly, official documents from this period are not dated by the regnal years of Belshazzar, either as king or co-regent, but are dated exclusively by the regnal years of Nabonidus. However, some deeds were sworn in the names of Nabonidus and Belshazzar jointly. Millard writes: 'this formula, swearing by the king and his son, is unattested in any other reign in any documents yet uncovered. This sug-

---

16 G.F. Hasel, 'The First and Third Years of Belshazzar (Dan 7:1; 8:1)', *AUSS* 15 (1977), 153-68.
17 BM 35382; ANET 303-307.
18 The entries for the eighth, and twelfth through to fifteenth years are missing.
19 Dougherty, *Nabonidus*, 93-98.
20 Dougherty, *Nabonidus*, 136.
21 Rowley, 'Historicity', 12-15.
22 cf. Thompson, 'British Museum', 20.
23 Rowley, 'Historicity', 13.

gests that Belshazzar may have had a special status'.[24] Secondly, the *Nabonidus Chronicle* records that the New Year festival did not take place while Nabonidus was in Tema. The New Year festival could only be performed by the king.[25]

These two factors mean that Belshazzar could not have been called *šarru* in Babylonian texts from this period, and official documents could not have been dated to his reign. However, as Young rightly noted, the book of Daniel is not an official Babylonian document. He writes:

> [Daniel] was written for Jews, the people of God, who had to deal with the man who ruled in Babylon . . . The man whose royal word could affect the Jews was Belshazzar. The man in regal status who desecrated the vessels of the Lord's temple was Belshazzar. Very properly, therefore, he is called 'king' and 'king of Babylon'.[26]

In addition, it should be noted that the book of Daniel does not call Belshazzar *šarru* but *melek*, and the two terms are not directly synonymous. Millard's work on the bilingual inscription at Tell Fekheriyah[27] has demonstrated that *melek* has a larger semantic field. An individual referred to as 'governor' in the Assyrian section of the text is referred to as 'king' (*melek*) in the parallel Aramaic section. Millard explains:

> Each inscription was aimed at a different audience, the Assyrian version to the overlords, and the Aramaic version to the local people. What to the Assyrian-speaking overlords was the governor was to the local Aramaic-speaking population the equivalent of king[28]

From the perspective of a Jewish exile Belshazzar was *de facto* king. Further, Shea has proposed that a Jewish exile would have interpreted the situation in Jewish political terms, i.e. as co-regency. '[Judah] was an environment in which, as opposed to the realm where they were exiled, co-regency was practiced'.[29] The fact that the datelines in Daniel 7:1 and 8:1 refer solely to Belshazzar is entirely consistent with Jewish practice for dating co-regencies.[30]

Nabonidus returned to Babylon in 540 BC and performed the New Festival at the beginning of the following year. When Cyrus began his campaign against the Babylonian heartland in the month of Tašrîtu it seems that Nabonidus led

---

[24] Millard, 'Belshazzar', 76.
[25] Rowley, 'Historicity', 15.
[26] Young, *Daniel*, 118.
[27] A.R. Millard & P. Bordreuil, 'A Statue from Syria with Assyrian and Aramaic Inscriptions', *BA* 45 (1982), 135-41.
[28] Millard, 'Belshazzar', 77.
[29] W.H. Shea, 'Nabonidus, Belshazzar, and the Book of Daniel: An Update', *AUSS* 20:2 (Summer 1982), 136.
[30] For further information on co-regencies in Israel and Judah see Thiele, *Mysterious Numbers*.

the army against the invaders. The *Nabonidus Chronicle* records that the Babylonian army was defeated at Opis and, on the fifteenth day of Tašrîtu (12 October 539), Sippar 'was seized without battle'. Whether Nabonidus sought refuge at Sippar after the defeat at Opis is unclear; the *Chronicle* simply records: 'Nabonidus fled'. The following day (13 October) Ugbaru, governor of Gutium, entered Babylon at the head of the Persian army.

It has been proposed that Nabonidus demoted Belshazzar upon his return in 540 BC.[31] This is not unlikely if Nabonidus resumed his governmental responsibilities, though it is nowhere stated. In light of explicit ascription of royalty to Belshazzar in Daniel 5, Shea has put forward the thesis that Belshazzar proclaimed himself king.[32] If news of Nabonidus' defeat had reached Babylon prior to its fall then with his father missing-in-action it is possible that Belshazzar might have assumed the throne. Shea sees the banquet described in the opening verses of Daniel 5 as a celebration of Belshazzar's accession. This thesis cannot yet be evidenced and the reality may be somewhat simpler. It is likely that the defense of Babylon was committed to Belshazzar when Nabonidus led the army against Cyrus. It is even possible that Nabonidus appointed Belshazzar regent at this time. In any case, Belshazzar was the highest ranking official in Babylon at its fall and, again, an unofficial document like the book of Daniel could reasonably have described Belshazzar as 'king' (*melek*) for this reason.

The Third Ruler

> The king cried aloud to bring in the astrologers, the Chaldeans, and the soothsayers. The king spoke, saying to the wise men of Babylon, 'Whoever reads this writing, and tells me its interpretation, shall be clothed with purple and have a chain of gold around his neck; and he shall be the third [תלתי *talti*] ruler in the kingdom' (Daniel 5:7 [NKJV]).

The standard interpretation of the reward promised by Belshazzar is that since he was the second ruler in the kingdom the highest office he could offer Daniel was the third.[33] The meaning of the term *talti* is straightforward: it is an ordinal derived from the cardinal *talt* ('three').[34] Thus, the most natural reading of the text is that Belshazzar offers the third highest office in the kingdom. Grabbe proposes that 'the most natural interpretation of the promise' is that it is related the three presidents appointed by Darius the Mede (6:3); 'Daniel is one of three "presidents" (*sarkin*) who rule under the king. Thus, the promise of Belshazzar

---

[31] Collins, *Daniel*, 32.

[32] Shea, 'Belshazzar', 141-42.

[33] Dougherty, *Nabonidus*, 196; also, see Baldwin, *Daniel*, 22; Mansfield, *Daniel*, 120; W. Keller, *The Bible as History* (London: Hodder and Stoughton, 1956), 300.

[34] Examples of the cardinal in biblical Aramaic: Ezra 6:4, Daniel 3:23, 24; 6:2, 10, 6:13; 7:5, 8, 20, 24. For examples of the ordinal in other Aramaic texts see *The Comprehensive Aramaic Lexicon* (Online: http://cal1.cn.huc.edu/).

is fulfilled under his conqueror, Darius the Mede.[35] Collins states that such an interpretation arises from "a mistakenly literal understanding of the rank".[36] Though the terms 'third' and 'three' are (necessarily!) related that is the extent of the connection between these verses. The appointment by Darius (6:3) reads as a fresh appointment, rather than a honoring of Belshazzar's rash promise. Montgomery argued that the word *talti* in this context should be understood as a reference to the Akkadian word *šalšu*, a title of a high official.[37] This proposal has not been universally accepted but is considered as 'probable' by many commentators[38] and is cited by Rowley as evidence that the meaning of *talti* is uncertain.[39]

Shea has argued against Montgomery's proposal on several grounds, most significantly on linguistic grounds. He writes: 'in order to get from *talti* to *šalšu*, one has to postulate a phonetic shift which ordinarily would not be expected, since Daniel should have used the Akkadian loan word for "*šalšu*-officer" instead of the Aramaic word for "third"'.[40] In Aramaic *šalšu* should have been rendered *šalšā*. Grabbe suggests that *talti* might be a 'loan translation',[41] however, since by this time *šalšu* had lost its original numeric significance it is not clear why the author should translate it using a numeric term. Further, Shea argues that Montgomery requires *talti* to be in the absolute state, but in fact, in 5:16 and 5:29 it is in the emphatic state.[42] This makes it likely that *talti* should be read as a numeral rather than an official title.

Aside from the linguistic arguments, the interpretation 'the third highest ruler' is also more consistent with the context. The rank of *šalšu*-officer was a relatively lowly one – lower than the rank of *mašennim*, which included the cupbearer and the overseers of the slave girls. It does not seem probable that the wise men of Babylon would have considered an appointment as a *šalšu*-officer as a particularly significant reward. It is also questionable whether such a *šalšu*-officer would have been 'clothed with purple and have a chain of gold around his neck' (5:7). Also, if there is a parallel here with the appointment of Joseph to second in the kingdom by Pharaoh (Gen. 41:40) then the interpretation 'third in the kingdom' seems required.[43] The objection that Belshazzar would have needed Nabonidus' permission to appoint the third-highest official in the kingdom[44] is moot when the king's state of agitation is borne in mind; a terror-struck king may make brash promises without regard to proper procedure.

---

[35] Grabbe, 'Belshazzar', 65.
[36] Collins, *Daniel*, 247.
[37] Montgomery, *Daniel*, 256.
[38] Young, *Daniel*, 121; Porteous, *Daniel*, 79; Collins, *Daniel*, 247.
[39] Rowley, 'Historicity', 18.
[40] Shea, 'Belshazzar', 139.
[41] Grabbe, 'Belshazzar', 64.
[42] Shea, 'Belshazzar', 138.
[43] See Shea, 'Bel(te)shazzar meets Belshazzar', 70.
[44] Rowley, 'Historicity', 19; Grabbe, 'Belshazzar', 65.

The Son of Nebuchadnezzar

Belshazzar was the son of Nabonidus, not Nebuchadnezzar, yet Daniel 5 describes Nebuchadnezzar as the 'father' [אַב *'ab*] of Belshazzar (vv.2, 11, 13, 18) and Belshazzar as the 'son' [בַּר *bar*] of Nebuchadnezzar (v.22). The simplest reading of this text would make Belshazzar the literal son of Nebuchadnezzar[45] and, thus, the text could be shown to be inconsistent with history.

However, the terms *'ab* and *bar* – and their Hebrew equivalents אַב *'ab* and בֵּן *ben* – have a larger semantic field that extends beyond the father-son relationship; *'ab* may also mean 'grandfather',[46] and in a wider sense 'ancestor'; *bar* may also mean 'grandson',[47] and in a wider sense 'descendent'. In fact, Aramaic does not have a separate word for 'grandfather' or 'grandson'; whether the author understood Belshazzar as the son or grandson of Nebuchadnezzar, he would have used the same terminology.

Many conservative scholars have hypothesized that Belshazzar was grandson of Nebuchadnezzar through a daughter; most of these follow Dougherty in identifying her with the queen 'Nitocris' mentioned by Herodotus. Rowley objects that, while *'ab* may mean 'paternal grandfather', Dougherty produces no examples of *'ab* as 'maternal grandfather'.[48] The fact that in Genesis 28:2 the phrase אֲבִי אֵם *'ab 'em* ('mother's father') is used for this relationship may support this conclusion. However, since certain prominent women are named as matriarchs – e.g. 'sons of Leah' (Gen. 35:23); 'sons of Zeruiah' (II Sam. 2:18) – there is reason to suppose that *ben* (and *bar*) could also be used 'descendants' from the female line.

Some conservative commentaries now assert as historical fact the parentage of Belshazzar from Nebuchadnezzar through Nitocris.[49] Yet Babylonian texts do not record the names of the wives of Nebuchadnezzar, Nabonidus or Belshazzar, and only preserve the name of one daughter of Nebuchadnezzar, 'Kaššaya', so the validity of this thesis cannot yet be definitively proved either way. However this thesis has been influential beyond the field of Danielic studies and so it is worth commenting upon in detail.

Nebuchadnezzar was succeeded by his son Amēl-Marduk,[50] who reigned for two years until he was assassinated by Neriglissar,[51] his brother-in-law.[52] A

---

[45] So LXX, 'θ, Vulgate, Baruch 1:11.

[46] cf. Genesis 28:13, 31:42, 32:9, II Samuel 9:7, 16:13; also see *The Comprehensive Aramaic Lexicon*.

[47] cf. Genesis 29:5, II Samuel 9:9, 19:24, II Chronicles 22:9, Nehemiah 12:23; also, see *The Comprehensive Aramaic Lexicon*.

[48] Rowley, 'Historicity', 20-21.

[49] cf. Mansfield, *Daniel*, 121.

[50] Hebrew: 'Evil-Merodach' (cf. II Kings 25:27, Jeremiah 52:31).

[51] Probably the same as Nergal-sharezer one of the Babylonian officials present at the fall of Jerusalem (cf. Jeremiah 39:3, 13).

[52] Berossus records '[Amel-Marduk] fell a victim to a conspiracy which was formed against his life by Neriglissoorus, his sister's husband' (Josephus, *Contra Apion*

cuneiform tablet records that Neriglissar was married to Kaššaya, the daughter of Nebuchadnezzar, which probably gave some measure of legitimacy to Neriglissar's accession. He was succeeded by his son, Labashi-Marduk, who in turn fell victim to a conspiracy after only nine months of rule. One of the conspirators was Nabonidus (Nabû-na'id) and he ascended to the throne, according to Berossus, 'by common consent' of the conspirators.[53]

We now know much about Nabonidus, and his mother, from their joint inscription at Harran.[54] Nabonidus was the son of Nabû-balatsu-iqbi and Adad-Guppi'. Nabonidus was not the son of Nebuchadnezzar, nor a blood-relation of the royal house. He describes his own humble beginnings:

> I (am) Nabonidus, who have not the honour(?) of (being a) somebody, and kingship is not within me, (but) the gods and goddesses prayed for me, and Sin to kingship called me.[55]

Nabonidus was a high official in the Babylonian court. Adad-Guppi' records how she 'caused him to stand' before Nebuchadnezzar and Neriglissar.[56] She even goes so far to say: 'my name he made (to be) favourite in their sight, (and) like [a daughter of] their [own] they uplifted my head'.[57] Given this close relationship with the preceding kings, it is not inconceivable that Nabonidus should have married a daughter of Nebuchadnezzar, though this is nowhere stated. As with Neriglissar, such a marriage would have strengthened Nabonidus' claim to the throne. This being said, Belshazzar' mother is not named in any cuneiform text and Daniel 5 is our only positive evidence that she may have been the daughter of Nebuchadnezzar. And if Nabonidus married Belshazzar's future mother after claiming the throne to legitimize his ascendancy then this would mean that Belshazzar could only have been seventeen at the fall of Babylon. While not impossible, this is extremely unlikely that Nabonidus would have entrusted the kingship to Belshazzar in his sixth year, i.e. when Belshazzar would have been aged seven.

Often conservative scholars have identified Nitocris, the queen of Babylon whose exploits are recorded by Herodotus, as the mother of Belshazzar. However, Herodotus does not preserve the name 'Belshazzar' and so this identification will always remain speculative. Herodotus describes Nitocris' relationship to the kings of Babylon as follows:

1:20). Megasthenes records he 'was slain by his kinsman Neriglisares' (Eusebius, *Praep. Evan.*, 10).

[53] *Contra Apion*, 1:20.
[54] C.J. Gadd, 'The Harran Inscriptions of Nabonidus', *Anatolian Studies* 8 (1958), 35-92.
[55] *Harran Inscription* H2 A.I.7-11 (Gadd, 'Harran Inscriptions', 57).
[56] H1 B.II.46 (p. 51).
[57] H1 B.II.49-50 (p. 51).

The expedition of Cyrus was directed against her son, who, like his father, was called Labynetus and was king of Assyria.[58]

Now if Herodotus meant Labynetus II to be identified with Nabonidus then consequently Nitocris would be identified with Adad-Guppi'. However, Adad-Guppi' was not queen of Babylon and it is questionable whether she would have ever held enough authority to implement the building work Herodotus ascribes to her.[59] This allows for the possibility that Labynetus II was intended to be identified with Belshazzar, who was regent in Babylon at its fall; on this basis Nitocris is identified as the mother of Belshazzar.

Dougherty, rather tenuously, argues that the fact that Herodotus names both father and son Labynetus is positive evidence that Herodotus intended Labynetus II to be identified with Belshazzar. Firstly, he reasons that the dual-usage of the names betrays some remembrance that the two kings were coregents.[60] Secondly, he links this dual-usage with the statement of Josephus that Belshazzar was also named 'Nabonidus' (*Antiquities* XX.11.2) as confirmation that Belshazzar shared his father's name.[61] Neither argument carries much weight; the statement of Josephus was likely made for apologetic reasons rather than being based on historical tradition.[62]

More recently the historicity of Herodotus' account of Nitocris has come into question. She is described as a queen in her own right and this is difficult to reconcile with known history. Though the reigns of both Nebuchadnezzar and Nabonidus contain periods when a regent would be needed – Nebuchadnezzar incapacitated by madness, Nabonidus in self-imposed exile – in both these cases there was an able crown-prince who could fulfill that role. Also, though the building-work of Nitocris – fortifying the entrance and banks of the portion of the Euphrates that flowed through Babylon – is known to have occurred, it is often ascribed to one of the kings; Berossus describes similar work occurring during the reigns of both Nebuchadnezzar and Nabonidus:

> [Nebuchadnezzar] also rebuilt the old city, and added another to it on the outside, and so far completed Babylon, that none, who might besiege it afterwards, should have it in their power to divert the river, so as to facilitate an entrance into it (quoted in Josephus, *Contra Apion* I.19).

> It was in [Nabonidus'] reign that the walls of the city of Babylon which defend the banks of the river were curiously built with burnt brick and bitumen (quoted in Josephus, *Contra Apion* I.20).

---

[58] Herodotus, *Histories* I.188. The word 'Assyria' is a misnomer common amongst the Greek historians for Babylonia.

[59] *Histories* I.185-86.

[60] Dougherty, *Nabonidus*, 187.

[61] Dougherty, *Nabonidus*, 66, 190.

[62] Rowley, 'Historicity', 23.

Modern archeology has now confirmed that these water-defenses were the design of Nebuchadnezzar.[63] Given these difficulties, it is probable that the account of Nitocris is, at least in part, legendary. For example, Lewy has suggested that Herodotus' account is based upon the combination of Assyrian traditions about the wife of Shamshi-adad V and the wife of Sennacherib.[64] Even if Nitocris is identified as the mother of Belshazzar, there is no evidence that she was the daughter of Nebuchadnezzar. Since Nitocris is an Egyptian name, at least one apologist has proposed that Nebuchadnezzar may have married an Egyptian bride as part of a peace agreement between his kingdom and Egypt. It is proposed that Nitocris was the daughter of this union. Apart from the mildly interesting fact that Necho II's sister, the priestess, was named 'Nitocris', this proposition is entirely speculation. While the historicity of Nitocris is in doubt, it would be unwise to impose Nitocris as the 'missing-link' between Nebuchadnezzar and Belshazzar.

One further issue of consideration is that the terms *'ab* and *bar* are not restricted to familial relations. The term *'ab* may also be used as 'chief' or 'master', or as 'founder'; *bar* may be used as 'disciple' or 'follower'.[65] It was not unusual for these terms to be use in a dynastic sense even when there was no direct descent. On the Tel Dan stela Hazael, king of Damascus, refers to his predecessor as 'father', though he was a usurper (lines 3-4). Jehu, another usurper, is called 'son of Omri' on Shalmaneser's Black Obelisk, though he was not his father. Similar situations can be found in Assyrian records regarding Tiglath-pileser III and Sargon II.[66] On this basis, *'ab* and *bar* may be translated 'predecessor' and 'successor', respectively.[67] In the case of Daniel 5, it is the dynastic relationship, rather than the familial, that is of significance to the author. The comparison is drawn between Nebuchadnezzar, who grew to reverence God, and Belshazzar, who desecrates the holy articles from the Temple. The author is drawing attention to the moral decline in the Babylonian Empire, which he believes led to its destruction. For his purposes 'successor' and 'predecessor' are the most relevant relationships.

In summary, Daniel 5 may provide evidence that Belshazzar was the maternal grandson of Nebuchadnezzar. As there is no evidence to the contrary, the historicity of Daniel 5 cannot be rejected on this point. The assertion that Nitocris was the mother of Belshazzar is unwarranted and cannot be supported unless further evidence comes to light. In any case, the terms *'ab* and *bar* would not be illegitimate were Belshazzar and Nebuchadnezzar not related.

---

[63] Wiseman, *Nebuchadnezzar*, 57.

[64] H. Lewy, 'Nitokris-Naqi'a', JNES 11 (1952) 264-86.

[65] *Comprehensive Aramaic Lexicon*; also compare Hebrew usage.

[66] Baldwin, *Daniel*, 22n; Kitchen, *Old Testament*, 37, 74, 510n; also, see G.L. Archer, *A Survey of Old Testament Introduction* (Chicago: Moody, 1973), 382-83.

[67] cf. NLT, HCSB, ESVn.

The Death of Belshazzar

The book of Daniel implies that Belshazzar was slain the night of the fall of Babylon to the Medo-Persian army (5:30-31). Over the years there have been several objections to this account, none which carry much weight. For instance, Rowley argues that 'it is wholly unlikely that Belshazzar, who had been for years in command of "the army of Akkad", would have been anywhere but in the field in this critical campaign'.[68] But this judgment is based upon fairly shaky guesswork. It is wholly unlikely that Nabonidus would have left his capital undefended. Since we know that Nabonidus was with the army in the field then it is entirely plausible that he delegated the defense of Babylon to his son. Grabbe has argued that it is unlikely that Belshazzar would have been killed in contrast to the kind treatment of Nabonidus (recorded by Berossus).[69] This objection is equally speculative. Nabonidus was captured alive because he surrendered; Belshazzar may well have died fighting.

Aside from these objections, it must be admitted that there is little external testimony for the death of Belshazzar. The silence of Berossus on this point is insignificant given that his account of the fall of Babylon is only five words long.[70] On the other hand, the omission of any reference to the death of Belshazzar in the *Nabonidus Chronicle* should be given some weight. Grabbe writes:

> Unless there has been a grave and otherwise unattested scribal lapse at this point, we can only conclude that Belshazzar was not killed at the time of the taking of Babylon.[71]

This objection cannot simply be dismissed as an argument from silence.[72] As crown-prince, and *de facto* regent of Babylon at its fall, one might reasonably expect Belshazzar's death to be mentioned in the Chronicle; earlier the Chronicle devotes several lines to death and morning of Adad-Guppi'. However, it is worth noting that the section of the Chronicle regarding the fall of Babylon is likely to have been written by a different hand than the earlier sections – a scribe under the guidance of the new Persian administration. The actual circumstances of the fall of Babylon, including the capture of Nabonidus, are only briefly recounted. The other cuneiform records in the *Cyrus Cylinder* and the

---

[68] Rowley, 'Historicity', 30.
[69] Grabbe, 'Belshazzar', 62; 'Nabonnedus delivered himself into his [Cyrus'] hands without holding out the place: he was therefore kindly treated by Cyrus, who provided him with an establishment in Carmania, but sent him out of Babylonia. Nabonnedus accordingly spent the remainder of his life in that country, where he died' (*Contra Apion*, 1:20). The *Nabonidus Chronicle* records that Nabonidus was arrested in Babylon when he returned there.
[70] Contra. Grabbe, 'Belshazzar', 61; 'Upon this Cyrus took Babylon' (*Contra Apion*, 1:20).
[71] Grabbe, 'Belshazzar', 61.
[72] Contra Shea, 'Belshazzar', 67-68.

Belshazzar

Verse Account are equally brief on this point. These texts demonstrate that Cyrus desired to be seen as the saviour of Babylon and a bringer of peace. Mention of the crown-prince may well have been considered an irrelevance for this purpose and his violent death was the sort of awkward detail that Cyrus would have been anxious to gloss over.

As it stands, there is no compelling reason to judge as unhistorical the proposition that Belshazzar died on the night of the fall of Babylon. Though we cannot rule out the possibility that Belshazzar had died previously,[73] in the absence of other evidence some weight must be given to the testimony of the book of Daniel. However, the historical records are not completely silent. Xenophon, in his *Cyropaedia*, does record that a king was slain in Babylon at its fall. Though its historical reliability is weak, in the absence of contrary evidence its testimony still carries some weight.

The *Cyropaedia* is generally recognized to be a work of historical romance, rather than a straight history. Some commentators have speculated that it was written in reaction to Plato's *Republic*, in praise of the virtues of monarchy. Xenophon, thus, must be suspected of taking some considerable liberties with history for polemical reasons. On the other hand, we know that the *Cyropaedia* is based upon historical traditions and has preserved some facts confirmed by other records.

Xenophon's account of the Persian campaign against the Babylonians (whom he consistently calls 'Assyrians') is far more detailed than that of the *Nabonidus Chronicle*, and he seems to have imaginatively interpolated historical traditions with narrative details and many long monologues. In brief, he mentions two kings of the Babylonians. One, the father, is slain in battle.[74] After this, 'an old Assyrian prince', named Gobryas, changes sides and allies himself to Cyrus.[75] Gobryas refuses to serve the king's son, recounting how he had slain Gobryas' own son in a fit of rage.[76] Cyrus accepts the allegiance of Gobryas, who in turn leads a detachment of men in the invasion of Babylon. It is this detachment of men who storm the palace and, finding the king with drawn sword, slay him and all his retinue.[77]

This account has some historical validity. The figure of Gobryas is now identified with Ugbaru, governor of Gutium, who, according to the *Nabonidus Chronicle*, did indeed lead the Persian army into Babylon. While we know that Nabonidus was not slain in battle prior to the fall of Babylon, if the kings mentioned by Xenophon are (loosely) based upon historical traditions then the for-

---

[73] 'Our documented evidence for Belshazzar ceases after Nabonidus' 14th year, several years before the fall of Babylon. While we cannot know for certain, we must allow for the possibility that Belshazzar was already dead by the time of Nabonidus' last year' (Grabbe, 'Belshazzar', 61).
[74] Xenophon, *Cyropaedia*, IV.1.8.
[75] *Cyropaedia*, IV.6.1.
[76] *Cyropaedia*, IV.6.2, also V.2.28.
[77] *Cyropaedia*, VII.5.26-30.

mer king should be Nabonidus, and his son, Belshazzar. This may suggest that Xenophon knew of some tradition that Belshazzar died in Babylon on the night of its fall.

In summary, the little evidence we have supports the proposition that Belshazzar was slain when Babylon was captured by the Persian army (13 October 539). Until further evidence bearing on this matter is discovered, we cannot say more.

Summary

Since the nineteenth century critical scholars have been pressed into retreat on the issue of Belshazzar as more evidence and more research is brought to bear on the topic. Though some scholars today still repeat the objections of earlier critics, others dismiss the validity of these arguments. Comments on this issue by P.R. Davies are telling:

> It has been clear since 1924 (Montgomery, pp. 66-67) that although Nabonidus was the last king of the neo-Babylonian dynasty, Belshazzar was effectively ruling Babylon. In this respect, then, Daniel is correct. The literal meaning of 'son' should not be pressed; even if it might betray a misunderstanding on the part of Daniel, a strong case against Daniel's historical reliability is not enhanced by the inclusion of weak arguments such as this.[78]

The book of Daniel is shown to be reliable on the issue of Belshazzar and, in fact, superior to the Greek historians who seem to have scanty information about Belshazzar. The author is right to describe Belshazzar as 'king' (*melek*) and correctly understands his position as second in the kingdom. His description of the relationship between Belshazzar and Nebuchadnezzar is perhaps misleading in English translation, yet in Aramaic may preserve some clue to Belshazzar's maternal-ancestry. If the author is correct regarding the circumstances of Belshazzar's death – and at present there seems no reason to doubt it – then he preserves intimate knowledge of these events, which are not even recorded in any extant cuneiform text.

Whether or not readers accept the miraculous events recorded in Daniel 5, the author has shown himself a capable and informed narrator and his testimony is worthy of the attentions of historians.

---

[78] Davies, *Daniel*, 30-31.

Chapter 7

The Fall of Babylon

In 549 BC the Median army revolted against Astyages, their king, and delivered him to Cyrus, king of the small kingdom of Persia. After his ascendancy to the head of the Medo-Persian Empire, Cyrus began to expand his empire westward. He did not immediately invade the Babylonian heartland but rather pushed westward to Lydia (in modern-day Turkey), defeating its king, Croesus. In 539 Cyrus advanced on and captured Babylon, bringing an end to the Neo-Babylonian Empire.

There is some disparity in the historical sources as to the sequence of events leading to Babylon's fall. Cuneiform tablets, written shortly after, record that Babylon was taken 'without battle', Cyrus being welcomed by the native population as a liberator, rather than a conqueror. On the other hand, the later Greek historians, Herodotus and Xenophon, record that the Euphrates, which runs through the city, was diverted to allow the Persian army to enter Babylon along the riverbed and that the city was taken by force. There is also disagreement regarding the chronology of Cyrus' campaign, the *Nabonidus Chronicle* gives the impression that the entire campaign was over within a month while Herodotus records that Babylon was taken after a long siege.

The book of Daniel is relatively silent as to the events leading up to the fall of Babylon, instead presenting an episode from within the city on the eve of its fall (cf. Dan. 5). Traditionally many conservative commentators have allied themselves to the narrative of Herodotus[1] – a fact that has been received with scorn by certain critics.[2] However, the narrative of Daniel 5 does not actually require the validity of Herodotus' account nor is it intrinsically inconsistent with any of the scenarios described by either the cuneiform or Greek sources.

In this section we will devote some time to analysis of the source material in the light of recent research to establish a probable history of the fall of Babylon. We will then consider any points of contact with the Danielic narrative.

---

[1] Dougherty, *Nabonidus*, 179-82; Boutflower, *Daniel*, 121-32; G.H. Lang, *The Histories and Prophecies of Daniel* (London: Oliphants, 1942), 78; E. Green, *The Prophecy of Daniel* (Birmingham: The Christadelphian, 1988), 47; Mansfield, *Daniel*, 126.

[2] Rowley, 'Historicity', 12-31; Porteous, *Daniel*, 76-77.

The Defenses of Babylon

The city of Babylon had formidable defenses. Babylon was surrounded by a 6km double-wall with eight gates, which enclosed the entire city. This wall was 11-14m high and 6.5m wide with a moat.[3] The half of the city on the eastern bank, which contained the majority of the temples and palaces, was also protected by a wall along the riverbank.[4] The city was also able to endure a long siege as on the eastern bank a second wall ran for 8.3km enclosing a large agricultural area. This external wall was 7.6-7.8m high and 3.72m wide, also having a moat.[5]

In addition to these defenses Nebuchadnezzar had constructed two further defensive walls which spanned the distance between the Euphrates and the Tigris. One was located to the south, near Kish; the other was to the north running 150km between the cities of Opis and Sippar. This wall was known to the Greek historian Xenophon as the 'Median wall'.[6] This was an earth wall lined with 3ft of brick and coated with bitumen; in total it was 16ft wide.[7] The Median wall also served as a flood barrier, protecting the area from the flooding of the rivers. It could also be used to deliberately flood the plain to hinder the advance of an invading army.[8]

Sources

Babylonian Chronicle
The Babylonian Chronicle is a series of cuneiform tablets recording the period from the reign of Nabonassar down to the reign of Seleucus III, though much of the Chronicle is no longer extant. The tablet for Nabonidus' reign is often known as the *Nabonidus Chronicle*, though it extends to the first year of Cyrus. The Chronicle was not written contemporarily but draws upon more extensive primary sources (no longer extant).

The first mention of the Persian invasion is in a damaged line at the end of the sixteenth year.

> . . . Tigris. In the month of Addaru [February/March 539] the image of Ištar of Uruk [. . .] The army of the Persians made an attack

The meaning of this line is not clear. The mention of the Tigris may refer to the crossing of the river by the Persian army. It is not clear where the Persian attacked but it is likely to have been to the north-east of Babylon, close to the

---

[3] M.A. Dandamaev, *A Political History of the Achaemenid Empire* (Leiden: Brill, 1989), 45.
[4] G. Tolini, 'Quelques elements concernant la prise de Babylone par Cyrus', *ARTA* (2005), 6; Wiseman, *Nebuchadnezzar*, 50-51.
[5] Tolini, 'la prise de Babylone', 6; Dandamaev, *Achaemenid Empire*, 45.
[6] *Anabasis*, I.7.15, II.4.12.
[7] Wiseman, *Nebuchadnezzar*, 60.
[8] Tolini, 'la prise de Babylone', 6; Dandamaev, *Achaemenid Empire*, 45.

Tigris. The Persian army was presumably delayed there for some reason as their next attack is recorded in the month of Tašrîtu (September/October).

In the intervening period the Chronicle records that 'the Sea Country made a short invasion' (around March 539). 'The Sea Country' refers to a territory south of Babylon, the area around the Persian Gulf. It may be that this territory took the threat of Persian invasion as an opportunity to gain their independence. This incident may indicate that Nabonidus was unpopular within his own empire.

The Chronicle records that, during the summer of 539, Nabonidus gathered the god-statues from the surrounding towns into Babylon. This action is later interpreted by Cyrus' own propaganda as being an act of sacrilege.[9] It is likely that Nabonidus removed the images for their protection from the Persian invasion. Precedents in Assyrian history demonstrate that god-statues were often removed from conquered cities and carried off as trophies. Beaulieu writes:

> Rather than incur the capture of their gods and the resulting implications of such capture, namely, that the gods were abandoning the city and calling for its destruction, cities often tried to prevent the transfer of the statues to enemy territory, since continued possession of them in the face of adversity proved that the gods were still protecting and supporting their people and native land.[10]

A letter from officials in Uruk details how soldiers and barley-offerings were sent with the statue of Ištar to Babylon. This letter explains the earlier reference to 'image of Ištar of Uruk', which means that Nabonidus' gathering of the cult-statues had already begun in February/March 539. Beaulieu notes that the movement of these cult-statues required specific rituals and a large retinue of priests and offerings.[11] Those cities from which statues were gathered, being those to the south of Babylon, were presumably still accessible and not yet threatened by the Persian invasion. This may explain why the images from Cutha and Sippar were not gathered to Babylon, as these cities are to the north of Babylon and this area may already have been under threat.

The Chronicle records the following sequence of events of the capture of Babylon:

early October	The Persian and Babylonian armies do battle at Opis. The inhabitants revolt and are massacred.
12 October	Sippar is seized 'without battle'. Nabonidus flees.
13 October	Ugbaru leads the Persian army into Babylon 'without battle'.
? October	Nabonidus returns to Babylon and is arrested.

---

[9] BM 90920, lines 9-11.

[10] P.A. Beaulieu, 'An Episode in the Fall of Babylon to the Persians', *JNES* 52 (1992), 242.

[11] Beaulieu, 'Fall of Babylon', 257.

29 October   Cyrus enters Babylon – 'green twigs were spread in front of him'.

From this sequence, it is clear that Nabonidus led that Babylonian army to meet the Persians in battle. The city of Opis (near modern-day Baghdad) was situated on the river Tigris and thus a key crossing point for the Persian army. The revolt of the citizens is significant and implies some dissatisfaction with Nabonidus' rule. The Chronicle is unclear who massacred them – Cyrus or Nabonidus.

That Nabonidus fled after the capture of Sippar may imply that he (and his army) was in Sippar prior to its fall. However, if this is the case then it is unlikely that it should have been captured without battle.

It is significant that it is Ugbaru who leads the Persian army into Babylon, not Cyrus. That Cyrus divided his forces is confirmed by the fact that Babylon falls the day after Sippar; a single day would not have been sufficient to move an army from Sippar to Babylon. This means that a siege cannot be ruled out on chronological grounds. Cyrus did not arrive at Babylon until sixteen days after it fell which would suggest that he (and part of the Persian army) was occupied elsewhere.

Cyrus Cylinder (BM 90920)
The *Cyrus Cylinder* is the propaganda of conqueror justifying his conquest. The opening paragraphs describe the tyrannies and impieties of Nabonidus. The text continues by describing how Marduk called out Cyrus, who is described as 'upright' and 'a righteous king', to liberate Babylon. (This record makes an interesting comparison with Isaiah 45, which declares that YHWH called out Cyrus to save his people). Its description of the fall of Babylon matches that of the Chronicle:

> He [i.e. Marduk] made him [i.e. Cyrus] enter his city Babylon without fighting or battle; he saved Babylon from hardship. He delivered Nabonidus, the king who did not revere him, into his hands. All the people of Babylon, all the land of Sumer and Akkad, princes and governors, bowed to him and kissed his feet.[12]

These two texts (Chronicle and Cylinder) are related. Though they are not from the same hand, they are both products of the same political climate. Cyrus is anxious to legitimize his rule and to win the allegiance of the Babylonian people. Therefore the assertion that Babylon was taken 'without battle' may not be strictly historical, so much as it is convenient.

The Verse Account
This text is damaged and does not record the actual fall of Babylon, yet the author's agenda is clear. He decries Nabonidus' preference of the Moon god accusing him of blasphemy against Marduk. The author also asserts that Nabonidus aroused the anger of the gods by removing them from their sanctuaries.

---

[12] BM 90920, lines16-18.

Cyrus, in contrast, is presented as a pious worshipper of Marduk and the author rejoices at his ascendancy. This account is indicative of the dissatisfaction against Nabonidus amongst certain of his own people.

One intriguing passage may provide evidence that Babylon was taken by force.

> To repair the city of Babylon he [i.e. Cyrus] conceived the idea and he himself took up hoe, spade and water basket and began to complete the wall of Babylon. The original plan of Nebuchadnezzar the inhabitants executed with a willing heart. He built fortifications on the Imgur-Enlil wall.

The *Imgur-Enlil* was the inner wall that encompassed the city.[13] If this wall was in need of repair shortly after the fall of Babylon then this would be strong evidence that Babylon was taken by force.

Herodotus, The Histories
The Greek historian Herodotus wrote his account about a century after the fall of Babylon. We know that he traveled in Mesopotamia and undoubtedly saw the defenses of Babylon for himself. He appears to have spoken to some Babylonians about these events.[14] Though Herodotus' account appears inconsistent with the cuneiform texts, his witness cannot be idly dismissed.

> After noting the provisions taken by Cyrus on his campaign, Herodotus notes how the Persian army was delayed at the crossing of the river Gyndes (=Diyala). He describes how one of Cyrus' horses raced into the river and attempted to swim across and was drowned. Cyrus swore that he would punish the river for the death of his horse and so the Persian army spent the whole summer digging three hundred and sixty channels from the river to drain it.[15]

It would be easy to dismiss this story as entirely fictitious except for the intriguing fact that it harmonizes with the Chronicle. As noted above, the Chronicle records some activity of the Persian army around February/March 539, possibly around the area of the Tigris. It is reasonable that Cyrus would have taken the route through the Diyala valley towards Opis. The Chronicle seems to indicate that Cyrus was delayed there for the whole summer but does not give explanation for this. G.C. Cameron, while dismissing the explanation provided by Herodotus as legendary, has proposed that Herodotus preserves a historical tradition that the Persian army spent summer 539 diverting the course of the river Diyala. Archeological research has revealed that the course of the river was altered near Opis. Also, there are some indications of an economic revival in the region of the Diyala basin during the Achaemenid period. Cameron sug-

---

[13] A.R. George, *Babylonian Topographical Texts* (Louvain, 1992) 141; Wiseman, *Nebuchadnezzar*, 46-48.
[14] 'The Babylonians themselves say . . .' (*Histories* I.191).
[15] *Histories* I.189.

gests that Cyrus had set his army irrigating the Diyala region.[16] An agricultural program of this kind by Cyrus may explain the revolt of the people of Opis in his favour when Nabonidus came to reassert his control over the region.

When Cyrus resumes his march towards Babylon, Herodotus records that the Babylonian army came out to meet him, though he states they attacked when 'he was within striking distance' of Babylon, not at Opis.[17] They are defeated but retire to Babylon confident of its defenses and the provision they had made to withstand a siege. Herodotus does not state how long the siege lasted, only that it 'dragged on'.[18] The siege was broken when 'somebody' devised the plan for one section of the army to divert the Euphrates upstream while other sections waited to enter the city along the riverbed when the water level dropped sufficiently. Herodotus previously records how a queen, whom he names Nitocris, had created an artificial lake into which she diverted the Euphrates for the purpose of lining the banks and bed of the river with stone and brick (*Histories* I.185-86). Herodotus states that it was this same artificial lake that Cyrus used to divert the river (I.191).The Babylonians were taken by surprise and so did not close the gates on the riverbank or man the walls. Herodotus explains:

> There was a festival going on, and even while the city was falling they continued to dance and enjoy themselves, until hard facts brought them to their senses.[19]

Xenophon, Cyropaedia
The *Cyropaedia* has long been recognized to be a historical romance, rather than a strict history. This being said, it does contain a historical core, manifesting several traditions that are confirmed by other sources.

Xenophon elongates Cyrus' campaign against Babylon, placing the capture of several Babylonian fortresses prior to the Persian campaign against Lydia.[20] In fact, Xenophon explains Cyrus' campaign against Lydia as a consequence of the Babylonian campaign, stating that Croesus was allied with the king of Babylon and sought to aid him against Cyrus.[21] After capturing Sardis, capital of Lydia, Cyrus subdues Phrygia, Cappadocia and Arabia before returning to lay siege to Babylon.[22]

Xenophon presents Cyrus as being concerned by the defenses of Babylon and describes how he spent much time preparing siege engines in readiness for the assault.[23] When Cyrus reaches the city he judges it to be invulnerable to assault[24] and, though his plan is initially to reduce the city through hunger, he

[16] G.C. Cameron (1974), cited by Dandamaev, *Achaemenid Empire*, 44.
[17] *Histories* I.190.
[18] *Histories* I.190.
[19] *Histories* I.191.
[20] Xenophon, *Cyropaedia* V.3.1-18.
[21] *Cyropaedia* VI.2.10.
[22] *Cyropaedia* VI.4.16.
[23] *Cyropaedia* VI.1.20-23.
[24] *Cyropaedia* VI.5.7.

finds the city too large to properly encircle.[25] He then proposes to feign construction of a blockade around the city, while the larger part of his army is set to digging gigantic trenches into which the Euphrates is to be drained. Cyrus chooses his moment carefully:

> Cyrus heard that it was a time of high festival in Babylon when the citizens drink and make merry the whole night long. As soon as the darkness fell, he set his men to work. The mouths of the trenches were opened, and during the night the water poured in, so that the riverbed formed a highway into the heart of the town.[26]

The Persian army entered the city. A detachment led by Gobryas and Gadatas, the eunuch, make their way to king's palace and slay the king with his retinue.[27]

Though Xenophon wrote later than Herodotus, there is no particular reason to suppose he is dependent (solely) on Herodotus for his information. There are several differences between the two accounts – the length of the siege, the feigned blockades, the location of the diversion, etc. – which indicate they knew separate traditions. In addition, Xenophon includes many peripheral details overlooked by Herodotus; the mention of Gobryas (=Ugbaru) is particularly significant. Xenophon traveled extensively with the Persian army and thus may have had greater access to the collective memory of the region than Herodotus did. Assuming the relative independence of Xenophon's narrative, then despite his romanticizing tendency we may regard the *Cyropaedia* as corroborating Herodotus' account on at least two key issues: that the day Babylon fell was a high day, and that the Persians diverted the Euphrates to gain access to the city.

Berossus
The writings of Berossus, being now only preserved in the quotations of other authors, are brief on the subject of the fall of Babylon. This being said, Berossus, as a Babylonian, probably had access to some traditions no longer available to us; he almost certainly had access to cuneiform texts. Thus, his testimony, though later, may be credited with greater trust than his Greek predecessors.[28]

Berossus[29] records that in the seventeenth year of Nabonidus, Cyrus came with a great army against Babylon. He notes that previously Cyrus had conquered 'all the rest of Asia', probably a reference to the Lydian campaign. Berossus continues that Nabonidus led his forces out to meet Cyrus but was defeated and fled to Borsippa and was 'shut up' there. The impression is that directly after this Cyrus took Babylon. In difference to the *Verse Account*, Berossus

---

[25] *Cyropaedia* VI.5.2.
[26] *Cyropaedia* VI.5.15-16.
[27] *Cyropaedia* VI.5.26-30.
[28] To explore the relationship between Berossus and the Greek historians see: Bichler, 'Greek Tradition'.
[29] Josephus, *Contra Apion* 1.20; Eusebius, *Praep. Evan.* 9.

records that Cyrus ordered that the walls of Babylon be destroyed after its fall because they were 'troublesome'. This strongly implies that Babylon was taken by force, and perhaps by a siege.

It is likely that Berossus was acquainted with the tradition of the diversion of the Euphrates.[30] Regarding the building works of Nebuchadnezzar, he writes:

> He also rebuilt the old city, added another to it on the outside, and so far complet-
> ed Babylon, that none, who might besiege it afterwards, should have it in their
> power to divert the river, so as to facilitate an entrance into it: and he affected this
> by building three walls about the inner city, and three about the outer.[31]

Bichler proposes that this is one of many instances in which Berossus was compelled by 'his duty to his Greek-speaking public'. Yet, significantly, in this instance Berossus appears to be departing from his Greek predecessors, implying that Babylon could *not* be taken by the diversion of the river. Such a statement probably indicates that Berossus was aware of some other explanation for the capture of Babylon, though he does not divulge this.

Daniel 5
The book of Daniel actually gives us little information about the events of the fall of Babylon. The focus of Daniel 5 is on the character of Belshazzar, rather than the downfall of a mighty nation. The author describes how Belshazzar held a 'great feast' during which praise was offered to various images (5:1-4). During the feast a hand appears that writes a cryptic message upon the wall. Daniel interprets this message as a judgment against Belshazzar and predicts that the same night Belshazzar would be slain. At the end of the story these predictions are fulfilled: the city falls to a Medo-Persian army, Belshazzar is slain and Darius the Mede receives the kingdom (5:28-31).

This narrative reveals little about the circumstances outside the palace. It makes no attempt to explain how the Medo-Persian army gained entrance to the city. The key factor in this account is the apparent confidence of Belshazzar. It seems improbable that he should have held a feast for his officials were the city surrounded by an invading army. His confidence may in part be explained by the strength of Babylon's fortifications, yet it may also imply that Belshazzar had not yet received news of the defeats at Opis and Sippar. These implications seem more consistent with the timetable laid out in the Chronicle, rather than Herodotus' account of a long siege.

The mention of Belshazzar praising many gods (5:4) takes on greater signif-icance when compared with the cuneiform accounts of the gathering of the lo-cal cult-images into Babylon. The author's description of 'the gods of gold and silver, bronze and iron, wood and stone' (5:4), though polemical,[32] is accurate.

---

[30] Bichler, 'Greek Tradition', 7, 20.
[31] *Contra Apion* 1:19; *Praep. Evan.* 9.
[32] cf. Deuteronomy 29:17, Isaiah 37:19, Ezekiel 20:32.

Like Herodotus and Xenophon, Daniel 5 records that there was a great feast in Babylon the night that it is captured.

Evaluation

The *Cyrus Cylinder*, though early, has a clear agenda. Its assertion that Babylon was taken 'without battle' can be given little weight. This text may be one of the sources for the *Nabonidus Chronicle* since it contains the same statement. Every other source evidences a forcible capture of Babylon. The phrase 'without battle' may be more explicable if the forced capture were judged to be a lesser conflict than, say, the battle of Opis. The Chronicle, Berossus, and Herodotus all state that prior to the fall of Babylon the Babylonian army was defeated by the Persians. If capture of Babylon did not involve direct confrontation with the Babylonian army then this may explain why the Persians felt the phrase 'without battle' was justified.

The question of a siege is more difficult. The chronology laid out in the Chronicle (of which there is no particular reason to doubt) rules out the long siege implied by Herodotus. If Cyrus did divide his forces, as seems likely, it is possible that a siege of Babylon could have already been in progress when Sippar fell. Berossus' statement that the walls of Babylon were 'troublesome' to Cyrus may imply a siege, though on the contrary it may imply that they prevented Cyrus attempting a siege (as Xenophon supposes). The concept that there was a siege may have arisen from Herodotus' observation of Babylon's defenses, rather than any historical tradition. If Herodotus judged that the defenses made a direct assault impracticable, he may have assumed that Cyrus judged the same and thus concluded that there must have been a siege.

The tradition that the river Euphrates was diverted has received some support from modern historians.[33] The support for this tradition is not weak, being preserved by both Herodotus and Xenophon. Some commentators have taken Jeremiah 50:38 ('a drought is against her waters, and they will be dried up') as support for this tradition.[34] Herodotus' record, at least, is based (in part) on oral testimony in Babylonia. Yet Berossus seems to explicitly contradict this tradition, saying that the defenses built by Nebuchadnezzar made this impossible. It is tempting to give greater weight to Berossus' testimony, yet this leaves unanswered the questions of how the diversion-tradition arose, and more importantly, how the Persian army gained access to the city.

---

[33] See H.G. Nesselrath, 'Herodot und Babylon: Der Hauport Mesopotamiens in den Augen eines Griechen' in *Babylon: Focus Mesopotamisher Geschichte, Wiege fruher Gelehrsamkeit, Mythos in der Moderne* (ed. J. Renger; Saarbrucjen, 1999), 189-206; also, J. Oates, *Babylon* (London: Thames & Hudson, 1986), 135: 'there is no particular reason to doubt this story'; E. Wright, *The Ancient World* (London: Hamlyn, 1979), 50: 'there may be some truth in Herodotus' story that Cyrus diverted the Euphrates'.

[34] Mansfield, *Daniel*, 126.

One hypothesis that was previously popular amongst historians is that the priests of Marduk, angered by the sacrilege of Nabonidus, betrayed Babylon into the hands of the Persians.[35] Though texts written after the fall of Babylon (*Cyrus Cylinder, Verse Account*) do describe Nabonidus as sacrilegious, he may not have been regarded as such during his reign. There is no record of revolts during his reign and, more significantly, there is no attempt to depose him during his ten-year 'exile' in Tema. While Nabonidus did have special reverence for Sin, the moon-god, he was not a monotheist and it is not recorded that he made any attempt to outlaw the worship of other gods.

Recent studies of a cuneiform text dating from this period have shed new light on this problem.[36]

> Nûrêa, son of Bêl-iqîša, descendant of the Priest of Nanaia received 19 sicles of silver in payment for the work on the rampart of the Great Gate of Enlil (carried out) from 14th Tebetu until 6th Addaru, by the hands of Marduk-rêmanni, son of Iddin-Marduk, descendent of Nûr-Sîn.[37]

This receipt is dated to the accession year of Cyrus. This text demonstrates that in January 538, which is within three months of the capture of Babylon, repair work was carried out on the Enlil Gate. This indicates that the Persians forced entrance to the city by breaking its gates. Tolini has further proposed that since this is the only receipt for such repair-work that we can reconstruct how Babylon fell.[38]

Tolini proposes that after the capture of Sippar the Babylonian army fell back and set up defensive positions between Babylon and the Persian army, blocking their route south. Cyrus, rather than engaging in a pitched battle, divided his forces. While the main strength of the Persian army held the attention of the Babylonian army, a contingent under the command of Ugbaru crossed the river Euphrates and marched along the western bank. Ugbaru led his contingent to the west part of the city, which is not protected by the external wall, and broke into the city through the Enlil Gate. With the element of surprise, the Persian troops were then able to penetrate to the eastern side of the city.[39]

This thesis is not only plausible, but explains several features of the various sources. The repairs to the Enlil Gate may explain the references in the *Verse Account* to repairs of the Imgur-Enlil. The division of the Persian army that Tolini describes explains why Cyrus did not arrive at Babylon until sixteen days after its capture. This hypothesis may also explain the origins of the legend that the Persian forces entered Babylon along the riverbed that was passed on to Herodotus and Xenophon:

---

[35] For example, H.W.F. Saggs, *Babylonians* (London: British Museum Press, 1995), 171; Wright, *Ancient World*, 50.
[36] Tolini, 'la prise de Babylone'.
[37] Cyr.10 Strassmaier.
[38] Tolini, 'la prise de Babylone', 3.
[39] Tolini, 'la prise de Babylone', 9-10.

One understands better the idea of a nocturnal and furtive passage along the bed of the Euphrates which these authors retell, if it is put in relationship to the surprise of the garrison of the eastern district in seeing Ugbaru's Persian soldiers arrive from the interior of the town, once they had secured the western district, when they believed them to be stuck in the neighbourhood of Sippar.[40]

As noted above, both Daniel and the Greek sources record that the city of Babylon was in the midst of a feast/festival on the night it was taken. In fact, Xenophon asserts that Cyrus chose the night to attack Babylon specifically to coincide with a high festival and thereby catch the defenders off guard. Such a scenario would help explain the apparent ease with which the Persian army captured the city. The evidence of the Greek historians has been strengthened by recent research which may identify this festival.[41]

In ancient near eastern cultures two New Years were celebrated: one in Nisannu (Nisan) and one in Tašrîtu (Tishri). In the month of Nisannu the *akitu* festival (New Year festival) was celebrated in Babylon, in honour of Marduk, the chief Babylonian god; this annual festival was recorded in the Babylonian Chronicles. Certain cuneiform inscriptions demonstrate that another *akitu* festival was celebrated in Harran in the month of Tašrîtu. The festival was in honour of Sin, the moon-god, whose temple was in Harran.[42]

Nabonidus was a zealous devotee of Sin and had restored the temple of Sin in Harran. There Nabonidus himself participated in the *akitu* festival to Sin. It is conceivable when Nabonidus returned to Babylon in 540 he transposed the festival from Harran to Babylon. We cannot rule out the possibility that the cult-statue of Sin was one of those gathered into Babylon prior to its fall.

The date of Babylon's capture is significant. In October there is a period of several days when the full moon appears to rise just as the sun sets; this phenomenon is termed the Hunter's Moon. It is, therefore, understandable that the *akitu* festival to the moon-god was celebrated in Tašrîtu (October), a period when 'the moon had an unusually prominent place at night'.[43] The *akitu* festival of Sin was celebrated on 17th Tašrîtu, though the festivities may well have been spread over days because of the Hunter's Moon. The Chronicle records that Babylon was captured on 16th Tašrîtu. It is conceivable, therefore, that Belshazzar was celebrating the preliminary festivities of the *akitu* festival. This hypothesis strengthens the idea that Babylon was captured at night when the moon would have been clearly visible.

Inasmuch as Daniel 5 is the only account of the events that unfolded within the Southern Palace during the evening of 13 October 539, there is no possible

---

[40] Tolini, 'la prise de Babylone', 12 [translated by K. Wilkinson].

[41] A. Wolters, 'Belshazzar's Feast and the Cult of the Moon God Sin', *Bulletin of Biblical Research* 4 (1995), 199-206; P.A. Beaulieu, *The Reign of Nabonidus King of Babylon 556-539 BC* (New Haven: Yale University Press, 1989), 226.

[42] Beaulieu, *Nabonidus*, 152.

[43] Wolters, 'Belshazzar's Feast', 203.

way of corroborating from other sources what is claimed to be an eyewitness account. Likewise, insofar as Daniel 5 is silent on the military strategy used to take the city, there are few areas of possible conflict with the other sources. To this extent, the question of the veracity of Daniel 5 will be judged largely on the merits of the book as a whole rather than on individual details. Yet we may make two observations, 1) allowing for the miraculous events, there is nothing implausible about the account offered in Daniel 5, and 2) where there are points of contact, Daniel 5 is consistent with the historical record. The confirmation that there is likely to have been a feast held in Babylon on the night of its fall is a case in point.

Previously the confidence and bravado ascribed to Belshazzar prior to the appearance of the hand had been the cause of some scorn amongst critics.[44] Surely Belshazzar had no cause for complacency or frivolity if the Babylonian army had recently been defeated at Opis (as per the cuneiform sources) or if the Persian army was camped outside the very walls of the city (as per the Greek historians). Yet, as we have seen, neither the cuneiform sources nor the Greek historians deliver the full historical picture. The reconstruction presented by Tolini, while giving the likely explanation for the fall of Babylon, incidentally also accounts for Belshazzar's confidence. Prior to Babylon's fall, the larger part of the Persian army was still many miles north of Babylon, probably being held in check by an entrenched Babylonian army. Belshazzar may have been reassured by the position of the army and by the city's considerable defenses – news may not yet have reached him of the fall of Opis or his father's flight. The furtive approach of Ugbaru's contingent and their dramatic entrance into the city would have come unheralded and would have taken Belshazzar completely by surprise. Before the Babylonians could muster any kind of defense, the Persian forces had crossed the river and entered the east side of the city – the regent of Babylon would have been one of their primary objectives.

Reconstruction

Having evaluated the source-material, let us draw together some speculative conclusions.

From 549 onwards Cyrus was consolidating his powerbase in Medo-Persia and expanding its territories. It appears that Cyrus did not immediately strike at Babylon but moved westward against Lydia, perhaps in an effort to isolate the Babylonians. Whatever the case, the threat of Persian expansion to the Babylonian empire was not immediately perceived by its king, Nabonidus, who did not return to Babylon until 540. We do not know when Cyrus made his first assault on Babylonian territory but it may well have been this initial blow that prompted Nabonidus' return.

---

[44] Rowley, *Historicity*, 20.

It is natural to assume that Belshazzar relinquished his authority to his father upon his return, though having governed Babylon for nearly ten years he would have been invaluable to Nabonidus. We may imagine that throughout 540-539 Belshazzar was employed overseeing various preparations for the Persian advance. We know that Nabonidus spent this time gathering the local cult-statues from their various towns to Babylon, partly for their protection and also to give 'divine' assistance to Babylon.

The Persian army approached the Babylonian heartland from the East, along the Diyala valley. They seem to have made some attack around this area but for some reason their advance was stalled. The difficulty of crossing the Tigris is a likely explanation. Some scholars have suspected that the tradition of the diversion of the Euphrates was born out of Persian attempts to cross the Tigris during this summer; however, it may be that they simply waited for the waters to subside. Yet they were not inactive; Cameron's thesis that they were engaged in some sort of public-relations irrigation program is inviting and may help explain the ready acceptance of the Persian conquerors by the Babylonian population.

In October the Persians successfully crossed the Tigris and moved into the vicinity of Opis. When Nabonidus received word, he mustered his army and marched north to meet the Persians in battle. It is likely that he left his regent, Belshazzar, in Babylon to watch over the defense of the city.

The Persian army successfully defeated the Babylonian army, perhaps aided by the citizens of Opis. The Persian army then moved westward to capture the strategic city of Sippar thus safeguarding their rear and as they prepared to advance upon Babylon. Rather than defend Sippar, the Babylonian army retreats to draw up defensive positions to block the Persian advance.

At some point during these events Nabonidus fled, but does not return to Babylon. It is possible that he despaired of victory. He may also have been shaken by the revolt of Opis and perhaps suspected that he was no longer safe even amongst his own countrymen.

Having captured Sippar, Persian forces were now able to cross the Euphrates and Cyrus sent a contingent under Ugbaru to approach Babylon along the west bank. The majority of the Persian army acts as a distraction for the Babylonian army, though there is no evidence that they engaged in further battle. Ugbaru reaches Babylon on the evening of 13th October, perhaps timed intentionally to coincide with the festivities to the moon-god. His forces penetrated the Enlil Gate and took the city by surprise. Before the alarm is raised, the Persians have crossed to the eastern bank and entered the Southern Palace where they find Belshazzar and slay him.

With the king missing, the regent dead and Babylon itself occupied, the Babylonian army has little reason to continue its campaign against Cyrus. It is likely that some negotiation took place and Cyrus may well have guaranteed the security and religious freedoms of the Babylonians. A little time later, Cyrus entered Babylon.

Chapter 8

A Median Kingdom

One of the key issues of dispute between critical and conservative scholars is whether the author of the book of Daniel believed that an independent Median kingdom succeeded the Babylonian Empire. We know that the Medes were a significant power in the region during the ninth to seventh centuries BC, halting the Assyrian advance eastward and allying with the Chaldean king Nabopolassar to bring about Assyria's downfall. Yet, prior to the fall of Babylon, Media had been annexed by Cyrus and was no longer an independent kingdom.[1]

The hypothesis that the author of Daniel believed in the succession of an independent Median kingdom is key to the critical interpretation of the Four Kingdom visions of Daniel 2 and 7: 1) Babylon, 2) Media, 3) Persia, and 4) Greece. These two propositions – the historical hypothesis and the interpretation of the Four Kingdoms – are used by critical scholars for mutual verification; whichever is disputed the other is used as justification. One cannot help notice the apparent circularity in this form of mutual verification. On the other hand conservative scholars are as equally zealous, if not more so, in defense of the 'Roman' interpretation, i.e. 1) Babylon, 2) Medo-Persia, 3) Greece, and 4) Rome. Either side the historical question is coloured by interpretative considerations.

Primarily this is an issue of historicity, and only secondarily an interpretative issue. The historical question should be considered independently, at least in the first instance.

Darius the Mede

Perhaps the cornerstone of the critical proposition is the figure of Darius the Mede.[2] The book of Daniel indicates that Belshazzar (the Chaldean) was succeeded by Darius the Mede who was in turn succeeded by Cyrus the Persian (5:31, 6:28, 9:1, 10:1, 11:1). This succession of kings is taken as indicative of

---

[1] Herodotus records that Media had to pay an annual tax to Persia (*Histories* 3.91-6). For further detail regarding the subordination of Media to Persia see E.M. Yamauchi, *Persia and the Bible* (Grand Rapids: Baker, 1990), 57f.

[2] H.H. Rowley, *Darius the Mede and the Four World Empires in the Book of Daniel: A Historical Study of Contemporary Theories* (Cardiff: University of Wales Press, 1935; repr. 1964), 146ff.

succession of kingdoms, and thus it is proposed that the author believed in an independent Median kingdom between the Babylon and Persian kingdoms.

There are several difficulties with the latter step in the argument. Firstly, the author clearly accounts for the predicate 'the Mede' as reference to Darius' ancestry (9:1) and is not (necessarily) any indication of his political allegiance. Secondly, Darius' kingdom is only ever described as that 'of the Chaldeans' (5:31, 9:1), and never as a Median kingdom or as being 'of the Medes'. It is true that Cyrus is once referred to as 'king of the Persians' (10:1), rather than the 'king of the Medes and Persians'.[3] It is questionable how significant this fact is. Since Cyrus was king of the Persians before he annexed the kingdom of Media it is not unreasonable that his title should be thus abbreviated.

While we cannot be sure as to the identity of Darius the Mede, many conservative scholars have speculated that he was a governor, or vassal-king, of Cyrus or even Cyrus himself (see below). Though the name 'Darius the Mede' is yet to be found in any cuneiform text, if any of these identifications were ever confirmed then the foundation of the independent-Median-kingdom hypothesis would be removed.

'The Law of the Medes and Persians'

It should go without saying that the author describes the government of Darius using Persian terminology (6:1-3). Yet the more significant factor is that Darius considers himself bound by the 'law of the Medes and Persians' (6:8, 12, 15). As one does not usually regard a nation as sovereign if it is bound by the laws of another kingdom, this fact has given pause to the critical scholars. Rowley tries to limit the damage to his case, saying:

> [The author] was aware of some connexion (sic) between them, and so could speak of them as under a common legal code. But that does not entail the supposition that he was unable to distinguish between them.[4]

In this case Rowley becomes the worst kind of apologist, arguing against evidence on a technical wrangle. Of course, Rowley is free to speculate how an author might have envisioned two separate kingdoms with a unified legal code, yet this is no kind of evidence that the author of Daniel did so. The historical reality is that this unified legal code dates from after the unification of the kingdoms under Cyrus.[5]

The Fall of Babylon

The account of the fall of Babylon in Daniel 5, though sparse on the details of the capture of the city, does identify for us to whom the city fell. Daniel, inter-

---

[3] Davies, *Daniel*, 28.
[4] Rowley, *Darius the Mede*, 148.
[5] Collins, *Daniel*, 268.

preting the writing on the wall states: 'PERES: Your kingdom has been divided, and given to the Medes and the Persians' (Dan. 5:28 [NKJV]).

Most commentators note the irony in the word 'Peres' (פרס 'divided'), which sounds like the word for Persians (פרס).[6] The author was well aware of the forces that came against Babylon and which nations succeeded to the kingdom of Belshazzar.

Rowley, again, objects:

> Against this, however, it is to be noted that in v28 it is said that the Babylonian kingdom shall be 'divided', and given to the Medes and Persians. Clearly, therefore, the author supposed that just as on the fall of Nineveh the Assyrian dominions were divided between the Medes and the Chaldaeans (sic), so the Babylonian empire was now divided, and part of it fell to the Medes and part to the Persians, as two separate but allied powers.[7]

But this proposition proves too much as no commentator is arguing in favour of two contemporary, yet sovereign kingdoms. In any case, the 'division' described in v28 is not that of the equal distribution of goods but implies destruction.[8]

The Ram

Having exhausted the narrative passages, we may turn to the vision of Daniel 8 for further evidence in the case. Daniel sees a ram with two horns, one higher than the other and the higher horn came up last. We are left in no doubt regarding the interpretation of these horns as we are told 'they are the kings of Media and Persia' (8:20). The application of the symbols is clear; the Persian kings only latterly became dominant but expanded the empire far beyond that of the Medes. The significant point is that the relationship between the Medes and Persians is represented by a single animal, i.e. the Medes and the Persians make up one unified kingdom.

P.R. Davies objects that this 'does not necessarily mean they are seen as a single empire',[9] though he does not provide any other explanation of the symbolism. Rowley also objects arguing that 'manifestly, then, our author did distinguish between the Medes and Persians' because there are two horns, though he concedes a 'connection'.[10] Rowley's own thesis that the single animal indicates an alliance, rather than a unified kingdom, appears to be entirely apologetic. The author's symbolism is more consistent with the historical facts than any fictional alliance.

---

[6] Porteous, *Daniel*, 81; Baldwin, *Daniel*, 125; etc.
[7] Rowley, *Darius the Mede*, 148.
[8] Young, *Daniel*, 127.
[9] Davies, *Daniel*, 28.
[10] Rowley, *Darius the Mede*, 149.

Summary

Davies judges the foregoing evidence to be 'ambiguous', yet his further proposition that the question should be settled by the interpretation of the Four Kingdoms reveals his hand.[11] If one examines the evidence impartially then two conclusions seem unavoidable:

1) There is no explicit reference in the book of Daniel to an independent Median kingdom as successor to the Babylonian kingdom.
2) There are strong indications that the Medo-Persian Empire was regarded by the author as a single unit, a) legally, b) militarily, c) symbolically.

The balance of evidence indicates that the author of Daniel believed that the Medo-Persian Empire succeeded to the Babylonian kingdom. In the absence of contrary evidence the independent Median kingdom thesis cannot be substantiated and the book of Daniel should not be considered at fault in this matter.

---

[11] Davies, *Daniel*, 28.

Chapter 9

Darius the Mede

In his seminal work, *Darius the Mede and the Four World Empires in the Book of Daniel*, H.H. Rowley wrote: 'the references to Darius the Mede in the book of Daniel have long been recognized as providing the most serious historical problem in the book'.[1] This assessment has remained pertinent as, to date, no extra-biblical source has been found bearing the name 'Darius the Mede' and, more significantly, the contemporary records appear to allow no chronological gap between the reigns of Belshazzar and Cyrus in which this Darius might have reigned. On this point the record in Daniel seems to stand at odds with our historical information.

This being said, the book of Daniel contains a considerable number of details about Darius the Mede. The book tells us that:

- he received the kingdom of Babylon after the death of Belshazzar (5:30-1, 9:1),
- he was sixty-two at the fall of Babylon (5:31),
- he appointed one hundred and twenty satraps with three presidents over them (6:1-2),
- he reigned as a king (6:2ff), made decrees (6:7-9, 25-27) and was (or behaved as) sovereign in his kingdom (6:7),
- he was bound by the law of the Medes *and Persians* (6:8, 6:12), therefore presumably ruled after the annexing of Media by Cyrus,
- he was the son of Ahasuerus and had Median ancestry (9:1),
- and only his first year is recorded (9:1, 11:1).

Now, some of these details are significant in their specificity; for instance, Darius is the only foreign king whose age is recorded in any OT text. It is a difficult problem to explain upon what basis the author of Daniel arrived at these detailed descriptions.

Rowley, following a large consensus of critical scholars, posits that Darius I Hystapis formed the basis for the character of Darius the Mede. Yet the sheer number of confusions necessary to arrive at the character of Darius the Mede makes this thesis unlikely. Rowley asserts that the author confused the conquest of Babylon by Cyrus (539 BC) with the defeat of Babylon by Darius Hystaspis

---

[1] Rowley, *Darius the Mede*, 9.

(520 BC) (hence 'Darius'); then he confused the number of satrapies under Darius Hystaspis (between 20 and 29[2]) with the number of satrapies attributed to Xerxes in Esther 1:1 (hence 120 satraps); then he confused the age of Darius Hystaspis in 520 with the age of Cyrus in 539 (hence 62);[3] then he confused the son of Darius Hystaspis, Xerxes, for his father (hence Ahasuerus); [4] then he confused Darius Hystaspis, who was a Persian, for a Mede (hence Darius *the Mede*).[5] That even a writer living many centuries after the events should make such a catalogue of historical blunders is difficult to conceive, especially one who is reliable on other historical details.

An alternative explanation is that the character of Darius the Mede is entirely fictional. The names 'Darius' and 'Ahasuerus' are suitably royal, being used by Persian kings and the activities ascribed to Darius appear fitting for his station. It is frequently asserted that the character was invented for polemical reasons. Jeremiah prophesied that the 'kings of the Medes' would be come to destroy Babylon;[6] also, Isaiah predicts that the Medes would come against Babylon.[7] It is plausible to suppose that a Jewish writer might invent an independent Median sovereign as conqueror of Babylon in an effort to fulfill these prophecies.[8] Yet, if this were his purpose why not choose known Median kings like the last king Astyages, recorded by Herodotus, or the (probably) fictional king Cyaxares II, recorded by Xenophon. In any case, other parts of Isaiah refer to the participation of Persia in the destruction of Babylon alongside Media;[9] the later chapters even name Cyrus as the conqueror of Babylon.[10] These references, coupled with implicit statements in other OT texts that Cyrus succeeded the Babylonian Empire,[11] make it highly unlikely that a second-century author would have felt any compulsion to insert a fictional Median king between Belshazzar and Cyrus.

---

[2] 'Herodotus tells us that he divided it into twenty satrapies, while his own inscriptions variously mention twenty-one, twenty-three, twenty-four and twenty-nine divisions of his dominions' (Rowley, *Darius the Mede*, 54).
[3] Rowley, *Darius the Mede*, 55-56.
[4] Xerxes is named Ahasuerus in the book of Esther.
[5] Rowley, *Darius the Mede*, 54-58.
[6] 'The LORD has raised up the spirit of the kings of the Medes. For His plan is against Babylon to destroy it' (Jer. 51:11); 'Prepare against her the nations, with the kings of the Medes, its governors and all its rulers, all the land of his dominion' (51:28)
[7] 'Behold, I will stir up the Medes against them' (Isa. 13:17).
[8] R.H. Charles, *A Critical and Exegetical Commentary on the Book of Daniel* (Oxford: Clarendon, 1929), 141ff; Davies, *Daniel*, 29.
[9] Isaiah 21:2.
[10] Isaiah 45:1ff. Many scholars ascribe this passage to the (hypothesized) Deutro-Isaiah, writing at a later time (e.g. Rowley, *Darius the Mede*, 58). In any case, these passages would have been completed by c.400 BC and known to the assumed second-century creator of Darius the Mede.
[11] II Chronicles 36:22-23; Ezra 1:1ff, 5:13ff.

Grabbe also dismisses the view that Darius the Mede is based upon a single historical figure and argues that that character is 'a creation from commonplace beliefs about Persian times'.[12] Following Sparks,[13] he proposes that the character is based upon a confused reading of other OT texts. The books of Zechariah and Haggai date the rebuilding of the Temple to the reign of Darius, yet also give the impression that this occurred shortly after the return of the captives. The naïve reader would suppose that the name of the king who conquered Babylon was 'Darius'.[14] In response, Colless demonstrated that any author with access to the OT would have known the role of Cyrus in the fall of Babylon.[15]

The most straightforward explanation for the presence of Darius the Mede in the book of Daniel is that its author believed Darius to be a real historical character, perhaps based upon acquaintance with some tradition no longer extant. The question, then, is how reliable was the information on which the author based this character. Was it a confused, inaccurate tradition? Or was the writer himself a contemporary witness to Darius the Mede? In this next section we will review the descriptions of Darius the Mede and test them for their historical validity.

Median Names

There are critics of the book of Daniel who, somewhat naïvely, rebut the writer for naming a Mede 'Darius', asserting '"Darius" is a Persian name'.[16] Now this assertion is accurate to the extent that 'Darius' is the name of three Persian kings (Darius I Hystaspis; Darius II Nothus; Darius III, also named Codomanus) but it errs in making a false distinction between Median and Persian names.

In fact, the languages used by the Medes and Persians were essentially the same: 'judging from the Median names that we know, and from the fact that Darius used the same Aryan language for the great Behistun inscription in Media as he did for those he had incised in Persia, we may assume that the Old Median language differed only dialectically from the Old Persian'.[17] Rawlinson notes that 'many Median names are absolutely identical with Persian', while others are 'plainly mere variants'. Though there are some Median names which

---

[12] L.L. Grabbe, 'Another Look at the Gestalt of "Darius the Mede"', *CBQ* 50.2 (April 1988), 211.

[13] H.F.D. Sparks, 'On the Origin of "Darius the Mede" at Daniel V.31', *JTS* 47 (1940), 41-46.

[14] Grabbe, 'Darius the Mede', 212.

[15] B.E. Colless, 'Cyrus the Persian as Darius the Mede in the Book of Daniel', *JSOT* 56 (1992), 116.

[16] Davies, *Daniel*, 27.

[17] *Encyclopaedia Biblica* (London: Adam & Charles Black, 1899-1903), 3663. Also, see *The Catholic Encyclopedia*, vol.10 (New York: Robert Appleton, 1911); M. Marashi, *Persian Studies in North America* (Ibex, 1994); G. Rawlinson, *The Seven Great Monarchies of the Ancient Eastern World*, vol.3 ('Media').

share no known roots with Persian (e.g. 'Astyages' and 'Cyaxares'), the majority are the same or similar.

There are some phonetic differences between the Median and Persian dialects. For instance, Marashi demonstrates that 'Old Persia /s/ = Median /sp/' on the basis that the Median for dog is *spaka* (as noted by Herodotus) and the Old Persian for dog is *saka*.[18] Such phonetic differences, if they did effect our pronunciation of 'Darius' (*dārayavahush*), are unlikely to have been distinguished in the Hebrew transliteration דריוש (*dryvsh*). There can therefore be no historical objection to the possibility of a Mede named 'Darius'.

The name 'Ahasuerus' is also generally viewed as a Persian name since it is used in Esther (and probably Ezra 4:6) of the Persian king Xerxes I.

The name 'Xerxes' (Ξερξης) is a Greek transliteration of the Old Persian *Xshayārshā*. The Hebrew 'Ahasuerus' (אחשורוש *'chshwrwsh*) probably derives from this name. Ware writes: 'if the Old Persian word *xshathrapāvan* becomes *'chshdrpnym* in Hebrew . . . and if Old Persian *dārayavaush* becomes Hebrew *drywsh*, then Old Persian *xshayārshan* (i.e. Xerxes) ought to become Hebrew **'chshyrsh*'.[19] Ware notes that the Hebrew forms recorded in the OT texts (*'chshwrwsh*, with variants *'chshwrsh* and *'chshrsh*) are different from his proposed transliteration, but explains that these are probably 'misspellings' on the basis that the letters *yod* and *waw* are often confused. Now, the name *Xshayārshā* means 'ruler of heroes', derived from the Old Persian word *xshayathiya*, meaning 'royal'. The linguist Igor Diakonoff proposes that *xshayathiya* was a Median loan-word, based upon its phonology.[20] This being the case, then the name *Xshayārshā* ('Ahasuerus') would be of Median derivation.

The phrase 'the son of Ahasuerus'[21] is generally interpreted as meaning that Ahasuerus was the father of Darius but the Hebrew word, *ben*, may equally mean 'grandson', and in a wider sense 'ancestor' (see above). The author of Daniel may refer to Ahasuerus as some notable forebear of Darius. However, we know of only four Median kings – Deioces, Phraortes, Cyaxares and Astyages – whose names are recorded by Herodotus. Only the latter two names are witnessed outside Greek histories on the Behistun inscription. Other sources for Median figures are sparse since there are no Median texts extant.

Though we have no independent record of *Xshayārshā* the father (or ancestor) of *Dārayavahush*, the existence of such a figure is, linguistically-speaking, entirely plausible.

---

[18] Marashi, *Persian Studies*, 260.

[19] J.R. Ware, 'Ahasuerus and Xerxes', *The Classical Journal* 20:8 (May 1925), 489.

[20] I.M. Diaknoff, 'Media', in *Cambridge History of Iran* vol.2 (ed. I. Gershevitch; London: Cambridge University Press, 1985).

[21] Daniel 9:1.

A Median king, not King of the Medes

Many critics of Daniel have erroneously asserted that the author of Daniel posited the existence of an independent Median Kingdom between the fall of Babylon and the accession of Cyrus the Persian (see above). In fact, the book of Daniel is entirely consistent with the historical facts that the Kingdom of Babylon was conquered by the Medo-Persian Empire. There is no reference to Darius reigning over the Medes; it is recorded that Darius reigned over 'the realm of the Chaldeans' (5:30-1, 9:1).

Given that Cyrus, and his Persian Empire, was ultimately the inheritor of the Kingdom of Babylon, it has often been suggested by conservative scholars that Darius was appointed by Cyrus as regent or vassal-king over Babylon. The Assyrian kings often appointed such a regent, for example when Sennacherib ruled the Assyrian Empire he appointed his son, Ashur-nadin-shumu, as king of Babylon.[22] Cyrus himself appointed his son, Cambyses, as king of Babylon at some point during his reign. Several of Cyrus' generals were Medes[23] and so there is nothing implausible about the idea that Cyrus should appoint a Mede to rule over Babylon.

The difficulty with this proposal is that there is little internal evidence that Darius was considered to be a subordinate ruler. The expression 'was made king' (9:1) is often taken to imply that Darius was appointed (by Cyrus), however this idea is doubtful. In Syriac this expression was used of the normal succession with no implication of subordination.[24] Cyrus is not referred to in this verse and if ordination is implied it is best understood as the divine ordination of earthly kings (cf. 2:21).[25]

Rowley asserts that 'the authority of Darius was conceived as real and absolute'.[26] Darius issues a decree to 'all peoples, nations, and languages that dwell in all the earth' (6:25), which is the same mode of address used by Nebuchadnezzar (4:1). Also, Darius issued a statute forbidding anyone to petition any man or god, except Darius, from thirty days (6:7). It is inconceivable that a subordinate ruler would have had the authority to forbid any man petitioning Cyrus. On the other hand, it is implied by the text that the statute of Darius came into effect the very day it was written (6:9-10), which may mean that the statue was localized to Babylon, and did not contradict degrees from Persepolis. In the narrative, the satraps appeal to Darius' vanity to urge him to sign their foolish decree. It may be that Darius had delusions of grandeur and was an insubordinate subordinate. Even so, it is easier to read Darius as absolute ruler.

---

[22] Boutflower, *Daniel*, 151.
[23] J.M. Cook, *The Persian Empire* (London: J.M. Bent, 1923), 42.
[24] Grabbe, 'Darius the Mede', 208n.
[25] Colless, 'Cyrus as Darius', 119.
[26] Rowley, *Darius the Mede*, 53.

Historiography

Early Identifications

The earliest identifications proposed for Darius the Mede are found in the Greek version of the Jewish books. The Old Greek of Daniel 5:31 identifies Darius the Mede with Artaxerxes, presumably on the basis that Artaxerxes succeeded Xerxes (Ahasuerus).[27] The Book of Tobit names the conqueror of Nineveh, Cyaxares I, as 'Ahasuerus' (Ασυηρος),[28] which might imply that he believed Darius the Mede to be his son, Astyages (assuming that Tobit had the Ahasuerus of Dan. 9:1 in mind). The identification with Astyages is also supported by *Bel and the Dragon*, the apocryphal addition to the book of Daniel.[29] Neither of these views has gained much support. Artaxerxes was a Persian king and reigned too late to be a credible candidate. The identification with Astyages has been supported by a few scholars, such as Lightfoot in the seventeenth century[30] and Alfrink in the twentieth,[31] but is made unlikely by the Greek and cuneiform records which make no reference to Astyages ever ruling Babylon. Astyages's age is also a problem as it is highly improbable that he was 62 in 539 BC. Astyages came to the throne in 585 BC, which means that were he 62 in 539 BC then he would have been only 16 when he became king. He was deposed by his grandson, Cyrus, in 550 BC. It is inconceivable that Astyages could have had an adult grandchild by the age of 51.

Cyaxares II

Regarding Darius the Mede, Josephus states that 'he was the son of Astyages, and had another name among the Greeks'.[32] The latter clause has been taken as justification for almost every identification that has been proposed; however, the most straightforward interpretation is that Josephus was referring to Cyaxares II, the son of Astyages, referred to by Xenophon. This identification was popular up to the nineteenth century amongst both scholars[33] and laity.[34] However, by the twentieth century this view was all but abandoned as it was impos-

---

[27]   cf. Ezra 4:6.

[28]   'But before he died he heard of the destruction of Nineveh, which was taken by Nebuchadnezzar and Ahasuerus: and before his death he rejoiced over Nineveh' (Tobit 14:15).

[29]   'And king Astyages was gathered to his fathers, and Cyrus of Persia received his kingdom' (Dan. 14:1).

[30]   J. Lightfoot, 'A Chronicle of the Times and the Order of the Texts of the Old Testament' in *Works* (1684), 1-147.

[31]   B. Alfrink, 'Darius Medus', *Biblica* 9 (1928), 316-40.

[32]   *Antiquities of the Jews* 10.11.4.

[33]   Rowley cites Prideaux, Lowth, Hengstenberg, Rosenmüller, Hävernick, Dereser, Kranichfeld, Kliefoth, Füller, Keil, Zöckler, Watson and Knabenbauer as supporters of this view (Rowley, *Darius the Mede*, 37).

[34]   For example, B.W. Saville, 'Darius the Mede and Darius Hystapes', *Journal of Sacred Literature and Biblical Record* 5:9 (April 1857), 163-70.

sible to maintain the historicity of Xenophon's *Cyropaedia*.[35] For instance, Xenophon gives the impression that Cyrus was subordinate to Cyaxares II during his campaign against the Babylonians, while the other Greek historians (Herodotus and Ctesias) record that Cyrus deposed the Median king, Astyages, long before the fall of Babylon. There is also no other record of Cyaxares II. In fact Herodotus records that Astyages had no son.[36] In recent years there have been some attempts to defend the historicity of the *Cyropaedia*. For instance, Douglas Waterhouse has argued that the histories of Herodotus and Ctesias were biased by pro-Persian propaganda against the Medes, and particularly, against the half-Mede, Cyrus.[37] However, this attempt is not ultimately successful since the Babylonian records, in particular the *Nabonidus Chronicle*, agree with Herodotus and Ctesias against Xenophon that Cyrus annexed the Median kingdom from Astyages after the revolt of Median army.

Gobryas / Gubaru

Following the discovery and publication of the *Nabondius Chronicle*, Babelon,[38] followed by a series of other commentators,[39] proposed that Darius was none other than Cyrus' general Gobryas. The Chronicle reads:

> The sixteenth day, Gobryas [*Ugbaru*], the governor of Gutium, and the army of Cyrus entered Babylon without battle . . .

> In the month of Arahsamna, the third day, Cyrus entered Babylon, green twigs were spread in front of him – the state of peace was imposed upon the city. Cyrus sent greeting to all Babylon. Gobryas [*Gubaru*], his governor, installed sub-governors in Babylon.

This thesis has several elements that recommend it: Gobryas was the general who captured Babylon (cf. Dan. 5:30-31); Gobryas appointed sub-governors (cf. Dan. 6:1-2); according Xenophon, Gobryas was old at the time of the fall of Babylon (cf. Dan. 5:31).[40] In addition there are several references in the cuneiform records to a Gubaru as governor of Babylon.

---

[35] 'Even in ancient times it was perceived that Xenophon's Cyropaedia was no more than a historical romance, written for didactic purposes' (Rowley, *Darius the Mede*, 41).

[36] Herodotus, *Histories* I.110

[37] S.D. Waterhouse, 'Why was Darius the Mede Expunged from History?' in *To Understand the Scriptures: Essays in Honor of William H. Shea* (D. Merling ed.; Berrien Springs: Andrews University Press, 1997), 173-89.

[38] E. Babelon, 'Nouvelles remarqyes sur l'histoire de Cyrus, in Annales de philsophie chretienne', *New Series* 4 (1881), 674-83.

[39] See Rowley, *Darius the Mede*, 19, for citations.

[40] 'While they were concerned with these matters, an old Assyrian prince, Gobyras by name, presented himself before Cyrus, mounted on horseback and with a mounted retinue behind him' (*Cyropaedia* IV.6.1).

Rowley objected to the Gobryas thesis, asserting that there was no evidence that a) he was called 'Darius', b) he was the son of Ahasuerus, c) he was a Mede, and d) he bore the title 'king'.[41] The strongest objection against the Gobryas thesis is that the *Nabondius Chronicle* appears to record the death of Gobryas shortly after the fall of Babylon: 'In the month of Arahsamna, on the night of the eleventh, Gobryas [*Ugbaru*] died.'[42]

In 1959, John Whitcomb revived the Gobryas thesis, arguing that Gubaru, governor of Babylon, should be distinguished from Ugbaru, governor of Gutium, and also from a later Persian Gubaru recorded on the Behistun inscription.[43] Whitcomb, using the cuneiform texts that name Gubaru, identified Darius the Mede as Gubaru, the governor of Babylon under Cyrus (and Cambyses). However, more recent research has demonstrated that the Gubaru of these texts did not become governor until the fourth year of Cyrus, far too late to be identified with Darius the Mede; prior to this the governor of Babylon was Nabû-ahhê-bullit.[44] In any case, it is difficult to suppose Gubaru was ever called 'king'. Cyrus had appointed his son, Cambyses, to be his regent in Babylon.[45]

Cambyses
It was consideration of the subordinate position of Gobryas that led Boutflower to reject the Gobryas thesis in favour of Winckler's proposition that Darius the Mede was Cambyses, king of Babylon.[46] Since Cambyses reigned as regent of Babylon, this proposition coheres suitably with the biblical data that Darius the Mede ruled over the kingdom of the Chaldeans. Boutflower argues that Cambyses is of Median descent through his mother Amytis, the daughter of Astyag-

---

[41] Rowley, *Darius the Mede*, 21-26.

[42] Rowley considered this reading of the damaged text to be 'very doubtful' because of references to Gobryas after this date (Rowley, *Darius the Mede*, 21). It is now generally held that the Gobryas of later texts is a different individual.

[43] J.C. Whitcomb, *Darius the Mede: A Study in Historical Identification* (Philadelphia: Presbyterian & Reformed, 1959). 'His unique contribution is in differentiating Gubaru from Ugbaru in the cuneiform document . . . the confusion between Gubaru and Ugbaru arose because in one of the original translation both names were transliterated Gobryas' (R.B. Dillard, *An Introduction to the Old Testament* (Zondervan, 2006), 335).

[44] 'Gubaru . . . was in office from the fourth year of Cyrus to the fifth of Cambyses (534-525 BC)' (W.B. Fisher, *The Cambridge History of Iran* (Cambridge University Press, 1985), 563); also, see Grabbe, 'Darius the Mede', 206.

[45] George Cameron in his review of Whitcomb's book argues: 'what we do know of Persian history tells us that the assumption by a satrap or governor of the royal title, whether it be in Aramaic, Babylonian, Elamite or elsewhere, would be tantamount to open revolt against the sovereign' (G.C. Cameron, 'Review: *Darius the Mede: A Study in Historical Identification* by John C. Whitcomb, Jr.', *JBL* 79.1 (March 1960), 70). Rowley writes that it would be impossible for 'the subordinate of a subordinate' to be called 'king' (Rowley, *Darius the Mede*, 24-28).

[46] C. Boutflower, 'The Historial Value of Daniel v and vi', *JTS* 17 (1915-6), 43-60, and Boutflower, *Daniel*, 142-67.

es[47] and so is the ancestor of Cyaxares I, whom he identifies with Ahasuerus, on the basis of the book of Tobit.[48]

Boutflower calculates that Cambyses may have been around the age of twelve when he became king of Babylon. He proposes that 'twelve' was the original reading of Daniel 5:31, rather than 'sixty-two', on the basis that the ancients represented numbers by letters of the alphabet and the original *yod* (representing 'ten') was mistaken for a *samekh* ('sixty').[49]

Rowley is not impressed by Boutflower's evidence for the use of letters as numerals, arguing that his examples are late and that there is no evidence that such a practice was customary in the sixth century BC. He concludes that Boutflower's proposed amendment to the text is 'merely dictated by the theory it is intended to accommodate'.[50] Rowley also casts doubt upon the authority of Ctesias, who is the only ancient source who records that Cambyses' mother was Amytis, daughter of Astyages; other sources name Amytis as the wife of Nebuchadnezzar.[51] These criticisms have stuck and there has been little attempt in recent years to recycle Boutflower's thesis.

Cyrus

A new identification for Darius the Mede was proposed by D.J. Wiseman in *Notes on Some Problems in the Book of Daniel*, where he suggested that 'Darius the Mede' was another name for Cyrus the Persian. The thesis rests on the dual-meaning of the conjunction *waw*, which is generally translated 'and' but may also be used to indicate identity.[52] For instance, I Chronicles 5:26 is translated 'so the God of Israel stirred up the spirit of Pul king of Assyria, *even* [*waw*] the spirit of Tiglath-pileser king of Assyria', as Pul and Tiglath-pileser were the same individual. Hence, Daniel 6:28 may be translated either as:

So Daniel prospered during the reign of Darius *and* [*waw*] in the reign of Cyrus the Persian[53]

or:

So Daniel prospered during the reign of Darius, *that is*, [*waw*] the reign of Cyrus the Persian[54]

---

[47] Boutflower, *Daniel*, 152
[48] Boutflower, *Daniel*, 155. Yet Boutflower admits: 'it is, however, a mistake to seek to identify the name "Cyaxares" with the name "Ahasuerus"'.
[49] Boutflower, *Daniel*, 156-67.
[50] Rowley, *Darius the Mede*, 13-15.
[51] Rowley, *Darius the Mede*, 16.
[52] D.J. Wiseman (ed.), *Notes on Some Problems in the Book of Daniel* (London: The Tyndale Press, 1965), 12. For further study of this usage see: D.W. Baker, 'Further Examples of the Waw Explicativum', *VT* 30 (1980), 129-36.
[53] cf. NKJV, ESV, etc.
[54] cf. NLT footnote, NIV footnote.

This identification is useful since it removes the problem of 'finding room' for Darius the Mede, between the fall of Babylon and reign of Cyrus. Some of the biographical data can also be matched. Cyrus was named 'king' and he did appoint governors.[55] Also, Herodotus records that Cyrus was the son of Mandane, daughter of Astyages, therefore Cyrus was half-Median. Also, the Harran Stele refers to a 'king of the Medes' years after the death of Astyages, who can only be identified as Cyrus.[56] As we have seen, Rowley asserted that Cyrus was around sixty-two at the fall of Babylon, on the testimony of Cicero who preserves a fragment from Dinon of Colophon (c.300 BC).[57]

Cyrus' father was named Cambyses, not Xerxes (Ahasuerus). Shea has argued that 'Ahasuerus' may be the Hebrew form of the Greek 'Cyaxares';[58] Cyaxares was the father of Astyages and hence Cyrus' maternal great-grandfather.

Wiseman's thesis has been criticized by Grabbe who brands it an 'exercise in apologetics' because, though it cannot be disproved, it does not appear to be prompted by positive evidence.[59] However, this thesis has more recently been defended by Bulmann[60] and Colless.[61] Bulmann marshals a variety of evidences to justify the claim that Cyrus was also known as 'Darius', including the fact that amongst many peoples Cyrus was regarded as a Median king.[62] Colless has argued that 'the reader is expected to understand, by the author's principle of dual nomenclature for many of the characters in the book, that Darius and Cyrus are one and the same person'.[63] One interesting observation is that it is stated that Daniel was in service till the first year of Cyrus (1:19-21) but his (Babylonian) service ended when Darius received the kingdom.

---

[55] 'It is probable that the satrapy system already existed in the time of Cyrus, since the title khshathrapanva is Median, and the organization was a development of the provincial governorships initiated by the Assyrians' (Wiseman, *Notes*, 14).

[56] Wiseman, *Notes*, 13.

[57] 'For Cicero preserves a tradition that he [Cyrus] lived to be seventy years old, having reigned thirty years in all. Since his death appears to have taken place in the ninth year of his reign, according to the Babylonian reckoning from the annexation of the Babylonian empire, if Cicero is to be relied on for his age at death, we should arrive at an age of sixty-one at the time of his overthrow of Nabonidus and Belshazzar' (Rowley, *Darius the Mede*, 55-56. For further references see Wiseman, *Notes*, 15 and Mitchell, 'Achaemenid History and the Book of Daniel, 75).

[58] W.H. Shea, 'Darius the Mede in his Persian-Babylonian Setting', *AUSS* 29 (1991), 235-57. Also, see C.C. Torrey, 'Medes and Persians', *JAOS* 66:1 (January-March 1946), 7-8.

[59] Grabbe, 'Darius the Mede', 207.

[60] J.M. Bulman, 'The Identification of Darius the Mede', *WTJ* 35:3 (Spring 1973), 247-67.

[61] Colless, 'Cyrus as Darius'.

[62] Bulman, 'Darius', 259.

[63] Colless, 'Cyrus as Darius', 116. The examples of double identity Colless cites include Daniel/Belteshazzar, little horn/king of the north and Ancient of Days/Most High (113).

Ugbaru

In series of articles W.H. Shea presented the thesis that for just over a year after the fall of Babylon a certain individual bore the title 'king of Babylon', who was neither Cyrus nor Cambyses.[64] The Neo-Babylonian kings bore the title 'king of Babylon' in documents dated to their reigns. The Persian kings, from Cyrus to Darius I, employed the title 'king of Babylon, kings of Lands'. However, Shea writes, 'it is clear from the contract tablet evidence that Cyrus did not take up the title "king of Babylon" during his accession year and most of his first year of rule there'.[65] Previously this gap in the titular usage was explained by the co-regency of Cyrus and Cambyses, which is witnessed by dual-references on some economic documents. However, in 1938 W. Dubberstein had proposed an alternative thesis that the co-regency occurred at the end of the reign of Cyrus.[66] This thesis was evidenced by Dubberstein from the peculiar titular use on one contract tablet: 'year 1, accession year, Cambyses king of Babylon and Lands',[67] and supported by Shea using comparisons with co-regencies of other Persian kings.[68] If this conclusion is sound then between the months Tasritu 539 and Tebetu 538, neither Cyrus nor Cambyses bore the title 'king of Babylon'. Shea proposed that Ugbaru, the general who captured Babylon, was 'king of Babylon' in these months.

As noted above the *Nabonidus Chronicle* records that Ugbaru died three weeks after the fall of Babylon. However, Shea has suggested a new reading of this record. After the fall of Babylon the Chronicle records events in this order:

> In the month of Arahsamna, the third day, Cyrus entered Babylon . . .

> From the month of Kislîmu to the month of Addaru, the gods of Akkad which Nabonidus had made come down to Babylon, were returned to their sacred cities.

> In the month of Arahsamna, on the night of the eleventh, Ugbaru died

Shea argued that these events should be considered consecutively,[69] in which case Ugbaru died the year after the fall of Babylon, a matter of weeks before

---

[64] W.H. Shea, 'An Unrecognized Vassal King of Babylon in the Early Achaemenid Period I', *AUSS* 9 (1971), 52-67; W.H. Shea, 'Darius the Mede: An Update', *AUSS* 20.3 (Autumn 1982), 229-47.

[65] Shea, 'Darius the Mede', 236.

[66] W.H. Dubberstein, 'The Chronology of Cyrus and Cambyses', *The American Journal of Semitic Languages and Literatures* 55.4 (October 1938), 417-19.

[67] TuM 203 92:11-14.

[68] Shea, 'Darius the Mede', 238-39.

[69] 'I surveyed the dated events in all ten known texts of the Babylonian Chronicle . . . I found that of the 318 chronological observations recorded in these ten texts, 313 are in consecutive order according to the dated events which precede or follow them' (Shea, 'Darius the Mede', 241); also, see W.H. Shea, 'An Unrecognized Vassal King III', *AUSS* 10 (1972), 102-108.

Cyrus adopted the title 'king of Babylon'.[70] Thus, Shea proposes that Darius the Mede is none other than Ugbaru, governor of Gutium.[71]

This thesis has much to recommend it. Firstly, Ugbaru may well have been king of Babylon. Though there is no record of the accession of Ugbaru, the fact that his name[72] (and his death[73]) is recorded on the Nabondius Chronicle may indicate that he was considered royal.[74] In any case, if Ugbaru ruled Babylon during the interregnum (before the accession of Cyrus) then he was *de facto* king. The length of his rule is consistent with the data recorded in Daniel for the reign Darius the Mede and Cyrus' succession. Secondly, Ugbaru was the general that conquered Babylon, which coheres with the statements in Daniel 5:30-31. Thirdly, though his age is not specifically mentioned, it is plausible that Ugbaru was elderly when he became king since he dies the following year. Shea comments that we cannot determine whether or not Ugbaru was a Median,[75] though the fact that he was governor of Gutium may recommend this. Diakonoff proposed that Gutium should be identified with Media; in the annals, the allies of Babylonia are recorded as 'Elam, Amurru (Syro-Palestine), Meluhha (Egypt) and Gutium' and we know that Media was one of the allies of Babylon at that time.[76] Dandamaev is more cautious but also asserts that Gutium was not a province of Babylon.[77] R. Zadok suggested that Gutium was 'an Achaemenid province comprising at least part of western Media and north eastern Assyria which bordered on Babylonia'.[78] Mitchell concludes 'to describe

[70] Shea, 'Darius the Mede', 243.
[71] cf. K. Koch, 'Dareios der Meder', in *The Word of the Lord Shall Go Forth* (C.L. Meyers & M. O'Connor, eds.; Winona Lake: Eisenbrauns, 1983), 287-99.
[72] 'only seven persons mentioned by name in the chronicles were not kings' (Shea, 'Darius the Mede', 244).
[73] 'of the twenty-two individuals for whom death dates are available from the chronicles, twenty were kings or queens while only two were non-royal persons' (Shea, 'Darius the Mede', 244).
[74] However, Dandamaev writes: 'not once in the Chronicle is Ugbaru called king; besides, there are no documents which are dated to his rule' (Dandamaev, *Achaemenid Empire*, 59).
[75] Shea, 'Darius the Mede', 247.
[76] I.M. Diakonoff, *The History of Media* (Moscow, 1956), 287-88.
[77] 'It is noteworthy that, having conquered Babylonia in 539 BC, Cyrus returned the gods and citizens deported to Babylon at Nabondius' order to their former abodes. According to the Cyrus Cylinder, these cities extended 'until the border of Gutium'. Consequently, Gutium did not belong to the Babylonian empire' (Dandamaev, *Achaemenid Empire*, 43).
[78] Zadok, cited Dandamaev, *Achaemenid Empire*, 43. Beaulieu notes that Gutium is listed separately from 'the Umman-mandi' (i.e. the Medes) on the Cyrus Cylinder (11-14) and concludes 'one can infer it was conquered by Cyrus, but that it had not been part of the Median kingdom' (Beaulieu, *Nabonidus*, 229). However, since the Umman-mandi is a people, not a region, these lines do not necessarily entail that the two are distinct and exclusive. The reading 'Gutium and all the Umman-mandi' may imply 'Gutium and all the other Medes'.

Gubaru as governor of Gutium therefore is in effect to name him governor of Media, and to open up the possibility that he was actually of Median birth him-self.[79]

Convenient as this thesis is, it depends upon the proposition that Cambyses was not king of Babylon during the first fourteen months after the fall of Babylon. This proposition has been shaken by the more recent research. For instance, Jerome Peat argues that the co-regency of Cyrus and Cambyses occurred in the first year after the fall of Babylon.[80] Peat examines the individuals named on the cuneiform tablets dated to the co-regency and demonstrates that one such individual, Kidin-Marduk, was bankrupt and possibly dead, by the fourth year of Cyrus. As such, the loan to Kidin-Marduk recorded on the tablet Camb.81 cannot be dated later than the fourth year of Cyrus. Since Camb.81 is dated according the co-regency, the co-regency cannot have occurred later than the fourth year of Cyrus.

A similar line of argument as Peat's was originally proposed by San Nicolò in 1941[81] and Shea does consider this possibility in his article. Shea attempted to cover his thesis stating that if the co-regency occurred in early in Cyrus' reign:

> I would suggest that it occurred in Cyrus' 2nd year, not his 1st, because of the chronology of the events narrated in the Nabonidus Chronicle, where Cambyses' participation in the Babylonian New Year's festival is placed at the beginning of Cyrus' 2nd regnal year.[82]

It is true that Cambyses had to be king of Babylon to participate in the New Year's festival and that, according to Shea's consecutive reading of the Nabonidus Chronicle, this occurred at the beginning of Cyrus' 2nd regnal year, but if this is the case then it inconsistent with Cyrus' use of the title 'king of Babylon' during his 2nd regnal year. However, if we place Cambyses' participation in the New Year festival at the beginning of Cyrus' 1st regnal year then this inconsistency disappears. In addition Peat notes that seven co-regency texts place the name of Cyrus first, i.e. 'the first year of Cyrus king of Lands, Cambyses king of Babylon', which seem to confirm that the co-regency occurred in Cyrus' 1st regnal year.[83] Therefore, the standard reading of the Nabonidus Chronicle seems required, which places the death of Ugbaru three weeks after he took the city.

---

[79] Mitchell, 'Achaemenid History and the Book of Daniel', 76.

[80] J. Peat, 'Cyrus "King of Lands", Cambyses "King of Babylon": The Disputed Co-Regency', *JCS* 41:2 (Autumn 1989), 199-216.

[81] M. San Nicolò, *Beiträge zu einer Prosoporagraphie neubabyloniscer Beamtender Zivil- und Tempelverwaltung* (Munich, 1941).

[82] Shea, 'Darius the Mede', 240.

[83] Peat, 'Disputed Co-Regency', 209; also, see Dandamaev, *Achaemenid Empire*, 58.

More recently Shea has returned to his Ugbaru-thesis.[84] He admits that his chronology was 'misguided' and agrees that the death of Ugbaru took place '25 days after he conquered Babylon and only 8 days after Cyrus arrived there'.[85] However, Shea argues that the activities ascribed to Darius the Mede could have occurred within a 25 day reign,[86] or even an 8 day reign (!)[87] Perhaps the most interesting detail of the thesis is Shea's proposal that the thirty-day embargo on prayers and petitions (Dan. 6:6-9) correlates with, and thus explains, the delayed return to their home cities of the Babylonian gods which Nabonidus had gathered into Babylon.[88]

It is interesting to note that as similar theory was proposed in 1942 by Herbert Owen, who proposed a seventeen day reign for Ugbaru assuming that his reign ended when Cyrus entered the city. Owen argues that it is possible for us to conceive of 'an individual like 'Ugbaru, the governor of Gutium', mentioned in the Nabonidus Chronicle tablet as entering Babylon with the troops of Cyrus seventeen days before the entry of Cyrus himself, being temporarily regarded and named as a king by a Hebrew prophet in high office, such as Daniel is described as being in the book of Daniel'. Owen goes further, proposing that 'Artaxerxes' in the LXX of Daniel 5:31 is a corruption of the name 'Ugbaru'. This portion of his paper is not particularly convincing.[89]

There is a difficulty with this thesis in that the book of Daniel dates the seventy-week prophecy to 'the first year of his [Darius'] reign'. Since Ugbaru's reign does not extend to the New Year, the short reign of Ugbaru would have all fallen within his accession year – he would not have had a 'first year'. Shea defends his thesis, arguing that 'co-regents do not have an "accession year"'.[90] A simpler explanation may be that a Jewish writer did not have a word to express 'accession-year'. For example, in Jeremiah 25:1 the regnal year of Nebuchadnezzar is incorrectly identified as his 'first year' [NKJV] when it was in fact his accession-year [cf. NLT footnote]. Elsewhere, Jeremiah identifies the

---

[84] W.H. Shea, 'Nabonidus Chronicle: New Readings and the Identity of Darius the Mede', *JATS* 7:1 (Spring 1996), 1-20; W.H. Shea, 'The Search for Darius the Mede (Concluded), or, The Time of the Answer to Daniel's Prayer and the Date of the Death of Darius the Mede', *JATS* 12:1 (Spring 2001), 97-105.

[85] Shea, 'Nabonidus Chronicle', 2.

[86] Shea, 'Nabonidus Chronicle', 2-4.

[87] Shea, 'Search Concluded', 98-99. In this article Shea argues that Ugbaru was appointed king by Cyrus when Cyrus entered the city on 3 Arahsamna.

[88] Nabonidus Chronicle 21-22; Shea, 'Nabonidus Chronicle', 11; Shea, 'Search Concluded', 100.

[89] H. Owen, 'The Enigma of Darius the Mede: a Way to its Final Solution', *JTVI* 74 (1942), 72-98.

[90] Shea, 'Search Concluded', 98. 'We have the example right from this same period of Cambyses, where only the first year of his co-regency shows up in the datelines on the tablets – no accession year texts. . . . There are also the double dated texts from the 12th dynasty in Egypt, which show the same phenomenon' (98n).

regnal years of Nebuchadnezzar correctly.[91] Another difficulty for this thesis is that the author of Daniel makes no effort to express the fact that the events of chapters 5-6 and 9 all took place within 25 days, something we might legitimately expect him to do.

We cannot test the Ugbaru thesis further since, apart from the brief references in the Nabonidus Chronicle, and Xenophon's shaky testimony about Gobryas, we know almost nothing about Ugbaru.

Summary

The work of conservative scholars has forced the reappraisal of the question by critical scholars. For instance, G.C. Cameron in reviewing Whitcomb's thesis conceded that the character of Darius the Mede may have been based on 'a faint remembrance'.[92] In Grabbe's latest assessment of the issue he states: 'Darius "the Mede" may well have elements of genuine historical memory behind him.'[93] Today few serious scholars would propose that Darius the Mede is entirely fictional. Nevertheless, despite the best efforts of conservative scholars, a definite historical identification still eludes us.

The two most likely candidates are Ugbaru and Cyrus.[94] Shea's proposal that the twenty-five day occupation of Babylon by Ugbaru prior to Cyrus' accession constitutes the first year of Darius the Mede is not inconceivable, though it appears unlikely. The identification of Cyrus with Darius the Mede is, historically-speaking, less problematic, though it depends on the idea that dual-nomenclature was an acceptable literary technique for an ancient Jewish writer – to the modern reader it can simply appear confusing.

The key piece of evidence is still missing – there is yet to be discovered any Babylonian, Median or Persian text that names any individual 'Darius the Mede'. Proponents for every candidate have suggested that 'Darius' may be a throne-name. Though reasonable in principle, this suggestion flounders in its application since if 'Darius' was his throne name then he should have been referred to as such in cuneiform texts dating from his reign, as Rowley rightly objects.[95] In the cases of Cyrus, Cambyses, and Gubaru, it is demonstrably false that they used 'Darius' as a throne-name. We do not have any cuneiform texts dated to the reign of Ugbaru so we do not know whether or not he adopted a different throne-name. However, his name is recorded on the *Nabonidus Chronicle* as Ugbaru, which implies that this was his official name. It is more

---

[91] Also see Thiele, *Mysterious Numbers*, 184-85 and Owen, 'Darius the Mede', 74.

[92] Cameron, 'Review', 71.

[93] L.L. Grabbe, 'A Dan(iel) for All Season: From Whom was Daniel Important?' in *The Book of Daniel: Composition and Reception* (vol.1; ed. J.J. Collins & P.W. Flint; Leiden: Brill, 2001), 233.

[94] Mitchell reminds his readers that Darius the Mede may turn out to be some third, as yet unknown, individual ('Achaemenid History and the Book of Daniel', 77).

[95] Rowley, *Darius the Mede*, 22.

credible to suppose that 'Darius the Mede' was a colloquial name, perhaps used only amongst the Jews.[96] If this is the case then it is less likely that we will ever discover a cuneiform text bearing that name.

The British Museum houses a collection of around 130,000 cuneiform texts, about a third of which have never been published. It is possible that one of the thousands of texts yet to be published will bear the name 'Darius the Mede'. Until this essential piece of evidence is discovered, Darius the Mede remains unknown to secular history. Though conservative scholars have been able to produce some credible hypotheses, definitive proof still eludes us.

---

[96] cf. Bulmann, 'Darius', 265.

Chapter 10

The Persian and Greek Periods

Whilst most of the narrative chapters of the book of Daniel are set in the Neo-Babylonian period, the book does refer to later periods especially in its vision chapters. Here, again, certain critical scholars have questioned the historical accuracy of the book. In this chapter we will explore a number of these alleged inaccuracies and demonstrate that these allegations prove false.

Satraps

Daniel 6:1 describes how Darius the Mede set one hundred and twenty satraps over his kingdom. This has often been seen as an inaccuracy since Herodotus records that Darius I Hystaspis divided the Persian empire into twenty satrapies (*Histories* III, 89). Rowley, who believed that the author had confused Darius the Mede for Darius Hystaspis, also comments that the inscriptions of Darius Hystaspis 'variously mention twenty-one, twenty-three, twenty-four and twenty-nine divisions of his dominions'.[1] The number of satrapies in Daniel 6:1 is closer to the number of provinces ascribed to Xerxes I in Esther 1:1 (i.e. one hundred and twenty seven). The book of Esther does not claim that there were one hundred and twenty seven satraps but that some of the one hundred and twenty seven provinces were governed by satraps (cf. Esther 8:9).

'Satrap' is an Iranian word of Median origin. The title existed long before Darius I divided his empire into twenty satrapies; it seems to have been used as a title of independent chiefs in northwestern Iran even prior to the emergence of the Median kingdom.[2] Millard argues that, whilst the Iranian word 'satrap' had a specific meaning in the administration of Darius I, the equivalent word in Babylonian and Aramaic texts (*pīhatu*) has a wider meaning 'embracing controllers of the vast territory of Babylonia and Transeuphratene . . . and of small regions such as Judah or Samaria'.[3] Therefore, he argues, 'the possibility may

---

[1]   Rowley, *Darius the Mede*, 54.

[2]   Muhammad A. Dandamaev & Vladimir G. Lukonin, *The Culture and Social Institutions of Ancient Iran* (Cambridge: Cambridge University Press, 2004), 100.

[3]   Alan R. Millard, 'Daniel in Babylon: An Accurate Record?' in *Do Historical Matters Matter to Faith?: A Critical Appraisal of Modern and Postmodern Approaches to Scripture* (eds. James K. Hoffmeier and Dennis R. Magary; Wheaton, IL: Crossway, 2012), 277.

be envisaged, therefore, that the term could be applied more widely than He-rodotus' report about the reign of Darius I implies'.[4] The word used in Daniel 6:1 and in Esther is *'achashdarpan* (cf. Ezra 8:36). This same word is used in Daniel 3 to refer to a post within the Babylonian administration under Nebu-chadnezzar (cf. Dan. 3:2, 3, 27).

Returning to Herodotus' report, Millard states that Darius I divided his em-pire into twenty satrapies. As observed above, Darius was not the first to coin the term 'satrap' but his division of the empire was new:

> There were almost certainly satraps before Darius, but Darius was the first sys-tematically to divide up the empire into provinces and put satrap in charge of them.[5]

If Daniel 6:1 had said that shortly after the fall of Babylon the new king (a.k.a. Darius the Mede) had divided the Persian empire into twenty satrapies then he would have committed an anachronism. A second century author, cribbing his historical information from Greek historians, is likely to have fallen into this trap. Prior to the reign of Darius I 'satrap' was not a restrictive term referring to only twenty persons:

> The post of strap was known from the beginning of the emergence of the Achae-menid empire, but under Cyrus, Cambyses, and in the first years of the reign of Darius I, the local kings, chiefs and civil servants were the governors of many countries. . . . The reforms of the Darius, in particular, were directed toward con-centrating the leading posts in the hands of Persians[6]

Assuming, then, that the author of Daniel uses 'satrap' in the broader sense, as suggested by Millard, then the description in Daniel 6:1 is entirely plausible in its historical setting.

Persian King-List

One frequent claim of critical scholars is that the author of Daniel had a limited knowledge of Persian history, knowing only four Persian kings.[7] This is based upon Daniel 11:2:

> Now then, I tell you the truth: Three more kings will arise in Persia, and then a fourth, who will be far richer than all the others. When he has gained power by his wealth, he will stir up everyone against the kingdom of Greece.

---

[4] Millard, 'Daniel in Babylon', 277.
[5] Samuel Edward Finer, *The History of Government from the Earliest Times: Ancient Monarchies and Empires* (Oxford: Oxford University Press, 1997), 303.
[6] Dandamaev & Lukonin, *Ancient Iran*, 101.
[7] E.g. K. Koch, *Das Buch Daniel* (Darmstadt: Wissenschaftliche Buchgesellschaft, 1980), 149.

Torrey takes this objection to the extreme, arguing that the book of Daniel forms part of a wider Jewish tradition that knew only four Persian kings: Cyrus, Artaxerxes I, Darius II and Artaxerxes II (Darius the Mede and Ahasuerus are counted as Median kings).[8] However, Torrey's thesis is handicapped by his overemphasis of the *Sedar Olam*, and other later Talmudic works, which inform his position. It need not be said that Ahasuerus is described as a Persian king in Ezra and Esther,[9] that Darius I is more probably the king referred to in the early chapters of Ezra,[10] and that Artaxerxes III and Darius III are correctly omitted as they reigned after the last events of the Old Testament. Since the books of Ezra, Nehemiah and Esther correctly identify six Persian kings, even a second-century author would have had sufficient information to know there were not only four kings.

Contrary to the critical assertions, Daniel 11:2 does not state that there were only four Persian kings in total, but that the fourth Persian king would stir up Greek aggression. This statement fits well with the history of the period as it was the Persian attacks on Greek territories at Marathon (490), Thermopylae (480), Salamis (480), and Plataiai (479) which were contributing factors in the unification of the Greek states against the Persian Empire.[11]

Jewish Chronology and the Sixty-Two Weeks

In Daniel 9:24-27 the angel Gabriel prophesies that from 'the word to restore Jerusalem' there will be seventy year-weeks till the consummation of transgression and establishment of everlasting righteousness. These seventy weeks are divided into three periods of seven, sixty-two and one weeks. The critical interpretation of this prophecy is that the seven weeks cover the period of the captivity, the sixty-two weeks last till the murder of Onias III and the one week covers the period of the Maccabean revolt. Setting aside the interpretative difficulties, the critical scholar is faced with the glaring fact that his sixty-two week period will not fit into our established chronology. The *terminus ad quem* (end-date) of the sixty-two weeks is predetermined to 170 BC as the murder of Onias III. The *terminus a quo* (start-date) is likewise predetermined to 539 as the end of the captivity. Thus the period proposed for the sixty-two weeks is 539-170; a total of 369 years (539 – 170 = 369). However, commentators are unanimous that the sixty-two weeks should total 434 years (62 x 7 = 434).

Many scholars attempt to answer this difficulty by claiming that it is the author of Daniel who is in error. For instance, Montgomery is forced to admit 'we can meet this objection only by surmising a chronological miscalculation on

---

[8] Torrey, *Medes and Persians*, 1-15.
[9] cf. Ezra 4:6, Esther 1:1-3f.
[10] Ezra 4:24ff.
[11] cf. A. Laato, 'The Seventy Yearweeks in the Book of Daniel', *ZAW* 102:2 (1990), 215-16.

part of the author'.[12] The reason for this miscalculation is the (assumed) 'absence of a known chronology'. Porteous comments: 'as the historical memory which the Jews retained of the period in question was very dim as regards facts, it may well be that they were equally vague as to the actual length of time that had elapsed since the return from exile'.[13] Yet the notion that our author's knowledge of the Persian and Hellenistic periods was 'vague' seems based on little more than critical rhetoric. The oft-cited example is Daniel 11:2, which demonstrates no error in knowledge at all (see above); had the author known only four Persian kings this would have shortened, not lengthened, his chronology.

The critical interpretation of the sixty-two weeks has often been defended by reference to Schürer's comment that ancient Jewish historians have a corresponding inaccuracy in their chronologies.[14] Schürer cites four examples; three from Josephus (1st century AD) and one from Demetrius (3rd century BC). Josephus states that:

a) from the second year of Cyrus (c.537) till the destruction of the Temple by the Romans (70 AD) there were 639 years and 45 days (there were actually 607 years);[15]

b) from the end of the seventy years captivity (c.538) till Antiochus V Eupator (164-162) here were 414 years (there were actually 374 years);[16]

c) from the return of the exiles (c.538) till Aristobulus I (105-104) there were 481 years and 3 months (there were actually 433 years).[17]

Demetrius states that:

d) from the captivity of the ten tribes of Israel (c.722) till Ptolemy IV (222) were 573 years and 9 months (there were actually c.500 years).[18]

Though none of these discrepancies is exactly equal to the proposed +65 year discrepancy in Daniel 9, they might appear strong evidence that a second century Jewish chronology might have contained such a discrepancy. Closer analysis reveals that the opposite is more likely.

[12] Montgomery, *Daniel*, 393.
[13] Porteous, *Daniel*, 141.
[14] E. Schürer, *Geschichte des jüdischen Volkes im Zeitalter Jesu Christi* (Dritter Band, Vierte Auflage, 1909), 266f. E.g. cited by Montgomery, *Daniel*, 393.
[15] Josephus, *The Jewish War* VI.48.
[16] Josephus, *The Antiquities of the Jews* XX.10.1.
[17] *Antiquities* XIII.11.1.
[18] Demetrius, quoted by Clement of Alexandria, *Stromata* I.21.141.

	a)		b)		c)		d)	
	53	B	53	B	53	B	72	B
	7	C	8	C	8	C	2	C
	+	A	-	B	-	B	-	B
	70	D	164	C	105	C	222	C
	60	y	37	y	43	y	50	y
	7		4		3		0	
	63	y	41	y	48	y	57	y
	9		4		1		3	
	-	y	-	y	-	y	50	y
	607		374		433		0	
discrepancy:	32	y	40	y	48	y	73	y

Table 1

The statement of Demetrius seems to indicate that there was a +73 year discrepancy between his and modern chronology. In the same quotation Demetrius also states that there were only 338 years and 3 months between the captivity of Judah and Ptolemy IV (there were actually 365 years). In this case there is a -27 year discrepancy in Demetrius' chronology. A. Laato points out that, according to Demetrius' figures, the time between the two captivities is exactly 100 years too long and so proposes that one of the figures is a typographical error. Laato proposes that 473 and 338 were the intended figures as they are closest to the accepted chronology.[19] If this is the case then both figures indicate that Demetrius' chronology was 27 years too short.

The three statements from Josephus appear to indicate +32, +40 and +48 discrepancies in his chronology. As these periods overlap we can calculate the discrepancies for various periods, assuming Josephus is consistent in his chronology. So the discrepancy for the period in question (539-170) is +40, while for the subsequent periods 164-105 and 105 BC-70 AD it is +8 and -16 respectively.

Table 2	Actual	b)	c)	a)*
538-164	374	414 (+40)	414 (+40)	414 (+40)
164-105	59		67 (+8)	67 (+8)
105 BC – 70 AD	175			159* (-16)
Total:	608	414 (+40)	481 (+48)	640* (+32)

---

[19] Laato, 'Seventy Yearweeks', 219.

* The *terminus a quo* of figures b) and c) is 538 BC, while that of a) is 537. To compensate a) is given as 640 (639+1).

These figures may be contrasted with the sum of the regnal lengths that Josephus records for the high priests during the periods 164-105, 105 BC-70 AD.[20]

Table 3 - High Priests (164-105 BC)	
Jacimus (Judas)	3
interregnum	7
Jonathan	7
Simon	8
Hyrcanus I	30
Total:	55 years

Table 4 - High Priests (105 BC-70 AD)	
Aristobulus I	1
Alexander	27
Hyrcanus II	7
Aristobulus II	3
Hyrcanus II	24
Antigonus	3
Herod till destruction of Temple	107
Total:	174 years

The sum totals for these periods are much closer to the actual figures, having a discrepancy of only -4 and -1 respectively. Therefore, to argue that the Jews had no 'known chronology' is simply false; the regnal figures of the High Priests would have provided a reasonably accurate basis on which to base chronological statements.

We should also bear in mind the textual variants that exist within the Josephus MSS. In 1851 Hooper noted:

> In each of 6 long chronometrical lines, which either have a *terminus* at or traverse this Division, there is a Various Reading reducing the amount by 100 years.[21]

The explanation for these variants is not immediately obvious. As Hooper states, 'the number of them forbids the hypothesis of *accidental* corruption';[22] whichever set of variants we take as original, the other must be explained as a deliberate alteration. For instance, Sir Isaac Newton asserted that the Jews had tampered with their chronology to preclude the Christian interpretation of Daniel 9. It is interesting to note that if we accept the shorter variant then the first year of Cyrus would fall approximately 483 years (sixty-nine weeks) prior to

[20] *Antiquities* XX.10.1.
[21] F.J.B. Hooper, *Palmoni: An Essay on the Chronographical and Numerical Systems in Use Among the Ancient Jews* (London: Longman, Brown, Green & Longmans, 1851), 334-5n.
[22] Hooper, *Palmoni*, 335n.

the traditional date for the birth of Jesus of Nazareth.[23] However, since the Josephus MSS were preserved by Christian scribes, we should perhaps be cautious of hastily making such accusations.

In summary, there is no basis to the critical assertions that ancient Jewish chronology is sixty-five years too long, as the critical interpretation of Daniel 9 requires. The chronological data provided by Demetrius has a -27 discrepancy compared with known history. The chronological data provided by Josephus contains varying discrepancies of +32, +40 and +48, with a possible set of variants indicating -68, -60, and -52 discrepancies. None of these are equal to the +65 discrepancy required by the critical interpretation; the proposition that a Jewish chronology with such a discrepancy ever is existed is without evidence. The regnal years of the High Priests recorded by Josephus provide a fair approximation for the periods 164-105 and 105-70. If a second century Jewish writer had access to the regnal-data for the period 539-164 then it is likely that his chronology would have been reasonably accurate. That the alleged inaccuracy in Jewish chronology is proposed without significant evidence perhaps betrays the *a priori* emphasis on the Maccabean period in the critical interpretation of Daniel 9.

Onias III

An intriguing element of critical interpretations of the book of Daniel is the prominence ascribed to the little known figure of Onias III, a high priest who was deposed around 175 BC. He is identified as the 'prince of the covenant' who is broken (Dan. 11:22). Perhaps more significantly, Onias is identified with the 'anointed' (or 'Messiah'), who is 'cut off, but not for himself' (Dan. 9:26).[24] In both cases, the focus is upon the murder of the individual as designating Onias. Yet the historicity of the account of Onias' murder is an open

---

[23] For instance, if we shorten figure c) by 100 years (381 years) and subtract this figure from 483 years, we are left with 102 years. Counting 102 years from the reign of Aristobolus I (c.105 BC) we are within the ballpark of 4 BC.

[24] There is no precedent in the OT for the use of משיח mashiyach ('anointed one', 'Messiah') as a title for the high priest. It is true that the word 'mashiyach' was used adjectively about the priests, (Lev. 4:3, 5, 16, 6:22; cp. χριστων ιερέων ('anointed priests'); II Macc. 1:10) but no priest is ever referred to as *the* anointed. The expression 'the anointed', and its equivalents ('the LORD's anointed', 'his anointed', etc.) is almost exclusively reserved for the king of Israel, specifically Saul (I Sam. 12:3, 5, 24:6, 10, 26:9, 11, 16, 23; II Sam. 1:14, 16, 21) and David (II Sam. 19:21, 22:51, 23:1; II Chr. 6:42; Pss 18:50, 20:6, 89:38, 51), and, more generally, as synonyms for the office of king (I Sam. 2:10, 35; Ps 2:2, 132:10, 17; also see Ps. 84:9; Lam. 4:20). The notable exception is the prophecy regarding Cyrus: 'thus says the LORD to His anointed, to Cyrus, whose right hand I have held . . .' (Isa. 45:1).

controversy and many scholars believe that Onias was not murdered at all, but died in his old age. [25]

The single account of Onias' murder is found in 2 Maccabees. Onias was deposed (c.175) and was succeeded by Jason, and then Menelaus. Menelaus wished to kill Onias and so Onias, fearing for his life, sought sanctuary in the temple at Daphne (4:33). Therefore, Menelaus gave some treasures from the temple at Jerusalem into the hands of Andronicus, who tricked Onias into leaving the safety of the temple and slew him (4:34). Upon hearing of the death of Onias, Antiochus Epiphanes (the tyrant who would later persecute the Jews) was moved with pity and wept and had Andronicus killed (4:38).

Other sources do not record this event, but ascribe a different fate to Onias. For instance, Josephus records that Onias went to Egypt and there received sanction from King Ptolemy to build a temple to rival that in Jerusalem (c.168).[26] Some scholars have proposed that Josephus incorrectly identifies Onias III as the builder of the temple at Heliopolis and assert that it was in fact Onias IV (c.164-3). However, as Solomon Zeitlin has argued, this second option is the most unlikely of the pair. By the time of Onias IV 'the Jews in Palestine, after the victories of the Maccabees, received religious freedom from Antiochus V . . . the Temple had been cleansed', there would be no reason to build a rival temple at such a time.[27] In 168 the high priest was an appointee of the Seleucid king, in 167 the Temple was defiled; there was every reason for a pious Jew to seek to reestablish Jewish worship in an alternative location. Also, as Parente notes, it is difficult imagine that Onias IV, who could not have been older that 25 and had never held office, would have been granted permission to build a temple by King Ptolemy.[28]

J.C. VanderKam, arguing against Parente, asserts that Josephus 'confused some characters in the story' and that 2 Maccabees is the more accurate account. He bases this assessment on the possible allusions to the death of Onias in the books of Daniel and Enoch, which he claims 'offer early testimony against Josephus' report'.[29] However, this assessment not only presupposes controversial interpretations of the passages in Daniel and Enoch but also over-

[25] *The International Standard Bible Encyclopedia* (Grand Rapids: Eerdmans, 1994), 605: 'The fate of Onias is disputed by scholars'; S.R. Johnson, *Historical Fictions and Hellenistic Jewish Identity: Third Maccabees in Its Cultural Context* (Berkeley: University of California Press, 2004), 14-16, 'the debate over the historicity of these events has continued to this day'.

[26] *The Jewish War* I.1.1; VII.10.2-3.

[27] S. Zeitlin, '"The Tobias Family and the Hasmoneans": A Historical Study in the Political and Economic Life of the Jews of the Hellenistic Period', *Proceedings of the American Academy for Jewish Research* 4 (1932-3), 195.

[28] F. Parente, 'Onias III' Death and the Foundation of the Temple of Leontopolis' in *Josephus and the history of the Greco-Roman Period: Essays in Memory Morton Smith* (F. Parente & J. Sieves eds.; Leiden: Brill, 1994), 83.

[29] J.C. VanderKam, *From Joshua to Caiaphas: High Priests after the Exile* (Uitgeverij van Gorcum, 2004), 206-207.

looks the other historical sources quoted by Parente. These include the account of Theodore of Mopsuestia, which follows 2 Maccabees *except for the death of Onias*, and Rabbinic literature, which records that Onias fled to Egypt to save his life.[30] Parente also refers to a papyrus, which may be addressed to Onias III c. 164 BC.[31] Now, admittedly Josephus is not a consistent witness, recording elsewhere that Onias III died prior to the construction of the temple in Egypt (c.175),[32] but these varied sources witness to a strong tradition that Onias fled to Egypt.

The account in 2 Maccabees is not unproblematic. For instance, Greek sources record that Andronicus was slain for killing the son of Seleucus IV Philopater; they do not mention Onias III.[33] Gera asserts that 'the story about the dismissal and murder of Onias III is fictional'.[34] Stern is more reconciliatory, proposing that the murder of Onias could have been used as a pretext by Antiochus to execute Andronicus but this apologetic proposal has yet to be evidenced.[35] On the one hand, it is not unreasonable to suppose that the author of 2 Maccabees inserted Onias III in to this story from the Greek accounts. On the other hand, it is improbable that Antiochus should have wept for Onias as 2 Maccabees records.

Several commentators have explained the account of 2 Maccabees as an attempt to glorify Onias III through martyrdom.[36] Johnson judges that there is much 'fictional or legendary material' worked into the book, the murder of Onias is just one example.[37] Freg objects that 'the passage in 2 Maccabees 4 is not a martyr tale but a short and restrained account which basically deserves historical credit'.[38] The same assessment cannot be made of the account of Onias' appearance to Judas Maccabaeus with Jeremiah in a vision, which is neither short nor restrained (2 Macc. 15:12ff). It is likely that this story was influential upon the formation of the later Christian martyr stories and comparison with this form may be use hermeneutic. The desire to use Onias as a saint-like figure, providing heavenly direction and comfort to the Maccabean rebels, would be strong motivation to elaborate the account of his death to conform to expectations of piety and sacrifice. The appearance of Onias to comfort the rebels is far more compelling if he himself was a victim of the unrighteous.

---

[30] Parente, 'Onias III', 76-77.
[31] Parente, 'Onias III', 84.
[32] *Antiquities* 12.5.1 (12.237).
[33] Diodorus 30.7.2-3; John of Antioch; see D. Gera, *Judaea and Mediterranean Politics: 219 to 161 BCE* (Leiden: Brill, 1998), 129; cf. Parente, 'Onias III', 74.
[34] Gera, *Judaea*, 129.
[35] M. Stern, 'The Death of Onias III', *Zion* 25 (1959-60), 3-5.
[36] Zeitlin, 'The Tobias Family', 196; Parente, 'Onias III', 98.
[37] Johnson, *Third Maccabees*, 14.
[38] J. Freg, *Temple and Rival Temple: The Cases of Elephantine, Mt. Gerzim and Leontopolis, in Gemeinile ohne Tempel* (H. von Beal Ego, A. Large & P. Pilifer, eds.; Mohr Siebeck, 1999), 188n.

The Diadochi

In Daniel's vision of the Ram and the Goat, he sees a goat with a notable horn. This horn is broken and in its place four horns grow 'toward the four winds of heaven' (Dan. 8:5, 8). Gabriel interprets these symbols: the goat represents Greece and the four horns represent four 'kingdoms' that shall come from this nation 'but not with its power' (Dan. 8:21-22). Daniel 11 also prophesies about a 'mighty king' who shall have a great dominion:

> And when he has arisen, his kingdom shall be broken up and divided toward the four winds of heaven, but not among his posterity nor   according to his domin-ion with which he ruled; for his kingdom shall be uprooted, even for others be-sides these (Dan. 11:4).

Identifying the historical referent for these words is fairly straightforward. The 'notable horn' and 'might king' of Greece was Alexander the Great, who con-quered from Egypt to India in the space of ten years. This horn was broken; whether through illness or treachery, Alexander died in Babylon in 323. The division of his kingdom amongst his generals, rather than 'among his posterity', also accords with historical fact. As such, Daniel 8:5-8 and 11:3-4 give neat synopsis of these events. There is, however, one historical quibble made by commentators regarding the numbering of the divisions. For instance, Grabbe notes in passing:

> The statement that Alexander's empire was divided four ways does not of course correspond to the historical reality, where the final division was between the Se-leucids, the Ptolemies, and the Antigonids.[39]

Since Daniel's account is both terse and (intentionally) veiled, few would con-sider this quibble to be of much significance. However, we have come to expect historical veracity in both the visionary and narrative passages and so it is per-haps worth pursuing Grabbe's incidental challenge.

The day after Alexander's death his generals met to discuss who should suc-ceed him. There were several amongst his prosperity who had claim: his broth-er Arridaeus, his son Heracles and the unborn child of his wife, Roxane. But Arridaeus was illegitimate, epileptic and probably mentally handicapped, and neither of his children was yet old enough to rule. In any case, the generals were reluctant to give the kingdom to half-caste children of foreign mothers. Perdiccas, the cavalry commander, had been selected by Alexander before his death and he intended to rule as regent for Roxane's child until he was of age. Meleager, commander of the Phalanx, preferred Arridaeus and there proceeded violence in which Meleager was slain. Following this incident, the generals reached the compromise that Perdiccas should serve as regent for both Arridae-us (named 'Philip III') and Roxane's child (who would be 'Alexander IV').

---

[39] L.L. Grabbe, 'A Dan(iel) for All Season', 234n.

This arrangement was short lived. The other generals grew suspicious of Perdiccas' power and in 321 Craterus, Antipater, Antigonus and Ptolemy formed a coalition against him. This was the First Diadoch War. The war was ended by the assassination of Perdiccas by his generals Peithon, Antigenes and Seleucus. In the subsequent agreements, Antipater became regent for Philip III and Alexander IV, and the other generals were appointed satraps of various provinces: Ptolemy in Egypt, Seleucus in Babylon, Antigenes in Elam, Lysimachus in Thrace and Antigonus in Pamphylia, Lycia and Phrygia.

Again, the arrangement did not last. Antipater died in 319 and appointed Polyperchon his successor, but his son, Cassander, felt overlooked and rebelled against Polyperchon with the aid Ptolemy and Antigonus. This was the Second Diadoch War. Polyperchon was defeated and fled (317). Cassander became regent and subsequently executed Philip III (316). Antigonus had ambitions of his own and, after defeating Eumenes (the former general of Perdiccas), proceeded to appoint his own satraps (315). Fearing the increasing power of Antigonus, Ptolemy allied with Cassander and Lysimachus to issue an ultimatum to Antigonus: give up his conquests or face a war. This led to the Third Diadoch War. In the peace treaty that followed (311) it was once again agreed that Alexander IV should become sole ruler of the entire empire when he came of age.

Cassander, pursuing his own ambitions, assassinated Alexander in 310, and later Heracles (309). With the heirs of Alexander dead, Cassander was closest to the throne (he was married to Alexander's half-sister, Thessalonica). To prevent Cassander becoming emperor, Antigonus invaded Greece, starting the Fourth Diadoch War (307). Ptolemy, attempting to aid Cassander, was defeated by Antigonus at Salamis. Following this victory Antigonus took the title 'king', intending to unite the former empire under his leadership. However, Antigonus' invasion of Egypt failed (306) and the other satraps, Lysimachus, Ptolemy and Seleucus, united against him. At the battle of Ipsus (301), Antigonus was defeated and slain. In the proceeding agreements, the victors abandoned the idea of ever unifying the empire and each took the title 'king'; Lysimachus in Thrace, Cassander in Macedon, Seleucus in Babylon and Ptolemy in Egypt.

The subsequent history of the Greek kingdoms is dominated by the kingdoms of the Ptolemies and the Seleucids, and the frequent wars between the two dynasties. The two kingdoms in Europe quickly disintegrated. In 298 Cassander died and his son, Philip IV died soon after. Cassander's brothers divided his kingdom between them leading to civil war.

Even this brief synopsis demonstrates the complexity of the political and military actions that followed the death of Alexander. The division of his empire did not take place immediately. The Diadochi were originally satraps, appointed either by Alexander himself or by Philip III (that is, by his regent);

there was no immediate attempt to become kings.[40] As we have seen, the original intention was for a sole regent to rule until Alexander IV was old enough take the crown. Even following the death of Alexander IV the Diadochi did not immediately try to claim the crown, presumably recognizing that they lacked legitimacy.[41] Only after his defeat of Ptolemy at Salamis did Antigonus feel confident to claim the kingship. Though four satraps followed suit and proclaimed themselves as kings (Cassander, Lysimachus, Ptolemy and Seleucus) this does not entail a fivefold division of the empire. Hölbl writes:

> An important distinction must be born in mind: while Antigonos (sic) laid claim to the entire kingdom of Alexander the Great, the others recognized each other as equals, even though they also based their kingships on their association with Alexander[42]

It is only following the defeat of Antigonus at Ipsus (301) that the idea of a unified empire is abandoned and the fourfold division of the empire is formerly recognized. The four ruled over independent kingdoms and none laid claim to the empire of Alexander as Antigonus had done.[43]

Grabbe's quibble is that the division of the empire that occurred at Ipsus was not the final division. This is true; there were subsequent battles and subsequent divisions. But this was the first division of Alexander's empire and it was divided into four kingdoms. Daniel's prophetic synopsis is entirely accurate for the level of detail it includes – it requires nothing more.

---

[40] R.A. Billows, *Kings and Colonists: Aspects of Macedonian Imperialism* (Leiden: Brill, 1995), 88-89.

[41] Billows, *Kings and Colonists*, 89.

[42] G. Hölbl, *A History of the Ptolemaic Empire* (trans. T. Saavedra; Routledge, 2001), 21.

[43] For example, Cassander declares himself 'king of the Macedonians' and Ptolemy is crowned as ancient Egyptian monarch; Hölbl, *Ptolemaic Empire*, 21-22.

Chapter 11

Is Daniel 11 a later Interpolation?[1]

The eleventh chapter, as Montgomery correctly judged, 'is the greatest stumbling-block to the "traditionalist" interpretation of the book'.[2] The difficulty presented by the chapter is not so much the accuracy of its predictions but its focus. The consensus of the majority of scholars, critical and conservative, is that the larger part of this chapter refers to the Hellenistic age, and more specifically, those events leading up to the Maccabean crisis. For Collins this calls into question the possibility that Daniel 11 was written by a sixth century prophet: 'There is no apparent reason, however, why a prophet of the sixth century should focus minute attention on the events of the second century.'[3] This difficulty is not lost on conservative commentators:

> This prophecy presents a problem the like of which occurs nowhere else in the Bible. In its detail it is *too* exact, *too* specific – and apparently *too* pointless. Verses 3-39, and possibly to the end of the chapter, read for all the world like a history written in the language of prophecy. For a short and otherwise unimportant period in Bible history, it deals with the inter-relations of the kings of the south (the Ptolemys of Egypt) and the kings of the north (the Seleucids of Syria), with only very slight mention of the consequent sufferings of the attenuated Judaean state.[4]

It was, perhaps, considerations of this kind that lead Rev. Charles Wright to propose that Daniel 11 in its present form is an interpolation, comparable with the later Targums. He theorizes that the original (Aramaic) was lost when holy books were destroyed during the Maccabean crisis and so this section was replaced with the only extant copy, a (Hebrew) paraphrase.[5] Similar theses had been proposed in the nineteenth century by Zockler and Lange.[6] Boutflower embraced Wright's thesis and thus criticized those scholars who used Daniel 11

---

[1]   An earlier version of this essay was published as 'Daniel 11', *CJBI* 2:4 (Oct 2008). Used by permission.

[2]   Montgomery, *Daniel*, 59.

[3]   Collins, *Daniel*, 26.

[4]   Whittaker, *Daniel*, 24.

[5]   Wright, *Daniel*, 242ff.

[6]   Zockler proposed that Daniel 11:5-45 was an interpolation, whilst Lange held that 10:1-11:44 and 12:5-13 were all additions to the original work: see R.D. Wilson, *The International Standard Bible Encyclopedia*, 1915.

as the mould for the interpretation of Daniel's other visions.[7] Montgomery, however, rejected Wright's thesis as 'pure assumption'.[8]

Since then, Wright's thesis has received little consideration. The consensus of critical scholars views the eleventh chapter of Daniel as an addition of a later recession of the book (one of many), but are not encumbered by the view that the book was in some way a complete literary unit before this. On the other hand, inerrantists generally reject the thesis (and other interpolation theories) outright. However, Wright's thesis can still be found amongst a handful of conservative commentaries.[9]

It might be tempting to dismiss Wright's thesis as an apologetic device. However, Wright himself believed that the interpolations were demonstrable by close analysis of the text.[10] In this analysis he draws attention to many particulars:

- some verses contain phrases which either have no clear referent or, according to Wright, are demonstrably unhistorical,
- some phrases are 'corrected' in OG-Dan to bring them into line with known history,
- significant events, and other relevant details, are omitted from the passage,
- particular characters or events that would have upset or enraged the Jews are ignored, while other details, seemingly irrelevant to a Jewish audience, are included.

This detailed 'cumulative' argument is worthy of critical examination. Wright's further proposition of how these interpolations were incorporated into the text may be simplistic, yet it is not integral to the thesis as other (more subtle) explanations can, and have, been, proposed. In this section we will explain the arguments of Wright, and of others, to assess the probability that chapter 11 is an interpolation.

General Considerations

Irrelevance

The principal difficulty with the prophecy, particularly vv5-20, is that it has no direct relevance either to Daniel's situation or the culmination of the prophecy. If, as 'Futurist' interpreters have claimed, vv40-45 refers to the Antichrist, or

---

[7] Boutflower, *Daniel*, 4-8. Boutflower proposes the Pseudagrapha, rather than the Targums, as a better model for the interpolations in Daniel 11 (8).

[8] Montgomery, *Daniel*, 60.

[9] Whittaker, *Daniel*, 24; *The Agora Bible Comentary: Daniel*, [Online: http://www.christadelphianbooks.org/agora/comm/27_dan/dan12.html]; P. Wyns, *The Revelation of Jesus Christ* [Online: http://www.carelinks.net/books/wyns/12-1.htm].

[10] Wright, *Daniel*, 252.

some other future aggressor, then the rest of the chapter becomes, at best, tangential. Even if this aggressor is identified with Antiochus Epiphanes the relevance of vv5-20 is questionable; comparison with Daniel 8 indicates that the level of detail in these verses is far greater than that required to set the scene. Rather, this section almost has the feel of prophetical showboating.

Character
Several scholars have commented that the prophecy of chapter 11 is uncharacteristic of other OT texts. Wyns judges it to be 'unlike any other Biblical prophecy' being 'extremely elaborate' and 'very political'.[11] Baldwin also comments, 'nowhere else is prediction as specific and detailed as here'.[12] While uniqueness is not a firm basis for accusations of fraud, these considerations have led many to conclude that this prophecy is really history.

Discontinuity
Several of the features displayed in chapters 10-12 are absent from chapter 11. Firstly, in chapter 10 the prophecy is manifested to Daniel through the medium of the angelic *dramas personae*, the 'princes'. The power-play between Persia and Greece is acted out by the angel-princes (10:12-14; 10:20-11:1). The angel-prince motif is repeated in chapter 12 when Michael the prince 'stands up' (12:1). Yet between 11:2 and 11:45 this motif is entirely missing, the prophecy being conveyed solely by direct speech.

Secondly, there is the *angelus interpreter* – the man clothed in linen (10:4-6) – who comforts Daniel and is sent to cause Daniel to understand (10:14). This figure recurs in chapter 12, with two other figures, to foretell the time-periods and to close the vision (12:5-13). Again, these figures are absent from chapter 11. Though it may be noted that it is the man clothed in linen who utters the prophecy (10:20-12:4), it is odd that he is allowed to such an extended speech without interruption from Daniel, either collapsing (10:8, 15) or responding (10:16-17, 19; 12:8).

Thirdly, Daniel's action (and reactions) are also absent from chapter 11, where elsewhere he is constantly describing how he felt or his failure to understand (10:2, 7, 11, 15, 19; 12:5, 8).

Now, all these features may be explained by the fact that the section in question is all in direct speech, yet it is this very feature that makes it discontinuous with the surrounding material.

The Vision of the Ram and the Goat
The comparison between chapter 8 and chapters 10-12 is also significant. In both sections we find presented the struggle between Persia and Greece, the notable career Alexander and the division of his empire, and the culmination of the vision in the Maccabean crisis and the figure of Antiochus Epiphanes. The

---

[11] Wyns, *Revelation.*
[12] 'Even when it is centred round the coming king, references are spasmodic and elusive'; Baldwin, *Daniel*, 184.

principal difference between the two sections, in terms of prophesied-events, is the discourse in chapter 11 regarding the King of the North and the King of the South. Though we should be careful of imposing our own expectations upon the text, we may question the addition of the two-kingdom discourse since, seemingly, it adds little to the purpose of the text. Why describe the fortunes of the King of the South if he does not feature in the crux of the prophecy?

Specific Considerations

a) *v5 – Capture of Jerusalem (omitted)*[13]

Josephus records that, after the division of Alexander's empire, Jerusalem was captured by means of 'deceit and treachery' (c.320 BC). Ptolemy I Soter entered the city on the Sabbath day on the pretense of offering a sacrifice and the citizens of Jerusalem allowed him entry unawares. Josephus also records that 'he reigned over it in a cruel manner'.[14]

Though this event was probably incidental in the fortunes of the Didachoi, the capture, and the subsequent treatment, of Jerusalem by Ptolemy I must have been of particular significance to the Jewish people. The fact that this event is omitted, while the marriage-alliance between Berenice (daughter of Ptolemy II) and Antiochus II is included, indicates a particularly partiality in the text.

b) *v5-6 – Seleucus I & Antiochus I (omitted)*[15]

While v5 informs us about the reign and dominion of Ptolemy I ('King of the South'), the accession and career of Seleucus I Nicator and his son Antiochus I Soter are entirely omitted. This cannot be because nothing of note occurred during their reigns – quite the contrary. Wright proposes that these events were omitted because they were of no direct concern of the Jews.

c) *v6 Impiety of Antiochus II (omitted)*[16]

Another significant event omitted by the author is the assumption of the title 'Antiochus II Theos' by the King of the North. One might imagine that such impiety would be frankly condemned by a Jewish author, but only his marriage is considered to be significant.

d) *v6 'she shall be given up and . . . he who fathered her'*[17]

The phrase 'she shall be given up' refers to the killing of Berenice. However, 'he who fathered her' would refer to Ptolemy II Philadelphus, who was not put to death by the Seleucids. OG-Dan and Th-Dan both omit reference to the father.

---

[13] Wright, *Daniel*, 249.
[14] Josephus, *Antiquities of the Jews* XII.1.4.
[15] Wright, *Daniel*, 249.
[16] Wright, *Daniel*, 250.
[17] Wright, *Daniel*, 251.

e) *v7 'a branch from her roots'*[18]
This phrase would most naturally refer to a child of Berenice, implying that her child became King of the South. In reality, the one who became king of Egypt was her brother, not her son. OG-Dan amends this phrase to 'a plant from his root'. This difficulty may simply result from pedantry on the part of Wright; most commentators allow that a brother is from the same 'roots'.[19]

f) *v10 'his sons shall wage war'*[20]
This phrase refers to the sons of Seleucus II, namely: Seleucus III (= Ceranus) and Antiochus III. Yet Seleucus III only reigned for three years and did not wage war against Egypt. OG-Dan amends the plural to a singular. At best this is an argument from silence and some commentators allow that the biblical author was party to better information than our own.[21] Young notes that while the first part of the verse is in plural, the latter part is singular; only one son 'overwhelms and passes through'.[22]

g) *v17 'with upright ones'*[23]
On the basis that the phrase 'upright one' would most naturally refer to a Jew, this verse implies that the king of the north would invade Egypt aided by a contingent of Jewish warriors. This is contrary to known history. On the other hand, 'upright ones' may not refer to people but may also be rendered 'fair terms'.[24]

h) *v21 'they shall not give him the glory of the kingdom'*[25]
This verse would imply that Antiochus IV Epiphanes was not given the status of king, contrary to history. OG-Dan gives 'the royal honour will not be granted to him', perhaps amending the text to imply that it is the honour, rather than the status, that was denied. It may that this phrase points to the fact that Antiochus was not the legal heir to the throne, but conspired against his brother Demetrius.[26]

---

[18] Wright, *Daniel*, 252.
[19] Young, *Daniel*, 236; Porteous, *Daniel*, 160; Baldwin, *Daniel*,187; cf. 'one of her relatives' [NLT].
[20] Wright, *Daniel*, 258.
[21] Porteous, *Daniel*, 161.
[22] Young, *Daniel*, 237.
[23] Wright, *Daniel*, 269.
[24] Young, *Daniel*, 240; Baldwin, *Daniel*, 188; cf. NKJVn, ESV, NLT; cf. 'an agreement' [OG-Dan].
[25] Wright *Daniel*, 279.
[26] Porteous *Daniel*, 165.

i) *v22 'the prince of the covenant'*[27]
Wright asserts that this phrase has no clear referent; it is omitted from OG-Dan. Most commentators identity this 'prince' as a High Priest, usually Onias III,[28] though few are definite on this point.[29]

j) *v28 Desecration of the Temple (omitted)*[30]
In v28 it is stated that 'his heart shall be moved against the holy covenant, so he shall do damage'. This is generally interpreted to Antiochus' desecration of the Temple on his return from his campaign in Egypt.[31] However, it is odd that this event is so lightly glossed over, especially when it is considered that not only did Antiochus remove the holy articles but massacred the people.

k) *vv33-35 The Cleansing of the Sanctuary (omitted)*[32]
The reaction of the author to the defilement of the sanctuary is, perhaps, quite unexpected. He does not concentrate on the uprising of the Maccabees (usually identified as the 'little help' of v34), but rather speaks of 'the wise' teaching the people, whilst some of 'the wise' stumble or fall 'to refine them'. Particularly unexpected is the omission of any reference to the cleansing of the sanctuary, especially when this very thing is predicted elsewhere in the book (8:14).

Analysis

Wright claims that the historical discrepancies he identifies signify that the full text cannot have been written in the second century. Rather, he proposes that the original prophecy was overwritten by the later author. Those phrases without clear historical reference as vestiges of the original preserved by the interpolator; why else would the author include inaccurate statements? The description of Antiochus (vv36-39) is a case in point:

> The text . . . does not contain any clear or distinct description of Antiochus. It does not possess those marked features which might well have been expected from a prophetic history written later than the events described. There are phrases which lead us to regard the prophecy as 'touched up' by a later parapharist.[33]

Yet, as we have seen, many of the historical issues raised by Wright are plausibly explained by other commentators; in some cases, it may be our limited knowledge of the period that is at fault. Also, Wright's thesis does not so adequately explain the omission of events of Jewish significance which he highlights. The first section especially (vv5-19) seems full of historical mentions

[27] Wright, *Daniel*, 283.
[28] Baldwin, *Daniel*, 192.
[29] Young, *Daniel*, 242, 'I do not know to what the reference is.'
[30] Wright, *Daniel*, 292.
[31] Cf. I Maccabees 1:20-28.
[32] Wright, *Daniel*, 293.
[33] Wright, *Daniel*, 278.

but absent of the events one might have expected a Jewish mind to focus upon. These (seemingly) irrelevant historical details cannot easily be explained either as original prophecy, for they are too accurate, or interpolations, for they are too irrelevant.

One plausible thesis, proposed by a number of scholars, is that the main portion of Daniel 11 derives from another text, a historical document that was rewritten into a prophetic format and embedded within the Danielic material.[34] This view draws plausibility from the richness of the historical material contained therein, such that historians use Daniel 11 as a primary source for the period. Grabbe declares, 'it is unthinkable that this [i.e. Dan. 11] is based on anything but a sophisticated historical document (or documents) of some sort'.[35] If, for instance, a short historical account of the affairs of the Didachoi were used as the basis of vv5-19 then this might explain the focus on marriage alliances and the like, rather than the ill-treatment of the Jewish people. The interpolation of this historical account into the text may also explain the apparent discontinuity caused by the sudden appearance of the King of the South in v5.

This, however, cannot be the whole story for while vv5-19 (perhaps 5-30a) may be based upon a non-Jewish historical source, vv30b-35 is Judeo-centric in outlook and likely of Jewish origin. The following section (vv36-39) also is not historical in character, lacking the specificity of the earlier sections. Many commentators interpret this section as a description of the archetypal 'antichrist', and it has been applied to various individuals including Herod the Great, Constantine, Napoleon and the Pope.[36] It is possible that this description was only secondarily applied to Antiochus IV and predates the composition of the text.

The final section (vv40-45) is inaccurate, if intended as a continuation of the events of the reign of Antiochus, and is interpreted by most scholars as a failed prediction of the author, thus pinpointing the date of composition (c.164 BC). A.S. van der Woude proposes that this prediction was not mere guesswork, but based upon contemporary rumours of a future Egyptian campaign and upon the eschatological framework provided by the OT prophets.[37] For instance, this section demonstrates clear parallels with Ezekiel 38-39.[38]

---

[34] R.G. Kratz, 'The Visions of Daniel' in *The Book of Daniel: Composition and Reception* (J.J. Collins & P.W. Flint (eds.), 2001), 108, 'It is widely-held now that an older source was incorporated into chapter 1.'

[35] Grabbe, 'A Dan(iel) For All Seasons', 234 ; Lebram, also, has suggested that Daniel 11 was based upon one or more source-texts, though he asserts that these sources as being Egyptian in origin – an assertion that Collins disputes (see Collins, *Daniel: With an Introduction to Apocalyptic Literature*, 100).

[36] For a good summary of the various interpretations of this section see: G.M. Harton, 'An Interpretation of Daniel 11:36-45', *Grace Theological Journal* 4.2 (1983).

[37] A.S. van der Woude, 'Prophetic Prediction, Political Prognostication, and Firm Belief Reflections on Daniel 11:40-12:3', in C.A. Evans, S. Talmon (eds.), *The Quest*

Table 5	Ezekiel 38-39	Daniel 11
northern invader	38:6, 15; 39:2,	11:40
allies: Ethiopia and Libya	38:5	11:43
horsemen and chariots	38:4; 39:20	11:40
gathering spoils	38:13; 39:10	11:43
destroyed on the mountains of Israel	38:21; 39:4;	11:45

It is perhaps significant that when these two accounts are integrated a geographical pattern emerges: the allies of Gog encircle those nations mentioned in Daniel 11. While Egypt is not named in Ezekiel, the bordering nations of Ethiopia and Libya are named as allies. Assuming that the King of the North is identified as Seleucid Syria, then, Togarmah borders it to the north and Persia to the east. Sheba and Dedan (Arabia) complete the circle, enclosing Edom, Moab and Ammon, who escape invasion.

If Wright's central proposition is correct, that the current text of Daniel 11 is an interpolation upon an original prophecy, then we may have some clues as to its form. We may tentatively propose that the original prophecy paralleled other OT prophecies of the eschatological battle over Israel; vv36-45 would represent a vestige of this prophecy. It is conceivable that in reaction to severe persecution, this prophecy was actualized by many textual additions to portray Antiochus as the eschatological antagonist; a non-Jewish account of the Didachoi was interpolated into the text to bridge the gap between Alexander and Antiochus.

Here, however, we reach the limits of the redaction-critical method. While this explanation of the present form for the Daniel 11 is plausible, it is based entirely on internal evidence. It is incumbent on proponents of such theories to provide some adequate explanation of how such interpolation arose and, if possible, provide manuscript evidence for the textual alteration. We shall see that both these criteria are difficult to fulfill.

Textual History

Generally, critical scholars presume that the textual transmission of texts like the book of Daniel was quite free, allowing for interpolations, expansions and additions. The textual history of the book of Enoch seems indicative of this

---

for Context and Meaning: Studies in Biblical Intertextuality in Honor of James A. Sander (Leiden: Brill, 1997), 64-66.
[38] Collins, *Daniel*, 100.

kind of transmission; various forms of the book are witnessed from disparate sources. On the other hand, the comparison between the MT and DSS demonstrates that once a book was accepted as sacred and canonical, its textual transmission was closed and no longer open to intentional alteration; this comparison holds true for the book of Daniel. If by the second century the book of Daniel was regarded as sacred scripture – and there are some good reasons to suppose this was the case – then it is difficult to explain how such an interpolation as proposed above could have occurred.

Wright answers this difficulty by proposing that the interpolation was not due to intentional alteration but was necessitated by the loss of the original text. Wright asserts that the original text of chapters 10-12 was written in Aramaic and that later a sort of Targum was written of this text in Hebrew. During the 'wholesale destruction of the sacred books' that occurred during the Maccabean period,[39] the original book of Daniel was lost or damaged. The missing portions were restored from this Hebrew Targum.[40]

Though the extant Targums are generally later and in Aramaic, the concept of a paraphastic and interpretative text based upon the scriptures is realistic, and were the sacred books destroyed these interpretative texts would have been the closest record of their original text. In addition, the proposition that chapters 10-12 are a Hebrew translation from an Aramaic original derives some support the detailed considerations of Frank Zimmermann.[41] However, the interpolations identified above are not targumic in character and there is no way to confirm whether such a text ever existed. Also, the completion of this Daniel-Targum would date after the destruction of the sacred texts.

Ellis updates Wright's explanation as it facilitates his own hypothesis of the canonization process of the book of Daniel. He proposes that it is 'intrinsically improbable' that the book of Daniel should have been composed in its entirety in the second-century and then, within a century, accepted as canonical without opposition.[42] Thus, he proposes that the book of Daniel was already regarded as canonical by the second century and that those elements that may reflect a second-century origin should be explained as the contemporization of the book which took place during the recopying of the Old Testament books and the widespread destruction of sacred books (see above). He proposes that this contemporization not only included updating orthography and terminology, but also 'explanatory elaboration'. The Septuagint is cited as an example of such 'elaboration' during textual transmission. Ellis argues that the canonical status of the book of Daniel would not have precluded this 'elaboration', stating that

---

[39] Cf. I Maccabees 1:56f; II Maccabees 2:14f; Josephus, *Contra Apion* 1.35f.

[40] Wright, *Daniel*, xix-xx, 46, 242.

[41] F. Zimmermann, 'Some Verses in Daniel in the Light of a Translation Hypothesis', *JBL* 58.4 (December 1939), 349-54; F. Zimmermann, 'Hebrew Translation in Daniel', *JQR* 51.3 (January 1961), 198-208.

[42] E.E Ellis, *The Old Testament in Early Christianity: Canon and Interpretation in the Light of Modern Research* (J.C.B. Mohr, 1991), 43.

such the same sort of elaboration was committed by the writers at Qumran and the New Testament writers.[43]

Ellis' examples of textual elaboration are problematic. Whilst earlier scholars viewed OG-Dan as elaborative, the growing consensus is that the errors of translation in OG-Dan are 'mechanical' rather than apologetic or contrived.[44] The New Testament writers are not an analogous example as, though at times they paraphrase OT, they do so to satisfy the requirements of their own writings, not (it must be assumed) with the intention of altering the received text. Again, the Qumran texts are not analogous since, while Covenanters felt free to compose a plethora of para-Danielic material, they did not take liberties with the book itself; their own copies of the book are largely consistent with MT. Even Wright's own analogy to the later Jewish Targums betrays his purpose, since the Targums were intentionally kept separate from the textual-transmission of the sacred texts. If the book of Daniel were regarded as canonical it is difficult to imagine that any pious Jew would consent to the drastic interpolations hypothesized above. Even if the text were damaged it is improbable that it should have been restored using a suspect text; the few analogous examples we have suggest the lacuna would have preserved.[45]

Paul Wyns responds that, whilst no pious Jew would consent to drastic interpolations of scripture, this consideration is only valid after the text was accepted as canonical. He argues that the different versions of Daniel, as represented by the Greek versions, indicate that the canonization process was still fluid in the second century; he says these differing versions are 'inexplicable' if the text was accepted as canonical in the Persian era.[46] It is true that there are differences between MT, Th-Dan and OG-Dan, but it is not obvious that this entails that the canonical status of Daniel was in dispute in the second century. The differences between MT and Th-Dan are better explained as due to transmission and translation. The differences between Th-Dan and OG-Dan probably indicate that OG-Dan relies on a different Vorlage, but at most that indicates some fluidity when that Vorlage was being composed and not during the translation stages. In any case the multiple versions of the book of Daniel (OG-Dan, Th-Dan, Hebrew/Aramaic) was the reality well into first century AD and beyond, yet these versions co-existed despite the fact that the book was regard-

---

[43] Ellis, *Canon and Interpretation*, 44.

[44] A.A. Di Lella, 'The Textual History of Septuagint-Daniel and Theodotion-Daniel' in in *The Book of Daniel: Composition and Reception* (J.J. Collins & P.W. Flint (eds.), 2001), 591-92.

[45] Comparison between MT and 4QSam[a] indicate that a paragraph has been omitted from the MT between I Samuel 10:27 & 11:1, which King Nahash is introduced [cp. NLT]. Rather than repair the lacuna, the Masoretes preserved the text as extant even though Nahash abruptly enters the text at 11:1. The absence of any formal greeting at the beginning of the Epistle to the Hebrews may also be due to this kind of lacuna.

[46] P. Wyns, *God is Judge: A Commentary on the Book of Daniel* (Biblaridion Media, 2011).

ed as canonical. So the translations of OG-Dan and Th-Dan in the second century do not indicate that the book was not yet regarded as canonical.

Perhaps the greatest difficulty for the hypothesized interpolations is absence of textual dispute. We do not possess a single variant manuscript that does not witness to the present form of Daniel 11.[47] Wright and Ellis require a watershed in the textual transmission of the book of Daniel such that all subsequent variants of the book originated from a single (hypothesized) elaborated version. The destruction of the sacred books during the Antiochene persecution would not have been such a watershed. Firstly, it is likely that the dissemination of the book of Daniel had already expanded beyond the borders of the Seleucid Empire if it was written in the sixth century. The Alexandrian origin of OG-Dan demonstrates that the book was present in Egypt by the second century. Wyns' conjectures that the persecution by Antiochus could have prompted the composition of the final form of the book (including Dan. 11), using materials rescued from the Jerusalem temple and carried to Egypt by Onias III.[48] Yet this doesn't explain the early acceptance of the book by the community at Qumran. The presence of copies of Daniel at Qumran from c.125 BC at the latest makes it unlikely that the book only reached its final (and canonical) form a few decades earlier. Secondly, it is unlikely that all copies of the book would have been destroyed during the crisis; pious Jews would have sought to preserve their sacred books from destruction. The obvious analogy with the texts preserved at Qumran during the Roman campaign 66-70 AD is indicative of the way zealous Jews are likely to have reacted in regard to the safety of their Scriptures. The community at Qumran seems to have preserved other texts during the Maccabean period so we can expect copies of Daniel, if present, to have also been preserved through the crisis. It is certainly significant that no similar watershed has been discerned in the transmission of the other OT books.

Not only are there no extant textual variants indicating the presence of interpolations, there is also no recorded dispute regarding the form of the text. Memories are long and even if the texts themselves were destroyed, it is probable that people would have remembered the original form of the book. Therefore it is difficult to accept that these individuals would have accepted a corrupted form of a sacred book, especially if its key prediction regarding the death of Antiochus had proved false (11:40-45). The interpolated text should have been rejected but instead it was universally accepted as Scripture.

We are admittedly dependent on later analogies in our efforts to conceive of the realistic treatment of sacred books by second century Jews; however, these analogies are not so late so as to render our conceptions implausible. Unless we are to concede that second century Jews took a dynamic, rather than static, view

---

[47] DSS witness to vv1-2, 11-39 (4QDan^a, 4QDan^c, pap6qDan). OG-Dan & Th-Dan contain Daniel 11 in its present form, though with variants.

[48] Wyns, *God is Judge*, 408-409.

of their scriptures then it seems impossible that the hypothesized interpolations would have been accepted.

An Alternative?

In his lecture, *The Background of Jewish Apocalyptic*, Lambert proposed that Daniel 11 parallels in style the genre of Babylonian Dynastic prophecy.[49] This proposition has been widely accepted amongst the commentators.[50] There are a number of cuneiform texts which record historical events as *vaticinia ex eventu*, these include several examples of annalistic history presented in the future tense and in veiled language. Lambert presents three texts, two whose composition date c.6-7th century BC[51] and one which probably dates from the Hellenistic period.[52] Each text uses phraseology reminiscent of Daniel 11. For instance the phrases 'a prince will arise and will exercise kingship for 13 years', 'after him a king will arise and will not judge the judgment of the land', 'after him a king will arise from Uruk', 'a rebel prince will arise', etc., find repeated parallel in Daniel (cf. 11:2, 3, 7, 20, 21; also cf. 9:26).[53] Lambert concludes, 'it is certainly possible, perhaps even probable, that the author of Daniel adapted the style of a traditional Babylonian genre for his own purposes'.[54]

If Lambert's conclusion is correct then whoever wrote Daniel 11 (and whenever they wrote it) they did so to conform to a specific genre. The chapter takes the form of a Dynastic Prophecy – from Alexander to Antiochus – including political details characteristic of the genre, though seemingly irrelevant to the modern reader. Thus, the fact that Daniel 11 is uncharacteristic of other OT prophecies is explicable. The apparent discontinuity with the surrounding text (10:1-19; 12:5-13) is probably best explained by the desire to make a distinction from the Babylonian texts; in this case the Dynastic Prophecy is uttered by an angel of God.

Conclusion

The eleventh chapter of Daniel provides traditionalists with a difficult problem: here in a book purporting to be a sixth century composition we find a chapter that is concerned with the political events of Hellenistic era and the Maccabean crisis, culminating with a predicted invasion of Egypt that never took place. Why should a sixth century Jew concern himself with such political minutiae?

---

[49] W.G. Lambert, *The Background of Jewish Apocalyptic* (London: Athlone, 1978; The Ethel M. Wood lecture, delivered at the University of London, 1977).
[50] E.g. Collins, *Daniel*, 99; Davies, *Daniel*, 71-72; etc.
[51] A.K. Grayson & W.G. Lambert, *JCS* 18 (1964), 12-16; H. Hunger & S.A. Kaufman, *JAOS* 95 (1975), 371ff.
[52] Grayson, *Babylonian Historical-Literary Texts*, 33.
[53] Lambert, *Jewish Apocalyptic*, 9-13.
[54] Lambert, *Jewish Apocalyptic*, 16.

And how can an inspired prophet make erroneous predictions? This chapter is the strongest argument in favour of late pseudonymous authorship.

The explanation advocated by Wright, though based upon critical analysis, was proposed to remove the foundation of the critical case for a late-date. By hypothesizing a second-century interpolation, he is able to extricate himself from much that he (as a traditionalist) finds uncomfortable. Yet, by playing the critical game he is in danger of proving too much. Upon his proposition almost any passage or phrase that causes interpretative difficulties can be excised from the text; in essence this is the modern critical approach.

The major challenge to any theory that proposes the deliberate alteration of the sacred text is sheer incredulity that such tampering could occur once the text was accepted as sacred ('canonical'). The ingenuity of Wright's thesis was to provide a mechanism for the incorporation of interpretative (uninspired) material into the text in good faith. Yet, the difficulties with this thesis make it unlikely and the weight of textual evidence is against it.

The alternative is to consider Daniel 11 to be intentional and inspired. If Daniel wrote in a Babylonian milieu, it is hardly surprising that his text should mirror this style. Could this be one more statement of God's superiority over the Babylonian gods, that his dynastic prophecy came true while their pseudo-prophecies did not?

This alternative only provides a beginning of a solution. It does not reveal why the period of Diadochoi was chosen for this Dynastic Prophecy, or why the prophecy culminates in an invasion that did not take place. Yet, whether we select a gap-theory, or a dual-fulfillment, or a conditional prophecy, as an explanation, we must accept the text as we have it. Appealing to interpolations is a red-herring and a dead-end.

Chapter 12

The Apocryphal Additions

In Protestant Bibles the book of Daniel has twelve chapters, following the context of the Masoretic text (MT). However, Catholic Bibles also include three additions to the book, which are found in the Old Greek (OG-Dan) and 'Theodotion' (Th-Dan) translations, and subsequently in the Latin. These are additions commonly known as 'The Prayer of Azariah and Song of the Three Holy Children' (Dan. 3:24-90), 'Susanna and the Elders' (Dan. 13) and 'Bel and the Dragon' (Dan. 14).[1] Though it is likely that the apocryphal additions to the book of Daniel were composed in Hebrew or Aramaic,[2] given the absence of the additions in the MT and the Dead Sea Scrolls (DSS),[3] it is unlikely that the additions were part of the autograph. This also seems confirmed by the fact that Th-Dan, and probably OG-Dan, were composed without the additions, as indicated by differences in the translation of those passages.[4]

Dating the three additions to the book of Daniel is not straightforward. The most we can say with confidence is that they must have been composed after the book of Daniel and prior to the Greek translations. If we date the Greek translations to the early first century, or late second century BC, then the additions must date from the second century at the latest. It has been suspected that the Prayer of Azariah was composed as prayer for the Maccabean martyrs and so was composed around this time.[5] If so, that would leave almost no time between the addition of the Prayer and the date ascribed by critical scholars to the composition of the autograph.

Given that the additions were not part of the autograph, we should not be surprised if they do not display the same historical awareness as the book of Daniel. If they do date from the Maccabean era then they serve as an appropriate example of the level of historical veracity we should expect from an author

---

[1]   In the Greek versions Susanna is placed before Dan. 1:1 and Bel immediately after Dan. 12:13. I will follow the chapter and verse of the Catholic Bibles.

[2]   Di Lella, 'Textual History', 598.

[3]   The fragmentary 4Q551 (also known as 4QDaniel-Susanna (?)) is not part of the story of Susanna in the Greek versions. It is not clear whether it is related to this story, or the book of Daniel, at all.

[4]   Di Lella, 'Textual History', 599.

[5]   Di Lella, 'Textual History', 599.

of that period writing about the Neo-Babylonian period. Assessing the historicity of the apocryphal additions forms the basis of a contrast with the rest of the book.

The Prayer of Azariah contains scant historical mentions and so is not suitable for assessment. In this chapter I will assess the historical details provided by Susanna and Bel.

Susanna

The story of Susanna regards an attractive young woman who is placed in a difficult situation by two lecherous elders. Taking their opportunity when she is alone, they demand that she lay with them or else they will testify that they caught her committing adultery with a young man. She faces a moral challenge either to stay chaste and face condemnation, or else sin against her husband and against God. She says:

> I am completely trapped. For if I do this, it will mean death for me; if I do not, I cannot escape your hands. I choose not to do it; I will fall into your hands, rather than sin in the sight of the Lord (Dan. 13:22-23 NRVSCE).

Brought before the assembly and accused of adultery, Susanna faces death. However, a young lad named Daniel stands up for her and, catching the elders in contradictory testimony, manages to prove her innocence.

The moral of the story is that you should stay faithful to God whatever the consequences. OG-Dan also focuses on the character of Daniel, saying, 'for this reason youths are beloved by Jacob, because of their simplicity' (Dan. 13:62 NETS). But the historical veracity of the story is questionable, as is its place in the book of Daniel.

In the Latin the story of Susanna is placed after chapter 12 but it clearly does not belong there. It is narrative, not a vision, so sits better with the first part of the book. In any case Daniel is described as being 'young' in the story (Dan. 13:45) so chronologically this story belongs earlier in the book. In the Greek versions, Susanna is placed at the beginning of the book but according to the first verse of the story it takes place in Babylon (Dan. 13:1 Th-Dan) and therefore is ill-suited to precede the story of Daniel's exile. (The first four verses are missing from OG-Dan but the reference to lawless elders 'from Babylon' in verse 5 strongly indicates that Babylon is the setting; cf. Dan. 13:28). It seems improbable that this story was part of the autograph.

Given the Babylonian setting for the story, many of the elements seem implausible. We argued earlier, from parallels with the Assyrian deportation, that most of the captives would have had to endure subsistence rations. The only exceptions were the literate elite, like Daniel and his friends. Yet Joakim, Susanna's husband, is described as being 'very rich', with his own house and fine garden (Dan. 13:4). Susanna is a lady of great refinement (Dan. 13:31), with maids to serve her and ointments to bathe with (Dan. 13:17). This all seems unlikely for the Jewish exiles. More significantly, the first captivity, when Daniel was taken to Babylon, was likely to have been very limited. Not the mass deportation of the later years. Yet the story implies there were many Jews living in Babylon (cf. 'assembly'; Dan. 13:28 OG-Dan; Dan. 13:60); OG-Dan implies that there were Jews leaving in nearby cities too (Dan. 13:6).

The other incongruous element is the depiction of independent judicial processes. The two elders in the story are appointed as judges. They try cases from the Jews in Babylon and, according to OG-Dan, other cities too (Dan. 13:5-6). It was their responsibility to administer justice (Dan. 13:9). When Susanna refuses to sleep with the elders, they convene an assembly of the people ('all the sons of Israel' Dan. 13:28 OG-Dan) and the assembly hears the testimony of the elders. This assembly also seems to have the power to enact executions based upon its own judgments (Dan. 13:45) and seems to be operating under the Law of Moses, quite independently of any Babylonian authority (Dan. 13:60-62). This is all very much improbable.

The story of Susanna then seems to have been written at long remove from the situation in the early years of the Babylonian captivity.

Bel and the Dragon

The story of Bel and the Dragon relates how Daniel demonstrated that the two titular objects of worship were not real gods. The idol of Bel appears to consume food. Daniel demonstrates that it is the priests and their families that are consuming the food making use of secret doors. The dragon is a living creature that Daniel slays 'without iron or club' by giving it cakes of pitch, fat and hair to eat. The Babylonians are indignant at Daniel's actions and demand that Daniel is thrown into a pit of lions for six days. On the sixth day the prophet Habakkuk is transported to Daniel with food. When the king finds Daniel alive, he has Daniel brought out of the pit and his accusers are thrown in and devoured. The story has a clear polemic against idolatry.

It is fairly obvious that this story was composed independently of the autograph. OG-Dan opens with the words 'From the prophecy of Hambakoum [i.e. Habakkuk] the son of Iesous of the tribe of Leui' (Dan. 14:1 NETS), implying that this was conceived as a story about Habakkuk and not part of the book of Daniel. (OG-Dan does identify the Daniel in this story with the Daniel of the book by naming him 'Baltasar' [i.e. Belteshazzar] – Dan. 14:34). Th-Dan tries to integrate the story into the book of Daniel, opening with the transition from the reign of Astyages to Cyrus. Nevertheless, it is clear that the story does not belong at the end of chapter 12, as it is placed, but (if anywhere) after chapter 6. The re-use of the lion's den is crude and is another indication that this story is a later composition.

In OG-Dan the king is identified only as 'the king of Babylon' (Dan. 14:2). Th-Dan, presumably in an attempt to lend weight to the account by adding historical detail, identifies the king as 'Cyrus the Persian' (Dan. 14:1). However, the writer describes Cyrus as receiving his kingdom from Astyages. This demonstrates a misunderstanding of history. Whilst Cyrus received the Median kingdom from Astyages, this was not a natural succession but Cyrus deposed Astyages. In any case these events took place in 550 BC, long before Cyrus conquered Babylon; Astyages was never king of Babylon. This attempt, by the writer of Th-Dan, to identify Darius the Mede and add historical detail to the story was not based on recollection of the events but on a clumsy reading of the Greek historians.

The name 'Bel' means 'lord' and could have been used for various Babylonian gods. In the Neo-Babylonian context, Bel would especially have been used for Marduk, the patron god of Babylon. The use of Bel in the story may be another indication of a reliance on Greek historians as opposed to firsthand knowledge. According to Th-Dan, Daniel destroys both Bel and his temple (Dan. 14:22); OG-Dan mentions only the destruction of Bel. The temple of Marduk in Babylon was the Esagila, which housed statues of Marduk and his consort. However, the Esagila was not destroyed during the reign of Cyrus, nor is there any record of the statue of Marduk being destroyed. Herodotus records that Xerxes removed a statue from the Esagila when he desecrated the temple and sacked the city in 482 BC. Yet the temple was not destroyed and was restored by Alexander the Great. The idea that Daniel was responsible for the destruction of the statue of Marduk or of the Esagila appears fanciful.

The second supposed god in the story, the dragon, seems also fanciful. Whilst the story does not record this δρακων breathing fire, the fact that it bursts when it consumes pitch and fat might imply this. The worship given to the dragon suggests that it is not some ordinary serpent but a distinctive and unique creature. This does not recommend the historicity of this account. In any case, there is no record of the Babylonians worshipping a live dragon.

Finally, we may think about the prophet Habakkuk. Of course, his transportation to Babylon to provide food for Daniel was miraculous, but laying that aside there are reasons to question the historicity of this account. Whilst the prophecy of Habakkuk is not precisely dated, it is written in anticipation of the Babylonian invasion (cf. Hab. 1:6), whereas the events of Bel and the Dragon date, according to Th-Dan, to the reign of Cyrus. There is a good seventy years dividing the two. Now, we must allow that if it is plausible that Daniel could have lived long enough for his life to span the whole Babylonian captivity then the same might be said for Habakkuk. But if Habakkuk is older than Daniel, as one might guess from the tenor of his prophecy, then it stretches credulity to believe him to be still living in the reign of Cyrus.

Summary

Neither the story of Susanna nor that of Bel and the Dragon were part of the autograph of Daniel. They were evidently added much later. They also are sorely lacking in historicity. These stories do not exhibit the level of accuracy one would expect from accounts written near the time. There exhibit the level of accuracy one would expect from a story teller with only a general grasp of the work of the Greek historians. The contrast between these stories and the book of Daniel is evident.

Chapter 13

Josephus and Daniel's Tower

Josephus was an admirer of the character of Daniel. He describes him as 'one of the greatest of the prophets'.[1] In his *Antiquities of the Jews*, Josephus recounts each of the six incidents recorded in the narrative chapters of the biblical book.[2] Yet, Josephus also records an additional story about Daniel, which is not recorded for us in Scripture:

> Now when Daniel was become so illustrious and famous, on account of the opinion men had that he was beloved of God, he built a tower at Ecbatana, in Media: it was a most elegant building, and wonderfully made, and it is still remaining, and preserved to this day: and to such as see it, it appears to have been lately built, and to have been no older than that very day when anyone looks upon it, it is so fresh, flourishing, and beautiful, and no way grown old in so long time; for buildings suffer the same as men do, they grow old as well as they, and by numbers of years their strength is dissolved, and their beauty withered. Now they bury the kings of Media, of Persia, and Parthia, in this tower to this day; and he who was entrusted with the care of it was a Jewish priest; which thing is also observed to this day.[3]

Now it would be easy to dismiss this story as apocryphal or legendary, but we should be cautious of making such an assessment. Firstly, this story is unlike any of the apocryphal stories about Daniel. It does not feature in the additions to Daniel found in the Greek versions, nor does it feature amongst the para-Danielic material amongst the Dead Sea Scrolls. Both the biblical and apocryphal Daniel stories are written with a polemic intention, whereas the account of Daniel building a tower is brief and unadorned. Secondly, Josephus is not prone to fiction. Though his historical methods are not impeccable, he does base his histories upon relevant sources whether the Bible itself, or other historians or oral tradition.

The tower briefly mentioned by Josephus would be of some significance if the connection to Daniel could be verified because it would supply historical evidence for the activity of Daniel. In this chapter we will explore the possible

---

[1] Josephus, *Antiquities of the Jews* 10.11.7 (10.266).
[2] Josephus, *Antiquities* 10.10.1-10.11.7 (10.186-281); cf. Dan. 1-6.
[3] Josephus, *Antiquities* 10.11.7 (10.264-5).

sources for Josephus' account of Daniel's tower and examine some archaeological sites that might fit Josephus' description of the tower.

Daniel 8:2

> I saw in the vision, and it so happened while I was looking, that I was in Shushan [Susa], the citadel, which is in the province of Elam; and I saw in the vision that I was by the River Ulai [NKJV].

F.F. Bruce, in an essay regarding Josephus and Daniel, presents the theory that Josephus' account of Daniel and tower is based upon 'a midrash on Daniel 8:2'.[4] He argues that the Hebrew word for 'citadel' (bîrâh) is rendered βάρις in the Th-Dan, which is the same word Josephus uses for Daniel's tower. Therefore, Bruce hypothesizes, some commentator on Daniel 8:2 might have misunderstood this verse to be speaking about a tower and connected it with Daniel. Josephus would have extrapolated his account from this commentary.

The immediate difficulty with this theory is that Josephus speaks of Ecbatana, not Susa. Bruce theorises that 'Josephus may have confused this city, where according to Ezra 6:2 there was also a bîrâ (LXX βάρις), with Susa.'[5] This explanation seems unlikely for a number of reasons. Firstly, according to Bruce's own hypothesis, Josephus is not taking his information directly from Daniel 8:2 or Ezra 6:2, but from a midrash. Secondly, Josephus knew very well that Susa was a distinct city from Ecbatana, as he refers to Susa in the very same chapter.[6] An alternative explanation is available in that a textual variant of this passage has 'Susa in Persia' instead of 'Ecbatana in Media'.[7] Presumably Bruce does not opt for this explanation because this variant is so poorly attested, being found only in a quote in the writings of Jerome.

It is not only the confusion of Ecbatana for Susa that would need to be explained. Almost nothing about Daniel 8:2 would give grounds for what Josephus writes. For example, how could Josephus take 'I was in Susa, the citadel' to mean 'I built a tower'? Furthermore, Daniel 8:2 mentions nothing about the burial of Persian kings or the observance of a Jewish priest. Also, Josephus places the construction of the tower in the reign of Darius the Mede, while Daniel 8:2 is dated to the reign of Belshazzar.

In essence the only link between Josephus' account and Daniel 8:2 is the word βάρις and that does not seem to provide sufficient justification for what Josephus writes.

---

[4] F.F. Bruce, *A Mind for What Matters* (Eerdmans, 1990), 21; cf. T. Stackhouse, *A History of the Holy Bible* (1836), 693.

[5] Bruce, *A Mind for What Matters*, 21.

[6] For example, 'he says that when he was in Susa, the metropolis of Persia' (*Antiquities* 10.11.7 [10.269]).

[7] Stackhouse, *History of the Holy Bible*, 693.

Other Sources

Three times in his account Josephus uses the phrase 'to this day'. He writes that the tower is 'preserved to this day', that the kings of Media, of Persia, and Parthia are buried in the tower 'to this day' and that a Jewish priest is caretaker of the tower 'to this day'. Assuming that this is not just speculation, the implication is that either Josephus has visited Ecbatana and observed the tower or, more probably, that he is citing the account of someone else. This being the case, then most of what Josephus has to say about the tower seems based on contemporary observation of a tower rather than an account dating for the time of Daniel.

Only one element of Josephus' account could plausibly have another source and that is the initial statement that 'when Daniel was become so illustrious and famous . . . he built a tower at Ecbatana'. Yet the greatest difficulty is that Josephus claims that he or his informer has seen the tower and observed the quality of its stones. However, such a cursory statement does not lend itself to the hypothesis that there was some other story or book about Daniel that Josephus was aware of. The most plausible explanation would seem to be that the connection between the tower and Daniel was contained in the same source upon which Josephus bases his description of the tower. The connection would be either a speculation from that writer or else a local tradition about the tower that the writer believed. Therefore, the source of Josephus' account is likely to be a local tradition associated with a specific building. In the rest of the chapter I discuss various options for the identity of that building.

The Tomb of Daniel

A common identification for the tower of Daniel mentioned by Josephus is the (so-called) tomb of Daniel, which is in Susa (modern Shush).[8] The 'tomb' is, in fact, an Islamic mosque, whose foundations may go back to the 7th or 8th century. It was presumably this structure that was observed by the Jewish travelers, Benjamin of Tudela (12th century) and Rabbi Pethahiah (15th century).[9] In these two accounts far greater detail is given to the elaborate suspension of the copper coffin of Daniel by iron chains from the bridge of the river Tigris.[10] Apparently, this was done to placate the local residents of the area who felt that the residents on one side of the river were being blessed because of the presence of the remains of the prophet. The Sultan, therefore, decreed that the coffin be suspended from the bridge and that no fisherman should catch any fish within a mile of the coffin. Unfortunately, we are furnished with no details as to what the tomb of Daniel might have looked like.

---

[8] W.A. Scott, *Esther: The Hebrew-Persian Queen* (H.H. Bancroft, 1859), 90; cf. Bruce, *A Mind for What Matters*, 21.

[9] S. Matheson, *Persia: An Archaeological Guide* (London: Faber and Faber, 1972), 150-51.

[10] *Benjamin of Tudela*, 52-53; W. Ainsworth, *The Travels of Rabbi Pethahiah* (Trubner, 1856), 39-41.

The reason why this structure is commonly identified with the tower of Daniel mentioned by Josephus is presumably the shared association with Daniel, but little else matches Josephus' description. The location of this structure (i.e. in Susa) might be admissible if we follow Jerome's variant (or if we suppose Josephus to be confused). Yet it would be strange if a tomb so strongly associated with Daniel's own burial should give rise to Josephus' description of a tower where many kings were buried.

Royal Persian Tombs

Josephus writes: 'they bury the kings of Media, of Persia, and Parthia, in this tower'. This statement is already problematic because Daniel's prominence in the Persian administration, as recorded in Daniel 6, post-date the fall of the last Median king. Whilst it is possible that Josephus intends to include Darius the Mede, it seems more likely that he is confused. The more significant difficulty is that the kings of Media, of Persia and of Parthia were not buried in the same place. The Median kings were, presumably, buried at Ecbatana, the capital of Media. Cyrus and Cambyses were buried in separate tombs at Pasargadae; other Persian kings (Darius I, Xerxes, Artaxerxes I, Darius II) were buried in separate tombs at Naqš-i-Rusham. The resting places of the last Persian kings (Artaxerxes II, III & Darius III) are uncertain, but it is probably that they were buried at Persepolis. The Parthian kings were buried at Nisa and Arbela.

These facts need not destroy all historicity in Josephus' account. Firstly, he does not say 'all the kings' were buried in the tower, though his statement would most naturally be taken to mean that this was the default burial location. Secondly, it is possible that when he says 'the kings of Media, of Persia, and Parthia', he does not mean to refer to three separate dynasties but one dynasty that ruled over all three territories (i.e. either the Persian or the Parthian kings). His statement that the kings are still buried there 'to this day' would, if accurate, entail that the Parthian kings were buried there.

Nasq-i-Rusham

Whiston, commenting on Josephus' account, seems to identify the tower of Daniel with the tombs at Naqš-i-Rusham (near Persepolis).[11] A series of Persian kings (Darius I, Xerxes, Artaxerxes I, Darius II) were buried in these tombs that were cut into the rock. The word βάρις refers to a tower or large building; it is not the natural word to describe these tombs carved out of the cliff side.

Pasargadae

The tomb of Cambyses long lost have recently been identified with the ruined stone monument Zendan-i-Suleiman ('the prison of Solomon').[12] However, this ruined structure provides little data for comparison with Josephus' description.

---

[11] Whiston, *Works of Josephus*, 284n.
[12] http://www.payvand.com/news/06/dec/1150.html [cited: 08 March 2009]

The tomb of Cyrus

A more promising structure is the tomb of Cyrus, which is still standing to this day. The tomb is a simple stone structure that sits atop a series of steps. The tomb is now empty, but the Greek historian Aristobulus gives us a description of what the tomb originally held:[13]

> Inside the chamber there was a golden coffin containing Cyrus' body, and a great divan with feet of hammered gold, spread with covers of some thick, brightly col-oured material, with a Babylonian rug on top. Tunics and a candys, or Median jacket, of Babylonian workmanship were laid out on the divan, and Medina trou-sers, various robes dyed in amethyst, purple, and many other colors, necklaces, scimitars, and inlaid earrings of gold and precious stones. A table stood by it, and in the middle of it lay the coffin which held Cyrus' body.

The most intriguing element of Aristobulus' account of Alexander's visit to the tomb of Cyrus is the mention of a small building within the enclosure, which was for 'the Magi' who guarded Cyrus' tomb. It is recorded that this duty had been 'handed down from father to son ever since the time of Cyrus' son, Cam-byses'. They had a grant from the King of a sheep a day, with an allowance of meal and wine, and one horse a month to sacrifice to Cyrus. The role of the Magi seems to parallel the role of the Jewish Priest described by Josephus, both being entrusted with the care of a royal tomb.

Now there seems little chance that the tomb of Cyrus is the structure that Jo-sephus describes. Even if Josephus had confused Pasargadae with Ecbatana, this tomb held only one king. It also seems unlikely that Josephus identified the Magi who guarded Cyrus' tomb as a Jewish priest, unless his encounter with the Magi was cursory. In fact, by Josephus' day there were probably no longer any Magi at Cyrus' tomb; Aristobulus records that Alexander had the Magi executed for allowing the body of Cyrus to be stolen. Nevertheless, the exam-ple of Cyrus' tomb gives us an example of how royal tombs of the Near East were treated, entrusted to the care of a religious figure. It is a credible possibil-ity that Josephus (or his informant) did observe a tomb that had a priest as care-taker.

Arbela

The Roman historian Dio Cassius records that some of the Parthian kings were buried at Arbela, though the exact location of the internment is unknown.[14] Now, there seems little to connect Daniel with Arbela, it is the wrong location and the wrong period. However, the city has an interesting Jewish connection.

Under the Parthians, the area around Arbela became the semi-independent kingdom of Adiabene. In the first century BC the Adiabenan royalty converted to Judaism. Now, it is conceivable that under the kings of Adiabene sponsored

---

[13] Aristobulus' account is preserved in the histories Arrian of Nicomedia (*Anabasis* 29.1-11).
[14] Dio Cass. LXXVIII.1.

a Jewish priest to care for the tombs of the Parthian kings in Arbela, in much the same way that the Persian kings employed the Magi to watch over the tomb of Cyrus. On the other hand, it is also conceivable that in the vibrant Jewish environment of Adiabene many a structure was constructed and associated with one or other of the Old Testament heroes. Indeed, in later years Arbela did become host to this sort of pseudo-tomb, such that the Jewish traveler, Isaac Cello, found there the tombs of Dinah, daughter of Jacob and of Seth, son of Adam! We must, therefore, entertain the possibility that the structure that Josephus (or his informant) visited was a similar forgery. One cannot help suspecting that this very possibility is betrayed by his words 'it appears to have been lately built'.

Having said all of this, it is unlikely that Josephus would have confused Ecbatana with Arbela. Josephus writes extensively about the kingdom of Abiabene,[15] so, we can be fairly sure that he knew where it was (and where it wasn't).

Ecbatana

This brings us finally to the city of Ecbatana, the capital of the Median kings and the summer residence of the kings of both Persia and Parthia. The modern city of Hamadan that was built on top of Ecbatana is home to the supposed tomb of Esther and Mordecai, which some have connected with the tower of Daniel,[16] but this structure is undoubtedly not ancient.

The severe limitation we face when discussing the city of Ecbatana is that so little of it has been excavated. An extensive archaeological survey is impossible due to the presence of modern buildings, and to date the limited excavations have only delved as far as the Parthian strata.[17] It seems that the Parthians, when digging the foundations of their own building projects, dug down to virgin soil and leaving little sign of Median or Persian periods.[18]

We have three descriptions of the city of Ecbatana available. Herodotus (fifth century BC) describes the construction of Ecbatana, which he ascribes to the Median king Deioces. He asserts that the palace of Ecbatana was encircled by seven walls, each painted a different colour, while the houses of the citizens of Ecbatana were built outside the walls.[19] The historicity of this account has been questioned and, in any case, these works of Deioces would predate the career of Daniel. Another account of the construction of the walls of Ecbatana is described in the book of Judith, this time ascribed to a king named 'Ar-

---

[15] *Antiquities* 20.2.1-4.3 (20.17-96).
[16] cf. Bruce, *A Mind for What Matters*, 22.
[17] P. Briant, *From Cyrus to Alexander: A History of the Persian Empire* (Eisenbrauns, 2006), 84.
[18] D. Stronach, 'Ecbatana (Hamadan)', *The Encyclopedia of Ancient History* (Wiley, 2012).
[19] Herodotus, *Histories* I.98.

phaxad'.[20] The historical value of the book of Judith is particularly dubious; certainly the supposed king Arphaxad is not known from any other source. The final account comes from the historian Polybius.[21] This account dates from the second century BC, and so it is likely that some of the features he describes are later than the Median/Persian period. Polybius describes two structures in Ecbatana, the palace and 'an artificial citadel, the fortifications of which are of wonderful strength'.[22] Neither structure fits Josephus' description of a tomb.

If, as the excavations suggest, Ecbatana was heavily rebuilt by the Parthians, it is very possible that no buildings from the time of Daniel were still standing in 1st century AD when Josephus is writing. Though he (or his informant) may have observed many impressive structures in Ecbatana, he is unlikely to have observed any tower dating from the time of Daniel. Since the tombs of the Persian and Parthian kings were elsewhere, the possibility that Josephus (or his informant) observed any royal tombs in the city is unlikely.

Conclusions

Because of the limitations of evidence, Josephus' account of the tower of Daniel looks highly dubious. It is difficult to explain away Josephus' account as a confusion based upon Daniel 8:2. Given the large number of para-Danielic writings extant amongst the apocrypha and the Dead Sea Scrolls it is possible that Josephus was aware of another apocryphal story about Daniel building a tower. Josephus does not seem to have based his account on a story but he seems to be describing a structure that can still be seen in his day (perhaps, a structure that he saw himself). And yet it seems impossible to identify the building Josephus describes with any known structure.

In fact, Josephus makes a number of statements that it is difficult to reconcile with the evidence. He claims that Daniel built a tower at Ecbatana that was still standing in his own day, and yet archaeological investigations reveal that it is unlikely that anything from the sixth century survived into the Parthian era. He claims that the kings of Media, of Persia, and Parthia were buried in that tower, and yet the Persian kings were buried at Pasargadae or Nasq-i-Rusham, whilst the Parthian kings were buried at Arbela. Further, Josephus also makes claims that seem implausible, such as that a Jewish priest was caretaker over the tombs of these pagan kings.

However, our examination of the various candidates for the tower of Daniel have revealed a number of elements that may go together to explain Josephus' report. Firstly, it is clear that Jewish populations did ascribe recent constructions to illustrious figures from the Old Testament. Arbela hosted the tombs of Dinah and Seth, modern Ecbatana contains the tombs of Esther and Mordecai, and there is even a tomb of Daniel. None of these structures is genuine, and

---

[20] *Judith* 1:1-4.
[21] Polybius, *Histories*, X.IV.27.1-13.
[22] *Histories* X.IV.27.6.

none should be identified as the tower of Daniel, but they are evidence of the pattern of famous biblical characters being associated with certain buildings.

Secondly, the example of the tomb of Cyrus illustrates the practice of the Persians to appoint wardens to tombs of special significance, whose service included sacrificing for the deceased. That a Jewish priest should serve as warden to a pagan tomb seems unlikely but the concept of priestly-warden is by no means incredible. Thirdly, Josephus himself says that the tower of Daniel appears to have been 'lately built' and one must suspect that this is because it was a recent construction.

Given the above, one may speculate plausibly about how Josephus arrived at his account. There was a building, presumably a tomb of some sort that the local population associated with Daniel. It was, perhaps, natural to assume that Daniel, as such an important figure in the government of Darius the Mede was responsible for some construction work. And it would seem obvious that Daniel must be responsible for the most illustrious building. Or perhaps the tower was a fake, specifically created in reverence for Daniel. In either case, there is nothing implausible about there being a building with such a story attached to it. That Josephus (or his informant) was taken in by the story may say more about his credulity than the plausibility of the story.

In sum, the story that Daniel built a structure at Ecbatana probably predates Josephus, but much of his account, including the identification with a certain structure in Ecbatana, is doubtful. We have no basis by which to connect this story with the historical figure of Daniel and so this account adds nothing to our evidence for Daniel or his works.

Chapter 14

Re-dating the Composition of the Book of Daniel

It is well known that opinion is divided on the dating of the book of Daniel. Whilst conservative scholars favour an early date ($6^{th}/5^{th}$ century BC), critical scholars since the nineteenth century have dated the book to c.165 BC. There have been numerous studies by conservative scholars (and laypersons) attempting to rebut the critical arguments for the late date. Perhaps the most important of these studies was *Notes on Some Problems in the Book of Daniel* (ed. D.J. Wiseman), which addressed historical and linguistic issues. This has been the precedent of many of the subsequent studies, which continue to focus on historical and linguistic issues to defend an early date.

Wiseman's book included four studies. The first, by Wiseman, concerned alleged historical discrepancies in the book of Daniel that might argue for a late date. This study discusses some of the issues that have been explored in greater detail in the present volume. The historical issues we have considered strengthen the case against the late-date. The book of Judith, probably composed around the second century BC, is a good example of the level of historicity we should expect from a late-author. The author is so far removed from historical reality that he believes Nebuchadnezzar to be the king of Assyria and have his capital in Nineveh. It hardly needs repeating that the author of Daniel demonstrates a far superior historical knowledge, not only superior to the author of Judith but superior to historians like Herodotus, who knew nothing of Belshazzar.

The other three studies in Wiseman's book each concern linguistic issues. In the nineteenth century, it was thought that the presence of Persian and Greek words required a second century date.[1] T.C. Mitchell and R. Joyce's study of the Greek loanwords in Daniel 3, all musical instruments, aimed to show that the presence of these words did not necessitate a late date for the composition of the book.[2] Subsequent studies have substantiated their conclusion. The early influence of the Greeks in the Near East is now well substantiated and the pres-

---

[1] Driver, *Introduction*, 508.
[2] T.C. Mitchell and R. Joyce, 'The Musical Instruments in Nebuchadnezzar's Orchestra' in *Notes on Some Problems in the Book of Daniel* (London: Tyndale, 1965).

ence of Greek loanwords in fifth/sixth century Aramaic is to be expected.[3] The presence of Persian words should never have been considered a significant criterion as it is consistent with any date of composition from the end of the sixth century. The fact that the translators of OG-Dan mistranslated some Persian words in Daniel is a clue to the antiquity of the book.[4] Analysis has demonstrated that the Aramaic sections are unlikely to have been composed later than 300 BC;[5] even proponents of the late-date concede that the Aramaic is archaic for a second century author.[6] Linguistic comparisons have also shown that the Hebrew sections are unlikely to be contemporary with second-century Hebrew texts.[7]

In principle, there is nothing wrong with these sorts of arguments. Since critical studies continue to be produced that repeat nineteenth century arguments in a remarkably uncritical manner. It is important to continue to emphasize their limitations. For example, the critical scholar who asserts that the Aramaic of Daniel is late or that the author had a poor knowledge of sixth century Babylon simply has not done their research. Yet historical arguments remain inconveniences for the critical scholar because, though the author clearly had better knowledge of sixth century Babylon than the Greek historians Herodotus and Xenophon, the critical scholar can always respond that perhaps the author had some form of historical tradition that we're not aware of or perhaps the historical bits were composed earlier than those troublesome predictive prophecies. There is, therefore, a need for new arguments and more rigorous criteria for dating the book that can categorically rule out an early date.

In this chapter I outline a new set of criteria for dating the book, identifying fixed starting points and the preceding stages from which a rigorous procedure for setting the latest possible date at which the book could have been written. I will identify several 'positions', which represent fixed markers against which the date of composition can be placed. I will also identify several 'periods', which represent lengths of time that must have occurred between the composi-

---

[3] For citations see E.M. Yamauchi, 'Greece and Babylon Revisited' in *To Understand the Scriptures: Essays in Honor of William H. Shea* (ed. D. Merling; Berrien Springs: Institute of Archaeology, 1997), 127-36.

[4] J. Burke, 'Linguistic Issues in Daniel', *CJBI* 2008, 123.

[5] K.A. Kitchen, 'The Aramaic of Daniel' in *Notes on Some Problems in the Book of Daniel* (London: Tyndale Press, 1965); E.Y. Kutscher, *Hebrew and Aramaic Studies* (Jerusalem: Magnes Press, 1977); also, see: P.W. Coxon, 'The Syntax of the Aramaic of Daniel: A Dialectal Study', *HUCA* 48 (1977), 107-22; R.I. Vasholz, 'Qumran and the Dating of Daniel', *JETS* 21 (1978), 315-21; Koch, *Das Buch Daniel*, 45-6; Z. Stefanovic, *The Aramaic of Daniel in the Light of Old Aramaic* (Sheffield: JSOT, 1992).

[6] Cf. J.C. Greenfield, 'Early Aramaic Poetry', *JANESCU* 11 (1979), 45-51.

[7] W.J. Martin, 'The Hebrew of Daniel' in *Notes on Some Problems in the Book of Daniel* (London: Tyndale Press, 1965); G.L. Archer, 'The Hebrew of Daniel compared with the Qumran Sectarian Documents' in *The Law and the Prophets* (ed. J. Skilton; Nutley: Presbyterian & Reformed, 1974).

tion of the book and one of the positions I identify. Combining the positions and periods, I propose a way to calculate the latest date for the composition of the book.

Manuscript Evidence

When it comes to dating the book of Daniel (as for any book of the Bible) the definitive piece of evidence would be the autograph, the original scroll on which the book was written. If we had the autograph there could be no dispute about date. But we do not have the autograph for the book of Daniel (or any other ancient text, for that matter). What we do have are manuscripts and manuscript fragments. These are important and tangible evidence for dating the book. It is worth emphasizing, as this will form a major part of the argument, that these manuscripts do not indicate a date of composition, they indicate the latest possible date of composition (*terminus ad quem*).

The oldest manuscripts of the Masoretic text (MT) are Leningrad Codex (1008 AD) and the Aleppo Codex (c.925 AD), which was damaged in 1948 during the fighting that took place when the State of Israel was founded. The oldest complete manuscripts of the Septuagint are found in the Codex Sinaiticus (4th century AD) and the Codex Vaticanus (4th century AD).[8] Though these are important textual witnesses, they do not provide manuscript evidence for dating Daniel.

Eight manuscripts of the book of Daniel were found at Qumran: 1QDan[a], 1QDan[b], 4QDan[a], 4QDan[b], 4QDan[c], 4QDan[d], 4QDan[e] and 6QpapDan.[9] None of these manuscripts are complete, but each contains a small section of the book of Daniel.[10] In 1953 the biblical texts from Qumran cave 4, including the five Daniel fragments, were allotted to Frank Cross, then Associate Professor of Old Testament at McCormick Theological Seminary (Chicago), for publication and study. In 1958 he published some of his findings. Of one of the Daniel fragments (4QDan[c]) he wrote:

> One copy of Daniel is inscribed in the script of the late second century BC; in some ways its antiquity is more striking than that of the oldest MSS from Qum-

---

[8] Small fragments of the Septuagint have been found which are far older, including John Rylands Papyrus 456 (2nd century BC) and Papyrus Fouad 266 (c.100 BC). Both these papyrus contain parts of Deuteronomy.

[9] These texts are also numbered as follows: 1Q71, 1Q72, 4Q112, 4Q113, 4Q114, 4Q115, 4Q116, 6Q7. The 'Q' signifies 'Qumran' and the preceding number is the cave number, so 4QDan[a] is the first of the Daniel manuscripts from cave 4 at Qumran. A full catalogue listing can be found in Vermes, *Complete Dead Sea Scrolls*, 639-56.

[10] These sections have been drawn together in a single English translation in *The Dead Sea Scrolls Bible* (ed. M. Abegg; San Francisco: HarperSanFrancisco, 1999), 482-502.

ran, since it is no more than about half a century younger than the autograph of Daniel.[11]

Cross' paleographical assessment was that 4QDan[c] was written 'in the script of the late second century BC', meaning that this fragment was dated sometime after 150 BC. A few years later he revised his dating of 4QDan[c] to around 100-50 BC.[12] Recent scholarship has dated 4QDan[c] to around 125 BC.[13] The other fragments are dated after this up to around 50 AD when the latest manuscript (4QDan[a]) was written. None of the Daniel fragments from Qumran have been carbon-dated as the process would result in the destruction of parts of the manuscript.

It is also possible that there is further manuscript evidence as yet discovered or held by private collectors.[14]

Position 1: 4QDan[c] fixes a *terminus ad quem* of c.125 BC for the book of Daniel

Working Backwards

Since 4QDan[c] is not the autograph, a certain amount of time must have passed between the date of the autograph and the date of this copy. Bruce Waltke has argued that the finds at Qumran should push back the date of Daniel prior to 165 BC. He writes:

> Equivalent manuscript finds at Qumran of other books where the issue of predictive prophecy is not in question have led scholars to repudiate a Maccabean date for their compositions.[15]

For example, some of the psalms were previously thought to date from the Maccabean period. However, the discovery of manuscripts at Qumran containing these psalms led to a revision in this theory. William Brownlee writes:

> Each song had to win its way in the esteem of the people before it could be included in the sacred compilation of the Psalter. Immediate entrée for any of them is highly improbable.[16]

Waltke also cites Millar Burrows who revised his dating of Ecclesiastes from the second to the third century BC based upon the discovery of two scrolls

---

[11] F.M. Cross, *The Ancient Library of Qumran and Modern Biblical Studies* (New York: 1958), 33.

[12] F.M. Cross, 'The Development of the Jewish Scripts' in G.E. Wright (ed.), *The Bible and the Ancient Near East: Essays in Honour of W.F. Albright* (London, 1961), 140.

[13] *Dead Sea Scrolls Bible*, 482.

[14] Waltke, 'Date', 321.

[15] Waltke, 'Date', 321.

[16] W.H. Brownlee, *The Meaning of the Qumran Scrolls for the Bible* (New York: Oxford University Press, 1964), 36.

found at Qumran, and Jacob Myers who ruled out a Maccabean date 'for any part of Chronicles' based upon a Chronicles fragment at Qumran.

Professor Waltke legitimately questions why scholars, such as Brownlee, have not revised the second century date for Daniel based upon equivalent evidence.[17] Brownlee's argument regarding the psalms that each needed a period of time before it could be accepted as sacred can surely also be applied to the book of Daniel. Given that Daniel was not written at Qumran, how is it that within forty years of its composition it could have been accepted as sacred (not to mention popular) amongst the community at Qumran? If we could give a plausible specification as to how long it would have taken a new composition to be recognized as sacred by the Qumran community then we could determine whether the manuscript evidence made a Maccabean date of composition impossible, and not just improbable.

Canonicity

Individual texts (e.g. letters) could be transported very quickly, even in the ancient world so, in theory, a book could be copied in another location shortly after its original composition. Therefore, the discovery of a single copy of Daniel does not, of itself, push back the date of composition. However, if a manuscript is being copied for religious purposes (i.e. if it is already regarded as canonical) then a significant lag time between original composition and reception (i.e. copying) is implied.

There is little dispute that by the end of the first century AD the book of Daniel formed part of the Christian Scriptures. The book is quoted by pseudo-Barnabas,[18] Clement,[19] and by the evangelists,[20] who name Daniel as a 'prophet'. The writer to the Hebrews cited Daniel as an example of faith.[21] There are also repeated allusions made in the book of Revelation.[22] The allusions in Paul are enough to indicate that Christian reverence for the book was early.[23] The NT witnesses to both OG-Dan and Th-Dan, but there are no allusions to the apocryphal additions, indicating that the additions were not regarded as scripture.[24]

---

[17] Waltke, 'Date', 321-22.
[18] Epistle of Barnabas 4:4-5; v4 is introduced as the words of 'the prophet'.
[19] I Clement 34:6, 45:6-7; Daniel and his three friends are cited as examples from 'the holy and true Scriptures' (45:2).
[20] Matthew 24:30, 26:64; Mark 13:26, 14:62; Luke 21:27.
[21] Hebrews 11:33.
[22] Revelation 1:1, 7, 13-15, 19, 2:10, 18, 3:5, 4:1, 7:14, 10:4, 5-6, 11:7, 15, 12:3, 14, 17, 13:1, 7, 8, 14:14, 16:18, 17:8, 18:10, 19:6, 20:4, 11-12, 15, 21:27, 22:5, 10.
[23] Daniel 2:44/I Corinthians 15:24; Daniel 2:47/I Corinthians 14:25; Daniel 6:21/II Timothy 4:17; Daniel 7:22/I Corinthians 6:2; Daniel 11:36/II Thessalonians 2:4; Daniel 12:1/Philippians 4:3; Daniel 12:3/Ephesians 2:15.
[24] One possible exception is Hebrews 11:12/Daniel 3:36 (OG-Dan).

Josephus also regarded the book of Daniel as Scripture.[25] His praise of Daniel is overflowing; he styles him 'one of the greatest of the prophets'.[26] Josephus devotes two chapters to the exploits of Daniel and his friends, recounting all six stories.[27] Though he knows an additional story in which Daniel builds a tower in Ecbatana, he makes no reference to the events of the apocryphal additions. Josephus believes that God inspired Daniel to a degree worthy of wonder[28] and accepts Daniel's visions as genuine prophecy.[29] Oddly, Josephus refers to 'several books' that Daniel wrote.[30] Koch suggests that this implies that the Greek versions were regarded as separate books, though there is no particular reason to accept this hypothesis over any other.[31] It is possible, for instance, that Josephus viewed the book of Daniel as a compilation of several works. The most likely explanation is that Josephus was aware of some para-Danielic text no longer extant. It is unlikely that Josephus counted these para-Danielic texts amongst the sacred books, which he numbers at twenty-two,[32] so however many books of Daniel Josephus knew, he only regarded one as canonical.

The inclusion of the book of Daniel in the Old Greek or Septuagint version is a strong indication that the book was regarded as canonical amongst the group in which the translation originated, generally recognized to be the Alexandrian Diaspora.[33] The Old Greek version of the Old Testament appears to have been an evolving entity, commencing with the translation of the Pentateuch in 3rd century. The book of Daniel was probably translated c.100 BC and was included amongst the Prophets, though it is not clear when the Old Greek books were first ordered in this way. The Old Greek version includes the apocryphal additions to the book of Daniel, indicating that these too were regarded as Scripture.

The other major witness from Alexandria is Philo. The majority of his works are commentary on sections of the Pentateuch which demonstrates his reverence for those books but we do not have a representative sampling for his attitude to the other OT books. When Philo refers to other OT books he does so with 'the same profound reverence as the Pentateuch'.[34] Philo does also regard

---

[25] '[L]et him be diligent in reading the book of Daniel, which he will find among the sacred writings' (Josephus, *Antiquities of the Jews* 10.10.4 (210)).

[26] *Antiquities* 10.11.7 (266).

[27] *Antiquities* 10.10.1-10.11.7.

[28] *Antiquities* 10.11.7 (277).

[29] *Antiquities* 10.10.4 (208-210), 10.11.7 (266-281), 12.7.6 (321-2).

[30] *Antiquities* 10.11.7 (267).

[31] K. Koch, 'Stages in the Canonization of the Book of Daniel' in *The Book of Daniel: Composition and Reception* (eds. J.J. Collins & P.W. Flint; Leiden: Brill, 2001), 2:442.

[32] *Contra Apion* 1.8 (38).

[33] N. Fernández Marcos, *The Septuagint in Context: Introduction to the Greek Version of the Bible* (Leiden: Brill, 2000), 53-64.

[34] R. Beckwith, *The Old Testament Canon of the New Testament Church and Its Background in Early Judaism* (London: SPCK, 1985), 22.

the teachings of Plato to be authoritative. From Philo's descriptions of the holy books, Ellis suspects that he had the same canon as Josephus, though the evidence is too scant to be conclusive.[35] In one fragment Philo does refer to the three divisions of the OT.[36] Whilst Philo does not explicitly mention Daniel, it is a reasonable supposition that Philo regarded the book as canonical.

In 1955 when the first transcription of the Daniel fragments from Qumran was published by Barthélemy and Milik it was asserted that the book of Daniel was not regarded as canonical there.[37] Barthélemy had two justifications for this assertion: 1) in the Daniel fragments the height of the text was approximately equal to its width, whereas in other biblical manuscripts the height was double the width, and 2) one Daniel fragment was written on papyrus (pap6QDan).[38] Further discoveries at Qumran revealed that, though there were general stylistic trends, one style was not followed exclusively for canonical books. Some fragments of Deuteronomy and Psalms also use the square format (4QDeut[n], 4QPs[g]) and there are fragments of Kings and Isaiah on papyrus (pap4QIsa[p], pap6QKg[s]).[39] Though Barthélemy's conjecture is occasionally repeated,[40] modern consensus is that the book of Daniel was regarded as canonical at Qumran.[41] The reverence for the book is evidenced by the eight copies found amongst the scrolls – surpassed only by Isaiah (12), Deuteronomy (14) and Psalms (10) – and also by the frequent allusions to the book.[42] It is possible that the threefold division of the Old Testament referred to by Josephus and Philo was known at Qumran.[43] Daniel is called a prophet.[44]

The above evidence indicates that by the early first century AD the book of Daniel was regarded as canonical by Christians, Rabbinic Jews, the Qumran sect and amongst the Jewish diaspora. Given this geographical distribution, it is likely that the book of Daniel had already been in existence for a long time previously. Koch argues that Daniel was not given canonical status before 50 BC,

---

[35] Ellis, *Old Testament in Early Christianity*, 8.

[36] '[T]he laws, the oracles uttered by the prophets, and hymns and the others' (Philo, *Hypothetica* 9, quoted Eusebius, *Praep. Evang.* 8:11).

[37] D. Barthélemy & J.T. Milik, *Qumran Cave 1: Discoveries in the Judaean Desert* 1 (Oxford: Clarendon, 1955).

[38] Barthélemy & Milik, 150.

[39] '[Barthélemy's] conjecture was insightful and judiciously worded, and he should not be faulted now that subsequent evidence indicates otherwise; but the conjecture should no longer be uncritically repeated' (E. Ulrich, 'Daniel Manuscripts from Qumran. Part 1: A Preliminary Edition of 4QDan[a]', *BASOR* 268 (1987) 19). Also, see W.E. Wegner, 'The Book of Daniel and the Dead Sea Scrolls', *Quartalschrift Theological Quarterly* 455 (1958), 103-16.

[40] D.N. Freedman & P.F. Kuhlken, *What Are the Dead Sea Scrolls and Why Do They Matter?* (Grand Rapids: Eerdmans, 2007), 4-5.

[41] Koch, 'Stages', 427-32; *Dead Sea Scrolls Bible*, 483.

[42] 11Q13 2:18; *War Scroll* 1:1, 11, 17:58; 4Q174 4:3.

[43] 4Q397 frgs 14-21.10.

[44] 4Q174 4:3.

proposing that there was 'a century of neglect' of the book of Daniel in mainstream Palestinian Judaism c.150-50 BC.[45] His evidence, however, is negligible comprising of the Psalms of Solomon solely. Koch admits likely dependence of I Maccabees on the book of Daniel, though argues that this dependence does not 'necessarily presuppose canonical status'. Yet the reference to 'the abomination of desolation' (I Maccabees 1:54) is most reasonably interpreted as an actualization of Daniel's predictions. This would presuppose that Daniel was regarded as a genuine prophet, which in turn would presuppose the canonicity of the book that records his predictions. Coupled with the appearance of Th-Dan during this period, the allusions in I Maccabees are strong indicators that the book of Daniel was indeed regarded as canonical prior to 50 BC.

The reception of the book of Daniel outside the community demonstrates that the book did not originate from Qumran (though this was never in doubt). As an exclusive sect, the dialogue with 'mainstream' Judaism would have been minimal and the likelihood of a book being accepted into the canon of the community from outside is likewise minimal. It is, therefore, probable that the canon of Qumran, apart from its own internal additions, represents the canon of 'mainstream' Judaism prior to their separation (c.150 BC).[46]

There is no established theory about how manuscripts received canonical status and how long that process might have taken. We can speculate that reception, particularly in the absence of an ecclesiastical hierarchy, would be dependent on circumstances. For example, we can hardly imagine that the book of Jeremiah had wide reception prior to the captivity but the book probably had wide acceptance once his predictions were realized. Ironically, we might reasonably suppose that a book written during the Maccabean revolt that failed to predict correctly the outcome of the conflict (as some scholars allege of the book of Daniel) would not receive wide canonical recognition and would swiftly be forgotten. What we can say, is that it is unlikely that canonical status is instantaneous and that the speed of reception is likely to be affected by circumstances, particularly the location of composition.

Period X: Time from composition to canonical reception

Textual History

The manuscript evidence from Qumran is not the only method for fixing a *terminus ad quem* for the book of Daniel. The complex textual history of the book, primarily its various translations, also provides a method for identifying the footprints of the book.

The earliest extant Greek translation (and almost certainly the first) of the book of Daniel is commonly known as the 'Septuagint' (LXX) or 'Old Greek' (OG-Dan). OG-Dan is only witnessed by three manuscripts: Chisian MS 88 (c.

---

[45] Koch, 'Stages', 424.
[46] Cf. Ellis, *Old Testament in Early Christianity*, 38-41.

9th-11th century AD), Syrohexaplar (c.615-7 AD)[47] and papyrus 967 (c. 2nd century AD). The former two MS are hexaplaric, both containing the text-critical symbols of Origen's text; pap. 967 predates the Hexaplar.

It is generally accepted that the OG-Dan translator worked from a Semitic Vorlage (source-text). This Vorlage differed in several important ways from MT. Firstly, OG-Dan contains longer versions of chapters 4-6 than MT. Secondly, OG-Dan contains the Apocryphal Additions (Susanna, Bel and the Dragon, the Prayer of the Three Children). The other differences between OG-Dan and MT, though previously explained by theological bias, are now understood to be due to the OG-Vorlage.[48] OG-Dan is generally dated to the late second century. The Additions, which undoubtedly were composed in Hebrew or Aramaic, predate this translation.

Around the second century AD the Old Greek text of Daniel was replaced in the Christian communities with the so-called 'Theodotion' version (Th-Dan).[49] Though ascribed to the eponymous translator, it is almost certain that Th-Dan predates his translation of the OT. The reason for this conclusion is that the NT citations of Daniel are often 'Theodotionic';[50] 'Theodotionic' citations also occur in *Epistle of Baruch* and the apostolic fathers. Several scholars have proposed that both the NT writers and Theodotion drew independently from a proto-Theodotionic version (cf. Barthélemy, Gwynn, etc.). Montgomery proposed that both were based upon an oral tradition.[51] More recently Schmitt, by close-analysis of the text discovered that many words that occur Th-Dan, occur rarely in other books of Theodotion but are attested in Symmachus.[52] Thus, the concept of a proto-Theodotionic version has generally been abandoned.[53] Rather, Th-Dan pre-dates the Theodotion and was incorporated wholesale into that translation.

It is generally recognized that OG-Dan is presupposed by Th-Dan;[54] Di Lella explains Th-Dan as one of several recensions of OG-Dan (inc. 'Proto-

---

[47] Syrohexaplar is Syriac translation from Origen's Hexaplar, which contained the OG. Though in Syriac, the MS is a useful witness to OG-Dan as the translation is 'slavishly literal' (Di Lella, 'Textual History', 586).

[48] Di Lella, 'Textual History', 592.

[49] Uncials: A, B, Q, Γ; Cursives: HP 62, 147; Lectionaries: HP 37, 45, 61, 132, 149 (chs 3-6), 105, 229; (cf. Montgomery, *Daniel*, 26-7).

[50] Matt. 21:44/Dan. 2:44; Matt. 28:56/Dan. 7:9; 1 Cor. 1:24/Dan. 2:20; Heb. 11:13/Dan. 6:22; James 1:12/Dan. 12:12; Rev. 1:7/Dan. 7:13; Rev. 1:19/Dan. 2:29, 43; Rev. 9:20/Dan. 5:23; Rev. 10:4/Dan. 8:26; Rev. 10:5-6/Dan. 12:7; Rev. 11:7/Dan. 7:21; Rev. 11:13/Dan. 2:19; Rev. 12:7/Dan. 10:20; Rev. 12:8/Dan. 2:35; Rev. 16:18/Dan. 12:1; Rev. 19:6/Dan. 10:6; Rev. 20:11/Dan. 2:35; (cf. Collins, *Daniel*, 9n; cf. Di Lella, 'Textual History', 593).

[51] Montgomery, *Daniel*, 50.

[52] Fernández Marcos, *Septuagint*, 89.

[53] Di Lella, 'Textual History', 595.

[54] Collins, *Daniel*, 8.

Lucian').[55] Th-Dan is frequently closer to MT than OG-Dan; significantly Th-Dan includes short versions of chapters 4-6 that are independent from Th-Dan. It is, therefore, likely that the translator had access to a Hebrew Vorlage, similar to MT. As Bogaret concludes, Th-Dan is sometimes a new translation and sometimes a revision of OG-Dan.[56]

Extant copies of Th-Dan contain the Additions, placing Susanna before chapter 1 and Bel and the Dragon after chapter 12. However, it is likely that Th-Dan did not originally contain these additions. Munnich has demonstrated that Th-Dan translates the divine names differently in the Additions than from the rest of the text, while OG-Dan translates them consistently. Di Lella writes:

> This difference proves that originally Th-Dan lacked the supplement in chapter 3 as well as the stories of Susanna, Bel and the Dragon. For these portions Th-Dan provides a recession of OG-Dan based on a substratum that itself is revised.[57]

Th-Dan is generally thought to have originated from Palestine, given its provenance, and so it was likely that the Additions were known in first century Palestinian Judaism.

Of the eight incomplete manuscripts of the book of Daniel that have been discovered at Qumran, the earliest dates from c.125 BC.[58] It is likely that each manuscript originally contained the complete book, except 4QDan[e] which may have contained only the prayer of chapter 9.[59] All twelve chapters are attested, though not in full; none of the Additions are attested. The three manuscripts containing chapters 4-6 witness to the shorter versions found in the MT.[60] The distribution of Hebrew and Aramaic matches that preserved in the MT. The text at Qumran is largely consistent with MT and there are few significant textual variants. Ulrich notes that 'the OG frequently agrees with the Qumran reading against the MT'.[61] This probably indicates that the DSS MS are earlier and closer to the autograph.

---

[55] Di Lella, 'Textual History', 595-96.

[56] P-M. Bogaert, 'Relecture et refonte historicisante du livre de Daniel attestées par la première version grecque (Papyrus 967)' in R. Kuntzmann & J. Schlossar, *Études sur le judaïsme hellénistique* (Paris 1984), 197-224.

[57] Di Lella, 'Textual History', 599.

[58] Ulrich, 'Part 1', 17-37; cf. E. Ulrich, 'Daniel Manuscript from Qumran. Part 2: A Preliminary Editions of 4QDan[b] and 4QDan[c]', *BASOR* 274 (1989), 3-26.

[59] *Dead Sea Scrolls Bible*, 482-83. This is not the only instance from Qumran where biblical prayers copied out apart from their source-text. It is likely that these prayers were used for liturgical purposes.

[60] 4QDan[a], 4QDan[b], 4QDan[d].

[61] E. Ulrich, 'The Text of Daniel in the Qumran Scrolls' in *The Book of Daniel: Composition and Reception* (eds. J.J. Collins & P.W. Flint; Leiden: Brill, 2001), 2:580.

If we collate these conclusions we arrive at an interesting and complex textual history for the book of Daniel (see Figure 1 below). This should not lead us to doubt the accuracy of our present text – as we have seen, the MT is likely to be very close to the Autograph, as confirmed by comparison with the DSS. It is the textual history of the Greek versions that interests us as these recensions imply the passage of years. We can fix the earliest NT citations of Th-Dan to c.55 AD (the composition of 1 Corinthians).

Figure 1

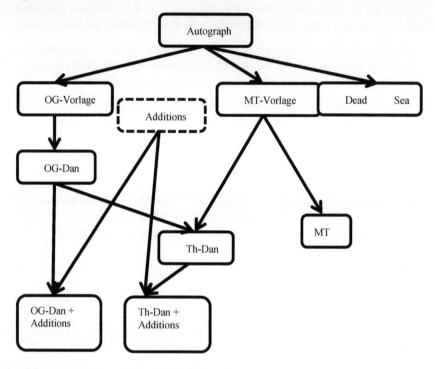

Figure 2

Looking at just the known recensions between the NT citations and the Autograph and we can identify at least four time-periods of undetermined length (A-D) that push back the date of the Autograph (see Figure 2, above).

Working backwards from the composition of 1 Corinthians (c.55 AD) and only fifty years for each period then composition of the Autograph around 165 BC is just plausible:

> 55 AD - Composition of 1 Corinthians by Paul
> 5 AD - Translation of Th-Dan
> 45 BC - Translation of OG-Dan
> 95 BC - OG-Vorlage semitic recension
> 145 BC - Composition of Autograph

However, we have good reason for considering this reconstruction to be overly optimistic. Paul is not the only NT writer to cite Th-Dan. Citations in Matthew (c.60 AD) and James (c.47?)[62] indicate that use of Th-Dan was widespread. Since Paul is unlikely to have carried copies of Th-Dan around with him, his citations may well have been made from memory. In which case, we cannot plausibly think that Paul was introduced to Th-Dan shortly before the composition of 1 Corinthians. On the contrary, it is more likely that his acquaintance with Th-Dan begins with his education in Jerusalem in the early part of the first century. Therefore, dating the composition of Th-Dan to 5 AD seems very optimistic.

The existence of Th-Dan not only requires that OG-Dan was already written and widely known, but also that it was widely deemed to be substandard. The fact that OG-Dan has survived at all makes it improbable that it had only a small circulation. Given that OG-Dan was likely composed in Egypt and Th-Dan was likely composed in Palestine then we need to factor in a period of dissemination and acceptance prior to the period of dissatisfaction that led to the new translation. The composition of OG-Dan has usually been dated to the late second or early first century BC.[63]

The OG-Vorlage recension upon the Autograph may require an even longer period. The OG-Vorlage is not a translation, but an adaption. If the explanation for this recension is not deliberate alteration then several iterations and copies are implied between the Autograph and the OG-Vorlage. Again, this all takes time.

If we allow an only slightly more generous 56 years for each period then a composition date of c.165 BC for the Autograph becomes impossible.

---

[62] John A.T. Robinson, *Redating the New Testament* (London: SCM, 1976).
[63] Di Lella, 'Textual History', 590.

Position 2: NT citations fix a *terminus ad quem* of 55 AD for Th-Dan

Period A: Time from composition to OG-Vorlage recession
Period B: Time from OG-Vorlage to OG-Dan translation
Period C:Time from OG-Dan to Th-Dan revision and translation
Period D: Time from Th-Dan to NT citations

Literary References

Another way of identifying a *terminus ad quem* for the composition of Daniel is to identify citations and allusions in other texts, assuming that the composition of these other texts can be dated with a degree of certainty. We have already noted that Daniel is cited frequently in the NT and by other Christian writers. It has sometimes been asserted that Daniel could not have been written in the sixth century because it is not referred to in Jewish works until the first century. It is, however, important to point out that we do not have copies of many Jewish works written between the fifth and second centuries so even if this were true it would not be a particularly strong argument against the early date. In fact, we will see that literary references that can be found in Jewish works attest to the wide popularity of the book of Daniel and make a second century date improbable.

Similar investigations as this have been previously undertaken. Roger Beckwith argues that a number of Jewish texts whose composition dates from before the Maccabean revolt were dependent on the book of Daniel. These include Tobit (Dan. 2, 7-9, 12), Book of Watchers (Dan. 4, 7-10, 12) and Ecclesiasticus (Dan. 8 or 11-12).[64] Wyns judges that these examples are 'not very convincing'.[65] Wyns cites more favourable the work of Glenn Miller, who finds allusions to the book of Daniel in *Apocalypse of Zephaniah, 1 & 2 Maccabees, Sibylinne Oracles, Testament of Levi, Testament of Benjamin, Ezekiel the Tragedian, Sirach, 1 Enoch* and *Baruch*.[66]

Dead Sea Scrolls

As well as the eight Daniel manuscripts found at Qumran, there were also discovered several other manuscripts that refer to the book of Daniel or that are based upon its stories.

> o   Florilegium (4Q174) – This text dates from c.25 BC.[67] It is a midrash about the Last Days. It writes of these times saying: 'This is the time of which it is written in the book of Daniel the Prophet: "But the wicked shall do wickedly and shall not understand, but

---

[64] R. Beckwith, 'Early Traces of the Book of Daniel', *Tyndale Bulletin* 53:1 (2002), 75-82.

[65] Wyns, *God is Judge*, 397.

[66] G. Miller, 'Was Daniel written after the events he foretold?', http://christianthinktank.com/qwhendan3x.html [cited August 2014]; Wyns, *God is Judge*, 416-17.

[67] *Dead Sea Scrolls Bible*, 484.

the righteous shall purify themselves and make themselves white". The people who know God shall be strong.'[68]

o The War Scroll (c.50 BC – 50 AD) – Several copies of the War Scroll were found at Qumran, both in cave 1 (1QM, 1Q33) and in cave 4 (4Q471, 4Q491-7), which demonstrates how popular this document was. The text itself describes the final battle against the Gentiles, particularly the Kittim, and also contains many rules about military preparation and conduct. The War Scroll makes many allusions to the book of Daniel. Vermes presents the thesis that this work drew its inspiration from Daniel 11:40-12:3, the final battle, and was later expanded with other material.[69] Vermes also refers to the fact that the several manuscripts of the War Scroll found at Qumran differ from one another. This shows that there wasn't a single version of the War Scroll. Over time changes had been made leading to the existence of several different redactions, or versions.

o Pseudo-Daniel in Aramaic (4Q243-5) – This is a collection of three small fragments that seem to be based upon the Daniel story.

o The Four Kingdoms (4Q552-3) – This Aramaic work is based upon the vision of Daniel 7. Here the four kingdoms are not represented by beasts, but by trees.

o Aramaic Apocalypse (4Q246) – A particularly significant text based upon the visions of Daniel 7. What makes this text so interesting is that it uses the words 'son of God', though it is not clear whether this figure is meant to be a saviour or a blasphemous tyrant.

o 4Q551 or 4Q DanSus? – This is very fragmentary text and is therefore difficult to interpret. It is probably not part of the apocryphal Susanna story preserved in the Septuagint. It may be based upon that story or may be an antecedent of the Susanna story.

o Melchizedek (11Q13) – This text (c.50 BC) is about a heavenly saviour identified as Melchizedek who is to come and proclaim freedom for the captives in the Last Days. He is described as 'the Anointed one of the spirit, concerning whom Dan[iel] said . . .'. Though the text is damaged, it is likely that it refers to Daniel 9:25.

The eight manuscripts of the book of Daniel attested to the popularity of the book with the Essenes living at Qumran between the second century BC and the first century AD. These other manuscripts give us a broader picture. The quotations in Melchizedek and Florilegium show that by the first century BC (at the latest) the Essenes regarded the book of Daniel as scripture. By the first century AD the Essenes had created many new stories and commentaries based upon Daniel, including several redactions of the War Scroll. The idea that the Essenes only read the book of Daniel for the first time in mid-second century is

---

[68] 4Q174.II; cf. Daniel 12:10.
[69] Vermes, *Complete Dead Sea Scrolls*, 164.

made improbable by the wealth of literature they produced in such a short space of time based upon it.

Second Century BC

The texts found at Qumran are not the only texts from this period that refer to the book of Daniel. The first book of Maccabees quotes explicitly from Daniel when it says:

> Now the fifteenth day of the month Casleu, in the hundred and forty fifth year, they set up the 'abomination of desolation' upon the altar, and built idol altars throughout the cities of Judah.[70]

And again:

> Daniel for his innocence was delivered from the mouth of lions.[71]

Scholars generally agree that I Maccabees was written around 100 BC. The last recorded event is when John Hyrcanus becomes king, which took place 134 BC, and so it is likely that I Maccabees was composed shortly after this date. References to the resurrection in 2 Maccabees seem to echo the language of Daniel and so may be dependent on the book.

OG-Dan (and Th-Dan) includes three additions to the book of Daniel not included in the Hebrew version, or amongst any of the manuscripts found at Qumran. These are called the Prayer of Azariah (sometimes called The Song of the Three Children), Susanna, and Bel and the Dragon. These stories are generally recognized to be additions to Daniel, not only because they are not found in the MT (or DSS) but also because they are inconsistent with the rest of the book and their addition disrupts the order of the other accounts. Scholarly consensus dates these additions before 100 BC, the approximate date of their translation into Greek in OG-Dan. Some scholars have looked for references to the crisis preceding the Maccabean revolt in these additions,[72] which would imply a date for these additions contemporary with the proposed date for Daniel itself.

In Baruch the author refers to Nebuchadnezzar and Belshazzar as being father and son and as living at the same time. This historical inaccuracy is probably based upon a misunderstanding of Daniel 5, which is sometimes taken to imply that Nebuchadnezzar was the biological father of Belshazzar. There is no consensus regarding the date of Baruch, though many scholars date it to the first century BC on the assumption that Daniel was composed in the second century. Were Daniel not dated so late then Baruch would be dated earlier.

---

[70] I Maccabees 1:54; cp. Daniel 12:11.

[71] I Maccabees 2:60; cp. Daniel 6.

[72] For example, 'you did deliver us into the hands of lawless enemies, most hateful forsakes of God, and to an unjust king, and the most wicked in all the world' (Prayer of Azariah 9).

Position 3: Citations and allusions in Jewish literature fix a *terminus ad quem* of late second century BC for the book of Daniel

Third/Fourth Century BC

Glenn Miller notes possible allusions to the book of Daniel in *Testament of Levi*, in *Testament of Benjamin* and in *Ezekiel the Tragedian*, texts dating from c.200 BC.[73] Both the allusions and the dating of these texts are far from certain so we must be cautious about putting much weight on this evidence.

One tantalizing piece of evidence from Qumran is the fragments that have been found of the book of Enoch. One of these fragments, 'Astronomical Enoch' (4Q208), has been carbon-dated to 186-92 BC.[74] Given 4Q208 has been dated paleographically to around 200 BC, these two methods agree on an early second century for this fragment.

What makes this fragment so significant is that the Ethiopic book of Enoch contains a lot of material that alludes to the book of Daniel, particularly its use of the imagery of 'the Son of Man' (Dan. 7:13). In this form, the book of Enoch must have been completed after the book of Daniel, and so *if* the fragments discovered at Qumran attested to this form then this would provide decisive evidence against the second century date for the book of Daniel.

Unfortunately, the fragments discovered at Qumran make up only a small amount of the text of the book of Enoch and many of the fragments are too small for translation.[75] The fragments do not contain any of the Son of Man material, while the Astronomical sections are much longer at Qumran than in the Ethiopic. Scholars speculate that the book, though perhaps originally composed as early as 400 BC, underwent several revisions over its history and did not take its final form until after the completion of the New Testament.[76]

Glenn Miller argues that Daniel 7 forms the basis of the throne theophany of 1 Enoch.[77]

Position 4: If discovered, allusions in Qumran Enoch would fix a *terminus ad quem* of early second century BC for the book of Daniel (tentative)

Fifth Century BC

The book of Nehemiah was written towards the end of the fifth century BC. Nehemiah is an exile in court of the Persian king Artaxerxes. Distressed by news from Jerusalem of those Jews who have returned, Nehemiah prays to God. One conservative commentator has written regarding this chapter:

---

[73] G. Miller, 'Was Daniel written after the events he foretold?', http://christianthinktank.com/qwhendan3x.html [cited August 2014].

[74] A.J.T. Jull, 'Radiocarbon Dating of the Scrolls and Linen Fragments from the Judean Desert', *Radiocarbon* 37:1 (1995), 14.

[75] Vermes, *Complete Dead Sea Scrolls*, 545.

[76] *Dead Sea Scrolls Bible*, 481.

[77] Miller, 'Was Daniel written after the events he foretold?'

When Nehemiah prayed for the peace of Jerusalem, he closely modeled his prayer on that of Daniel, so presumably he already had a copy of the Book of Daniel included in *his* Bible![78]

Comparison of the two prayers demonstrates their connection:

And I said, 'O LORD God of heaven, the great and awesome God who keeps covenant and steadfast love with those who love him and keep his commandments . . .' Nehemiah 1:5 (ESV).

And I prayed to the LORD my God, and made confession, and said, 'O Lord, great and awesome God, who keeps covenant and steadfast love with those who love him and keep his commandments . . .' Daniel 9:4 (ESV)

Both men confess their sin and the sins of the nation of Israel. Both men refer to the curses laid down in the Law of Moses. And both men pray for the restoration of the nation of Israel.

Nehemiah did not copy his prayer word for word from Daniel; he tailored it to his own situation. His prayer is also shorter than Daniel's, which probably indicates that Daniel's is the original. However, it is possible that both men based their prayers upon a traditional prayer-format, which may explain their similarities.

Position 5: Parallels in Nehemiah may indicate a *terminus ad quem* of late fifth century BC for the book of Daniel (tentative)

Sixth Century BC
The prophet Zechariah was one of the Jews who returned to Jerusalem after the exile with Zerubbabel to rebuild the Temple.[79] In the book named after him there are recorded the account of a series of visions which Zechariah received. One of these seems based upon Daniel's vision of the four beasts.

And I lifted my eyes and saw, and behold, four horns! And I said to the angel who talked with me, 'What are these?' And he said to me, 'These are the horns that have scattered Judah, Israel, and Jerusalem.' Then the LORD showed me four craftsmen. And I said, 'What are these coming to do?' He said, 'These are the horns that scattered Judah, so that no one raised his head. And these have come to terrify them, to cast down the horns of the nations who lifted up their horns against the land of Judah to scatter it' Zechariah 1:18-21 (ESV).

As in Daniel's vision, and the Four Kingdoms from Qumran, here we have a series of four kingdoms of the Gentiles. The use of horns as a symbol of kingdoms is the equivalent to the use of this symbol in Daniel. Whilst the connec-

---

[78] H.A. Whittaker, *Exploring the Bible* (Wigan: Biblia, 1992), 34 (original emphasis).
[79] Ezra 5:1.

tion between Daniel 7 and Zechariah 1 is not textual or literary, one might plausibly think that the one was based upon the other.

Position 6: Parallels in Zechariah may indicate a *terminus ad quem* of late sixth century BC for the book of Daniel (tentative)

Initial Findings

In this study we have aimed to identify fixed points (*terminus ad quem*) from which to calculate the latest possible date for the composition of the book of Daniel. We have identified at least two fixed points that provide a *terminus ad quem* for the book itself:

> Position 1: 4QDan^c fixes a *terminus ad quem* of 125 BC for the book of Daniel
>
> Position 3: Citations and allusions in Jewish literature fix a *terminus ad quem* of late second century BC for the book of Daniel

Both these fixed points presuppose the canonical reception of the book of Daniel and implies the following time-period:

Period X: Time from composition to canonical reception

Therefore, we can define the calculation for the latest possible date for the composition of book of Daniel as follows:

> (position 1 or position 3) – (period X) = the latest possible date

In other words, if period X is longer than around forty years then the late date (165 BC) for the composition of the book of Daniel is impossible.

We have also identified a fixed point that provides a *terminus ad quem* for a Greek translation of Daniel:

> Position 2: NT citations fix a *terminus ad quem* of 55 AD for Th-Dan

As we have seen, this date presupposes four time periods between the recessions that led to Th-Dan translation of Daniel:

Period A:	Time from composition to OG-Vorlage recession
Period B:	Time from OG-Vorlage to OG-Dan translation
Period C:	Time from OG-Dan to Th-Dan revision and translation
Period D:	Time from Th-Dan to NT citations

Therefore, we can define a second calculation for the latest possible date for the composition of the book of Daniel as follows:

> (position 2) – (period A) – (period B) – (period C) – (period D) = the latest possible date

In other words, if these four periods were longer than an average of 56 years then the late date (165 BC) for the composition of the book of Daniel is impossible.

We have also identified three tentative *terminus ad quem* any one of which, if confirmed, would necessarily rule out the late date.

Position 4: If discovered, allusions in Qumran Enoch would fix a *terminus ad quem* of early second century BC for the book of Daniel (tentative)

Position 5: Parallels in Nehemiah may indicate a *terminus ad quem* of late fifth century BC for the book of Daniel (tentative)

Position 6: Parallels in Zechariah may indicate a *terminus ad quem* of late sixth century BC for the book of Daniel (tentative)

It is hoped that future research will identify a sound methodology upon which to calculate the probably length of periods A-C and period X, which would provide definitive proof against the late date hypothesis and force critical scholars to consider the historical and linguistic evidence upon which the early date is established.

Conclusion

Goldingay wrote that it was misguided to evaluate the book of Daniel on historical criteria (see Introduction) yet having done so we have found that the book is able to weather the test. Many of the problems previously identified by critics, such as the dateline in Daniel 1:1, can now be answered; other objections have now fallen by the wayside.[1] Even those problems where definitive proof still eludes us, such as the figure of Darius the Mede, the account cannot be lightly dismissed as ahistorical. Few scholars would now share Davies' baseless assertion that 'the discrepancy between historical fact and the Danielic stories is of such a scale as to make the squabbling over individual points of error rather trivial'.[2]

Today critical scholars are more willing to admit that in many points the book of Daniel accurately reflects the Neo-Babylonian milieu in which its stories are set.[3] This is due to a significant number of historical details that are recorded accurately. The author correctly portrays the experiences of foreign captives at court, rightly characterizes Nebuchadnezzar as the great builder of Babylon (Dan. 4:30) and rightly records that Babylon was at feast the night it fell. Perhaps more significantly, the author knows the name 'Belshazzar', a name that was unknown to the Greek historians.[4] These facts have fed the growing consensus amongst critical scholars that the author of the book of Daniel had access to an abundance of historical sources including the Greek histori-

---

[1]   For instance, regarding the phrase 'the books' (Dan. 9:2) S.R. Driver asserted that 'the expression used implies that the prophecies of Jeremiah formed part of a collection of sacred books, which nevertheless, it may safely be affirmed, was not formed in 536 BC' (Driver, *Introduction*, 500). However, the word translated 'books' (ספר *cepher*) does not necessarily refer to the Scriptures but can refer to any piece of writing. This term is used in the book of Jeremiah to describe the very letter to which Daniel refers (Jer. 29:1).

[2]   Davies, *Daniel*, 31.

[3]   Van der Toorn, 'Mesopotamian Background', 37f; Paul, 'Mesopotamian Background', 55f; etc.

[4]   'The fact that the name of Belshazzar, which was not preserved in classical sources, is found in Daniel 5 strongly suggests that the ultimate origin of this story comes from a neo-Babylonian milieu' (Paul, 'Mesopotamian Background', 64).

ans,[5] ancient near eastern court tales,[6] and a 'sophisticated' account of the Dia-dochi.[7] (This is not to mention the Babylonian literature that influenced the later chapters of the book).[8] This has led several scholars to the conclusion that the narrative chapters (at least) must have been written amongst the Eastern Diaspora, rather than in Palestine.[9] You will seldom hear today that all of the book of Daniel was written during the Maccabean crisis. Most critical scholars will propose that the final form was composed at that time but the narrative chapters were in circulation as independent stories long before this date. Even a few conservative scholars, who otherwise maintain the unity of the book, have theorized that Daniel 11 may be a later interpolation. This is illustrative of the fact that it is the apparently Maccabean-centric visionary details, like Daniel 11, that are the sticking-points for dating the book. The narrative chapters, taken in isolation, do not suggest a late-date; on the contrary their historicity far exceeds apocryphal books known to have been written in the second century.

Conservative scholars still maintain that the book of Daniel was written in the sixth or fifth century and that the author was eyewitness to the events. Certainly, there are some accuracies that suggest a close intimacy with the court setting. For instance, the writer knows that the king should be addressed 'O king, live forever' (cf. Dan. 2:4, 3:9, 5:10, 6:7, 22) [10] and that the wall facing the throne in the Southern Palace was coated with white gypsum plaster (cf. גיר *giyr* 'chalk' or 'plaster'; Dan. 5:5).[11] However, it is not clear that even these details require an eyewitness, though this level of detail makes a late Palestini-an authorship unlikely. The difficulty is that those details that could only be known to an intimate witness, such as the scenario in the Southern Palace at the fall of Babylon (cf. Dan. 5), are impossible to corroborate from the sources available to us. Nevertheless, the level of historical detail makes a strong case for an early and eastern authorship.

Yet exactly when and where the book of Daniel was composed is a side-note to the crux of the historical debate: is the book of Daniel historiography or his-torical-fiction? Did these events actually occur, as conservative scholars claim? Or are these fictional events told in a historical setting? The wider political events referred to in the book of Daniel can be corroborated. The captivity of select Jews in 605, the regency of Belshazzar and the emergence of the Medo-

---

[5]   P. Niskanen, *The Human and Divine in History: Herodotus and the Book of Daniel* (JSOTsupp 396; London: T&T Clark, 2004).

[6]   Van der Toorn, 'Mesopotamian Background', 52.

[7]   Grabbe, 'A Dan(iel) for all seasons', 234.

[8]   cf. Lambert, *Jewish Apocalyptic*; cf. E.C. Lucas, 'Daniel: Resolving the Enigma', *VT* 50:1 (Jan 2000), 66-80.

[9]   Van der Toorn, 'Mesopotamian Background', 38; Lucas, 'Enigma', 79.

[10]   Paul, 'Mesopotamian Background', 63; S.M Paul, 'A Traditional Blessing for the Long Life of the King', *JNES* 31 (1972), 351-55.

[11]   Boutflower, *Daniel*, 184; R. Koldewey, *Excavations at Babylon* (A. Johns trans.; London 1914), 104.

Persian empire are the sort of issues that can easily be demonstrated from our sources. It is the intimate personal events of Daniel and his friends, and their relationships to a succession of kings that are more difficult to evidence from ancient sources. Though there is some possible evidence for the insanity of Nebuchadnezzar and the fate of Belshazzar, we do not have definitive proof. On the other hand, there is a question about how much evidence we should expect to find. The fates of Daniel and his friends, though significant for Jewish readers, can hardly expect to be of note for Babylonian scribes. The illness of Nebuchadnezzar would have been an obvious embarrassment and for good reason may have been omitted by Nebuchadnezzar's biographers. Perhaps the conversion of Nebuchadnezzar, if it occurred, may have been worthy of mention, but even in the book of Daniel Nebuchadnezzar is not portrayed as an exclusive worshipper of YHWH (cf. Dan. 2:47, 3:28). As a pious Jew, Daniel would have instructed Nebuchadnezzar against building a temple to YHWH in Babylon, if he ever desired to do so, and so we are unlikely to find archaeological evidence of Yahwist religion in Babylon even if it did occur.

Despite all these limitations, there is strong reason to believe that these stories are rooted in historical events and are centered on real individuals. Even critical scholars acknowledge that it is easier to explain the Danielic narratives as rooted in a historical figure.[12] Ezekiel provides us with significant evidence that Daniel was an actual person, who was celebrated for his wisdom and righteousness. There is also an intriguing and exciting proposition from Shea that Hananiah, Mishael and Azariah are named as Babylonian officials upon the *Istanbul Prism*, though it is difficult to see how these identifications could ever be proved conclusively. In the absence of an inscription or tablet naming Daniel as a high court official or describing the actual events the book of Daniel records, the narrative chapters will always be open to skepticism. Nevertheless, it is no longer possible to regard the book of Daniel as fanciful; the level of historicity is too significant for that.

Once it is conceded that the Danielic narratives are based upon historical events form-critical approaches to the question of its historicity become somewhat irrelevant. The fact that the author has a clear polemic agenda – and he does – has little bearing upon whether his material is historical or fictional. The polemic may turn historical events to his purpose as easily as fictional ones, perhaps more easily as it adds a level of realism to his moral. We may still debate over individual historical issues and further research is always warranted, but there is no justification for disregarding the historical question or for dismissing the book as fiction.

---

[12] 'The stories were most likely based on an actual historical figure, though the memory of his real historical context was often hazy and inaccurate. Whether this figure was named Daniel is uncertain' (Grabbe, 'A Dan(iel) for all seasons', 243).

Implications

One of the implications of these conclusions is the impact on the date of composition. A book that has a high degree of historical accuracy, especially when contrasted with the Greek historians and with apocryphal works is more easily explained by an early composition date. This, when combined with other considerations (see chapter 14), makes the oft-defended late date for the book of Daniel difficult to maintain. But this is not the only implication of the historical issues in the book of Daniel.

Interpretation

For the critical scholar interpretation determines date and date determines interpretation. Once it is assumed that the book of Daniel (or its final redaction) was written in the Maccabean era then it becomes necessary to interpret the book's various visions as a product of this milieu (whether it is suitable to the imagery or not). Thus the fourth world-empire must be Greek, both Little Horns must be Antiochus Epiphanes, the 'anointed one' must be Onias III and Daniel 11:40-45 must be a failed prophecy. On the other hand, if we allow that the book arose in a different milieu and/or if we allow that the author could see beyond his own circumstances then none of these interpretations is necessary. We can look again at the four world-empires and ask whether the second empire is Media or Medo-Persia without *a priori* constraint. We can look again at the Little Horns of Daniel 7 and Daniel 8 and give due attention to their differing descriptions and designations. And we can look again at the 'anointed one' and search for an individual who was actually 'cut off'. Rather than try to interpret the visions of Daniel as though they all must fit within a Maccabean context, we can let the symbols speak from themselves.

Some of the historical issues considered in this book have interpretative implications. Contrary to the aspersions made by certain scholars, it seems evident that the author of the book of Daniel did not believe that there was an independent Median kingdom between the Babylonian and the Persian. Consequently, by the internal logic of the book as well as the facts of history, the second beast of Daniel 7 should be Medo-Persia, not Media. This would be consistent with the traditional interpretation that views the fourth beast as the Roman Empire.

Given the likelihood that Onias III was not murdered, as has been previously supposed, then he fits none of the criteria for the 'anointed one' of Daniel 9. Similarly, since the critical assumption that the Jewish chronology must be in error has proved to be groundless, we should look for an 'anointed one' who appears at the end of the time-period that Daniel 9 describes. Traditionally Christians have identified the 'anointed one' of Daniel 9 with Jesus Christ and, on one interpretation at least, the specified time-period matches exactly. This is either a coincidence, a remarkably convenient interpretative contrivance, or else truly predictive (uncomfortable as that may be).

This does not mean that there are no problems with traditional/conservative interpretation. Can the eschatological Little Horn still be identified with Roman Christendom when the papal temporal power has waned? How are we to understand the last half-week of the seventy if this was not fulfilled by Jesus of Nazareth? Can we legitimately interpret Daniel 11:40-45 eschatologically when its context is historical? Yet these and other problems do not fatally undermine the traditional interpretations, but should be the subject of further discussion and research unrestrained by the strait-jacket of the Maccabean mould.

Faith

In the nineteenth century, E.B. Pusey declared:

> The book of Daniel is especially fitted to be a battlefield between faith and unbelief. It admits of no half-measures. It is either Divine or an imposture.

[. . .]

> Either then we have true miracles and true prophecy, or we should have nothing but untruth. An apology for the supposed forger, such as those put out by some Germans and lately in England, is utterly untenable and immoral.[13]

While some maintain that the battle still rages, the majority of modern scholars have left the field. The late-date and pseudonymity of the book of Daniel, especially of its prophecies, is everywhere proclaimed but few, save the hardened skeptics, seem interested in exposing the book as an imposture. For many believers, the pseudonymity of the book sits quite happily with their faith and they think nothing of making the kind of 'apology for the supposed forger' that Pusey so despised. After all, as Goldingay has argued, if God inspired other works of fiction why should the pseudonymity of Daniel be a stumbling block to the believer?

Jesus, however, took Daniel seriously. He regarded Daniel as a prophet. He expects the words spoken by Daniel to be fulfilled. Jesus incorporates the predictions of Daniel into his own prophecy (Mark 13:14). For many Christians, then, it is going to be problematic, to say the least, to regard Daniel as a fictional character. The problem for the believer is that a fictional prophet cannot utter factual prophecy (or, in the case of Daniel, receive factual visions). If there never was an individual named Daniel then the visions he allegedly received must also be fictional and thus worthless. It is pointless to argue that history-written-as-prophecy can have polemic value if their predictions of future blessings are nothing more than pipe-dreams. If there is no assurance in the promise of 'everlasting righteousness' (Dan. 9:24) or of the resurrection from the dead (Dan. 12:2) then it is small comfort to reinterpret these predictions as polemic-fiction. To rob these visions and prophecies of their authority is to rob them of their purpose.

---

[13] E.B. Pusey, *Daniel the Prophet* (New York: Funk and Wagnalls, 1886), 75.

The first step to reclaiming the book of Daniel for the believer is to reestablish the historicity of its hero. That is why the historical issues of the book of Daniel are so important: they justify the believer in taking the book seriously.

Appendix 1: Genealogies[1]

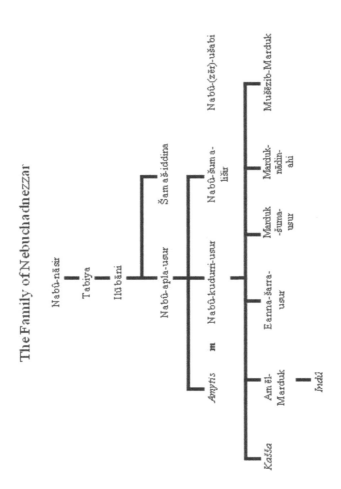

The Family of Nebuchadnezzar

Nabu-apla-usur	=	Nabopolassar
Nabu-kudrri-usur	=	Nebuchadnezzar
Amel-Marduk	=	Evil-Merodach

---

[1] See Wiseman, *Nebuchadrezzar*, pp7-12.

The Family of Neriglissar

Nergal-sarra-usur	=	Neriglissar
Nabu-kudrri-usur	=	Nebuchadnezzar

The Family of Nabonidus

Nabu-naid	=	Nabonidus
Bel-sarra-usur	=	Belshazzar

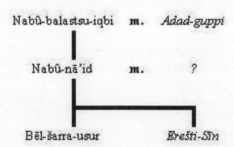

162

Median Dynasty

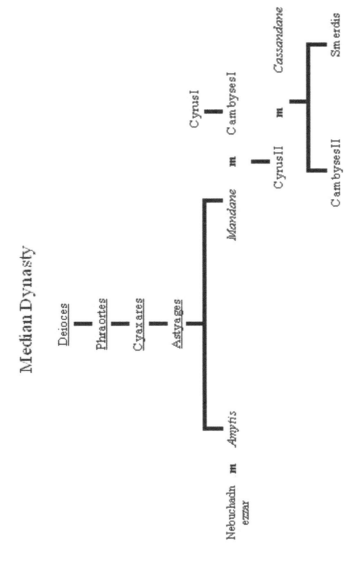

Persian Dynasty

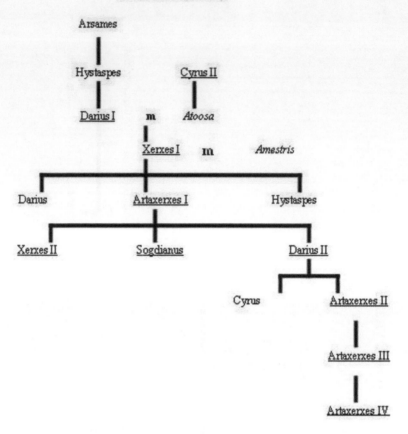

Appendix 2: King Lists

Neo-Babylonian Dynasty

Nabopolassar	626-605
Nebuchadnezzar II	604-562
Evil-Merodach	561-560
Neriglissar	559-556
Labashi-Marduk	556
Nabonidus	555-539
(Belshazzar	549-539)

Persian Empire

Cyrus II	559-530
Cambyses II	529-522
Bardiya	522
Darius I	521-486
Xerxes I	485-465
Artaxerxes I	464-424
Xerxes II	424
Sogdianus	424
Darius II	423-405
Artaxerxes II	404-359
Artaxerxes III	358-338
Artaxerxes IV	337-336
Darius III	335-331

Appendix 3: Chronology

605			
		May/June	? battle of Carchemish; Nebuchadnezzar conquers the entire region, including Judah; Daniel, Hananiah, Mishael and Azariah are taken captive
	15	August	Nabopolassar dies
	7	September	Nebuchadnezzar returns and ascends to the throne of Babylon
605-1			Nebuchadnezzar marches opposed through "Hatti-land"
601		?	Jehoiakim rebels against Babylon
		Nov/Dec	Nebuchadnezzar invades Egypt and is repelled
598		Nov/Dec	Nebuchadnezzar sets out to Judah with his army; Jehoiakim dies
			Nebuchadnezzar seizes Jerusalem and captures Jehoiachin; Zedekiah is appointed vassal-king of Judah
595			Nebuchadnezzar's army rebels against him
			?possible date of events of Dan 3
588	15	January	Nebuchadnezzar lays siege to Jerusalem
	18	July	Walls of Jerusalem are penetrated; Zedekiah flees but is captured
	14	August	Nebuzaradan, captain of the guard, burns the Temple
561	2	April	Amel-Marduk releases Jehoiachin from prison
c.550			Median army revolts against Astyages, Cyrus appointed king
c.549			Nabonidus in Tema
546			Mother of Nabonidus dies
		April/May	Cyrus marches against Lydia and conquers it
539		March/April	Nabonidus performs the New Year festival in Babylon
		July/August	Nabonidus gathers city-gods into Babylon
	11	October	Sippar is seized without battle
	12	October	Ugbaru, governor of Gutium, enters Babylon
	29	October	Cyrus enters Babylon in peace
	6	November	Ugbaru dies
			city-gods are returned to their cities
538		Feb/March	The wife of the king dies
			Cambyses becomes regent of Babylon
		Dec/Jan	Cyrus becomes "King of Babylon"
537			Daniel's final vision (Dan. 10-12)

Appendix 4: "We Shall Fight on the Beaches": A Critique of Criticism

Introduction

Traditionally the *We Shall Fight on the Beaches* text has been ascribed by scholars to the pen of the wartime hero Winston Churchill. Modern textual criticism has thrown doubt upon this conclusion positing that the text is more likely the product of a so-called Churchillic circle. In this paper I will demonstrate that *Beaches* originates several decades after the War from a nationalistic group designated in the text by the term 'Island', the text itself being based around a pre-war conquest-hymn. Further we can discern within the text three distinct stages of redaction: 1) the pseudonymous monograph, written as vainglorious boast in reaction to the pressures of immigration, 2) the apologetic revision made in response to internal criticism, and 3) the eschatological additions made by splinter-Islandite group.

The Text

1. I have, myself, full confidence that if all do their duty, [if nothing is neglected,
2. and if the best arrangements are made, as they are being made,] we shall prove
3. ourselves once again able to defend our Island home, to ride out the storm of
4. war, and to outlive the menace of tyranny, if necessary for years, if necessary
5. alone.
6. [At any rate, that is what we are going to try to do. That is the resolve of His
7. Majesty's Government – every man of them. That is the will of Parliament and
8. the nation.]
9. The British Empire, [and the French Republic,] linked together in their cause and in
10. their need, will defend to the death their native soil, aiding each other like good
11. comrades to the utmost of their strength.
12. Even though large tracts of Europe and many old and famous States have fallen
13. or may fall into the grip of the Gestapo and all the odious apparatus of Nazi rule,
14. we shall not flag or fail.
15. We shall go on to the end, [we shall fight in France,]
16. *we shall fight on the seas* [and oceans,]
17. *we shall fight* [with growing confidence and growing strength] *in the air,*

18. we shall defend our Island, whatever the cost may be,
19. *we shall fight on the beaches,*
20. *we shall fight on the landing grounds,*
21. *we shall fight in the fields* and in the streets,
22. *we shall fight in the hills*;
23. *we shall never surrender* (and even if, which I do not for a moment
24. believe, this Island or a large part of it were subjugated and starving, then our
25. Empire beyond the seas, armed and guarded by the British Fleet, would carry on the struggle,
26. until, in God's good time, the New World, with all its power and
27. might, steps forth to the rescue and the liberation of the old.)

Words in *italics* represent the original conquest-hymn, words in [ ] mark additions of the second redaction, words in ( ) mark additions of the third redaction.

The Conquest-Hymn
The discontinuity between the preceding lines and the 'we shall fight . . .' couplets (lines 16-17, 19-20, 21-22) indicates this section of the *Beaches* text was formerly a separate hymn that was adopted by the writer. Each couplet is formed by the juxtaposition of two differing locations. Line 18 does not conform to this structure and is clearly a later addition.

The proactive confidence embodied in the hymn is dissimilar to the defiant reactionism of the rest of the text, yet it is also uncharacteristic of the War period. Such buoyant enthusiasm for battle is unlikely to have been manifested after the early defeats to the German *Blitzgreig*. It is more probable that these lines represent a pre-war conquest-hymn composed by pro-war activists to encourage support for further expansion of the Empire. We may legitimately speculate that this conquest-hymn dates to the height of the British Empire around 1900.

The Islandite Revision
In the opening lines of *Beaches* demonstrates the distinct isolationist *Tendentz* of the writer. Words such as "myself" (line 1) and "alone" (line 5) are employed to instill a separatist ideal. Phrases such as "native soil" (line 10) and "good comrades" (line 11) emphasize the merits of isolationism and nationalism; the xenophobia of the author(s) is apparent. The repetition of the term "Island" (lines 3, 18, 24) is distinctive and clearly cannot denote the United Kingdom as this is made up of many isles. Rather the exclusivity in the term's usage indicates that "Island" was used to designate the circle or group from which *Beaches* originates. The absence of external witness to a group of this name indicates that this group was secretive and highly sectarian.

The historical anomalies in the text require a date for the text long after the War period. Particularly the use of the term "Gestapo" (line 13) presupposes the influence of post-war satire. (It can hardly be supposed that this German term was in common usage in the early years of the War.)

The aggressive nationalism portrayed in the text indicates that this text was composed in response to the increased immigration in the post-war decades. It is likely that Wartime hero – Churchill – was selected as a suitable figurehead for this movement, given his defiance of the German invader. The pseudonymous text was undoubtedly composed as rallying-call for British nationalism, which seems to have been the key Islandite ideal.

The Apologetic Revision
In many sects, expansion leads to the expression of views differing from that of the established leadership. Often a new generation seeks to question the group's original ideals. This 'watershed of rationalism', as we may call it, requires the justification of old concepts to contemporary standards. The glosses and additions to the *Beaches* text demonstrate that such a watershed occurred within the Islandites. New historical information led to questions being asked about the validity of the group's founding documents, particularly the *Beaches* text.

The role of the French, though previously omitted for obvious reasons, had to be conceded within the text due to the historical realities of the war-period (lines 9 & 15). Also the role of Parliament, and the collaborative nature of the war-effort, needed to be recognized (lines 6-8), even though it creates a clear inconsistency in the text with the isolationism of the opening lines. The apologetic phrases in lines 1b-2 were added to balance the bravado of the text against the facts of wartime defeats.

There is also an interesting gloss that occurs in line 17, where the limits of the British airforce were noted despite the damage it does that couplet. The redactor was at pains to preclude further historical criticism of the text.

The Eschatological Revision
The *Beaches* text would most naturally finish on the word "surrender" (line 23a). However, the present form of the text includes an additional paragraph, which is not only inconsistent with the style of the preceding text but also is inconsistent with its outlook being distinctly defeatist. The religious terminology of this paragraph demonstrates that it was added for didactic reasons.

It is probable that as the Islandites expanded their membership they developed a quasi-religious, neo-apocalyptic fringe, which being dissatisfied with the group's lack of progress in its nationalistic goals looked for the realization of those ideals in an eschatological renewal. It need not be said that this apocalyptic outlook would be inconsistent with an early date for the text.

Conclusion
This last form of the text, though probably composed by a splinter-group, was the enduring form. Its optimistic vision of the future disguised its nationalistic and xenophobic origins and led to the great popularity of the text. It is undoubt-

edly from these popularist audiences that the tradition of the text's historical
authenticity arose.

******

Epilogue
The preceding article is, of course, entirely spurious. However, any humour that
it engenders is founded solely on the sure knowledge that the *We Shall Fight on
the Beaches* speech was penned by Winston Churchill in June 1940. Were the
circumstances of the speech's origins unknown or obscured then the conclusions presented above might appear plausible within critical circles.

This is the inherent danger of redaction criticism. Where external evidence is
unavailable internal criteria, such as discontinuity, is (over)emphasized and the
idiosyncrasies of the author become indicators of redaction, revision and disu-
nity. This is not to say that critical methods are necessarily invalid, but it does
mean that dogmatism on the part of critical will rarely be warranted.

This consideration has important implications for the field of biblical studies. For instance, many critical scholars believe that the final redaction of the
book of Daniel was penned around 164 BC by a group known as the Maskilim
(literally 'the wise'), which is otherwise unknown to history. It is also asserted
that the apocalyptic sections of the book were appended to an already extant
compilation of court-tales. These conclusions are reached in the absence, and at
times in the face of, external evidence. The limitations of the critical method
should be considered before accepting these conclusions.

Bibliography

Abegg (ed.), M., *The Dead Sea Scrolls Bible.* San Francisco: HarperSanFrancisco, 1999.

Ainsworth, W., *The Travels of Rabbi Pethahiah.* Trubner, 1856.

Alexander, J.B., 'Critical Notes: New Light on the Fiery Furnace', *JBL* 69.4 (1950), 375-376.

Alfrink, B., 'Darius Medus', *Biblica* 9 (1928), 316-340.

Archer, G.L., Jr., *A Survey of Old Testament Introduction.* Chicago: Moody, 1973.

—. 'The Hebrew of Daniel compared with the Qumran Sectarian Documents' in *The Law and the Prophets.* Ed. J. Skilton; Nutley: Presbyterian & Reformed, 1974, 470-481.

—. 'Modern Rationalism and the Book of Daniel', *Bibliotheca Sacra* (April-June 1979), 129-147.

—. *The Expositor's Bible Commentary: Daniel – Minor Prophets.* vol.7; Grand Rapids: Zondervan, 1985.

Argubright, J., *Bible Believer's Archaeology* (vol.2): The Search for Truth. Xulon, 2003.

Avigad, N., 'Seals of Exiles', *Israel Exploration Journal* 15:4 (1965), 222-232.

Babelon, E., 'Nouvelles remarqyes sur l'histoire de Cyrus, in Annales de philsophie chretienne', *New Series* 4 (1881), 674-83.

Baker, D.W., 'Further Examples of the Waw Explicativum', *VT* 30 (1980), 129-136.

Baldwin, J.G., *Daniel: An Introduction and Commentary.* TOTC; Leicester: Inter-Varsity Press, 1978.

Ball, C.J., 'Inscriptions of Nebuchadnezzar II: 1. The India House Inscription', *PSBA* 10 (December 1887), 87-129.

Barthélemy, D. & J.T. Milik, *Qumran Cave 1: Discoveries in the Judaean Desert* 1. Oxford: Clarendon, 1955.

Beaulieu, P.A., *The Reign of Nabonidus King of Babylon 556-539 BC.* New Haven: Yale University Press, 1989.

—. 'An Episode in the Fall of Babylon to the Persians', *JNES* 52 (1992), 241-261.

Beckwith, R., *The Old Testament Canon of the New Testament Church and Its Background in Early Judaism.* London: SPCK, 1985.

Berger, P-R., *Zeitschrift fur Assyriologie* 64 (1975).

Bichler, R., 'Some Observations on the Image of the Assyrian and Babylonian Kingdoms within the Greek Tradition' in *Melammu Symposia V: Commerce and Monetary Systems in the Ancient World: Means of Transmission and Cultural Interaction.* Stuttgart, 2004, 499-518.

Billows, R.A., *Kings and Colonists: Aspects of Macedonian Imperialism.* Leiden: Brill, 1995.

Black, J.A., A. Green & T. Rickard, *Gods, Demons and Symbols in Ancient Mesopotamia.* University of Texas Press, 1992.

Bogaert, P-M., 'Relecture et refonte historicisante du livre de Daniel attestées par la première version grecque (Papyrus 967)' in R. Kuntzmann & J. Schlossar, *Études sur le judaïsme hellénistique.* Paris 1984, 197-224.

Boutflower, C., 'The Historical Value of Daniel v and vi', *JTS* 17 (1915-16), 43-60.

—. *In and Around the Book of Daniel.* London: SPCK, 1923; repr., Grand Rapids: Kregel, 1977.

Briant, P., *From Cyrus to Alexander: A History of the Persian Empire.* Eisenbrauns, 2006.

Brown, J., *A Dictionary of the Bible.* Edinburgh: William Oliphant, 1866.

Brownlee, W.H., *The Meaning of the Qumran Scrolls for the Bible.* New York: Oxford University Press, 1964.

Bruce, F.F., *A Mind for What Matters.* Eerdmans, 1990.

Bulman, J.M., 'The Identification of Darius the Mede', *WTJ* 35:3 (Spring 1973), 247-67.

Burke, J., 'Linguistic Issues in Daniel', *CJBI* 2008, 122-127.

Cameron, G.C., 'Review: *Darius the Mede: A Study in Historical Identification* by John C. Whitcomb, Jr.', *JBL* 79.1 (March 1960), 70-1.

Carroll, R.P., 'Exile, Restoration, and Colony: Judah in the Persian Empire' in *The Blackwell Companion to the Hebrew Bible.* L.G. Perdue ed.; Oxford: Blackwell, 2001, 102-115.

Charles, R.H., *A Critical and Exegetical Commentary on the Book of Daniel.* Oxford: Clarendon, 1929.

Colless, B.E., 'Cyrus the Persian as Darius the Mede in the Book of Daniel', *JSOT* 56 (1992), 113-126.

Collins, J.J., *Daniel: with an Introduction to Apocalyptic Literature.* Eerdmans, 1984.

—. *Daniel: A Commentary on the Book of Daniel with an essay, 'The Influence of Daniel on the New Testament' by Adela Yarbro Collins.* Minneapolis: Fortress, 1993.

—. '4QPrayer of Nabonidus ar', in *Qumran Cave 4. XVII: Parabiblical Texts, Parts 3.* Ed. J.C. Vanderkam; DJD XXII; Oxford: Clarendon, 1996, 83-93.

—. 'Daniel' in *Dictionary of Deities and Demons in the Bible.* Ed. K. van der Toorn, B. Becking & P.W. van Horst; Eerdmans, 1999, 219-220.

Cook, J.M., *The Persian Empire.* London: J.M. Bent, 1923.

Coxon, P.W., 'The Syntax of the Aramaic of Daniel: A Dialectal Study', *HU-CA* 48 (1977), 107-122.

Cross, F.M., *The Ancient Library of Qumran and Modern Biblical Studies.* New York: 1958.

—. 'The Development of the Jewish Scripts' in G.E. Wright (ed.), *The Bible and the Ancient Near East: Essays in Honour of W.F. Albright.* London, 1961, 160-166.

—. 'Fragments of the Prayer of Nabonidus', *IEJ* 34 (1984), 260-264.

Dandamaev, M.A., *A Political History of the Achaemenid Empire.* Leiden: Brill, 1989.

Dandamaev, M.A. & Vladimir G. Lukonin, *The Culture and Social Institutions of Ancient Iran.* Cambridge University Press, 2004.

Davidson, S., *An Introduction to the Old Testament* (vol.3). London: William & Norgate, 1863.

Davies, P.R., *Daniel.* OTG; Sheffield: JSOT, 1985.

Davies, W.D. & L. Finkelstein, *The Cambridge History of Judaism* (vol.1): Introduction; The Persian Period. Cambridge University Press, 1984.

Day, J., 'The Daniel of Ugarit and Ezekiel and the Hero of the Book of Daniel', *VT* 30.2 (1980), 174-184.

—. 'Foreign Semitic Influence on the Wisdom of Israel and its appropriation in the Book of Proverbs' in *Wisdom in Ancient Israel: Essays in Honour of J.A Emerton.* Ed. J. Day, R.P. Gordon & H.G.M. Williamson; Cambridge University Press, 1995, 55-70.

Diakonoff, I.M., *The History of Media.* Moscow, 1956.

—. 'Media' in *Cambridge History of Iran* vol.2. Ed. I. Gershevitch; London: Cambridge University Press, 1985, 36-148.

Di Lella, A.A., 'The Textual History of Septuagint-Daniel and Theodotion-Daniel' in *The Book of Daniel: Composition and Reception.* J.J. Collins & P.W. Flint (eds.), 2001, 568-607.

Dillard, R.B., *An Introduction to the Old Testament.* Zondervan, 2006.

Dougherty, R.P., *Nabonidus and Belshazzar.* New Haven: Yale University Press, 1929.

Down, K.K., *Daniel: Hostage in Babylon.* Grantham: Stanborough, 1991.

Dressler, H.H.P., 'The Identification of the Ugaritic Dnil with the Daniel of Ezekiel', *VT* 29:2 (April 1979), 152-161.

—. 'Reading and Interpreting the Aqhat Text: A Rejoinder to Drs J. Day and B. Margalit', *VT* 34.1 (1984), 78-82.

Driver, S.R., *An Introduction to the Literature of the Old Testament.* 1st ed., 1891; 7th ed., Edinburgh: T&T Clark, 1898.

Dubberstein, W.H., 'The Chronology of Cyrus and Cambyses', *The American Journal of Semitic Languages and Literatures* 55.4 (October 1938), 417-419.

Ellis, E.E., *The Old Testament in Early Christianity: Canon and Interpretation in the Light of Modern Research.* J.C.B. Mohr, 1991.

Eshel, E., 'Possible Sources of Daniel' in *The Book of Daniel: Composition and Reception.* Ed. J.J. Collins & P.W. Flint; Leiden: Brill, 2001, 387-394.

Farrer, A., *The Expositor's Bible* (1895).

Fernández Marcos, N., *The Septuagint in Context: Introduction to the Greek Version of the Bible.* Leiden: Brill, 2000.

Finer, Samuel Edward, *The History of Government from the Earliest Times: Ancient Monarchies and Empires.* Oxford University Press, 1997.

Fisher, W.B., *The Cambridge History of Iran.* Cambridge University Press, 1985.

Flint, P.W., 'The Daniel Traditions of Qumran' in *The Book of Daniel: Composition and Reception.* Ed. J.J. Collins & P.W. Flint; Leiden: Brill, 2001, 329-367.

Freedman, D.N., 'The Prayer of Nabonidus', *BASOR* 145 (1957), 31-32.

Freedman, D.N. & P.F. Kuhlken, *What Are the Dead Sea Scrolls and Why Do They Matter?* Grand Rapids: Eerdmans, 2007.

Frey, J., 'Temple and Rival Temple: The Cases of Elephantine, Mt. Gerzim and Leontopolis' in *Gemeinile ohne Tempel.* H. von Beal Ego, A. Large & P. Pilifer, eds.; Mohr Siebeck, 1999, 171-203.

Gadd, C.J., 'The Harran Inscriptions of Nabonidus', *Anatolian Studies* 8 (1958), 35-92.

George, A.R., *Babylonian Topographical Texts.* Louvain, 1992.

Gera, D., *Judaea and Mediterranean Politics: 219 to 161 BCE.* Leiden: Brill, 1998.

Gifford, E.H. (trans.), *Eusebius of Caesarea: Praeparatio Evangelica (Preparation for the Gospel)* vol.3 (1903).

Goldingay, J.E., *Daniel.* WBC 30; Dallas: Word Books, 1989.

— 'Daniel in the Context of Old Testament Theology' in *The Book of Daniel: Composition and Reception* vol.1 (J.J. Collins & P.W. Flint, eds.; Leiden: Brill, 2001), 639 –660.

Grabbe, L.L., 'The Belshazzar of Daniel and the Belshazzar of History', *AUSS* 26:1 (1988), 59-66.

—. 'Another Look at the Gestalt of "Darius the Mede"', *CBQ* 50.2 (April 1988), 198-213.

—. '"Canaanite": Some Methodological Observations in Relation to Biblical Study' in *Ugarit and the Bible: Proceedings of the International Symposium on Ugarit and the Bible – Manchester, September 1992.* Ed. G.J. Brooke, A.HW. Curtis & J.F. Henley; Münster: Ugarit-Verlag, 1994, 113-122.

—. 'A Dan(iel) for All Season: From Whom was Daniel Important?' in *The Book of Daniel: Composition and Reception.* Ed. J.J. Collins & P.W. Flint; Leiden: Brill, 2001, 229-246.

Grayson, A.K. & W.G. Lambert, *JCS* 18, (1964).

Grayson, A.K., *Assyrian and Babylonian Chronicles.* Locust Valley, 1975.

—. *Babylonian Historical-Literary Texts.* Toronto: University of Toronto Press, 1975.

Green, A.R., 'The Fate of Jehoiakim', *AUSS* 20:2 (Summer 1982), 103-109.

Green, E., *The Prophecy of Daniel.* Birmingham: The Christadelphian, 1988.

Greenfield, J.C., 'Early Aramaic Poetry', *JANESCU* 11 (1979), 45-51.

Harper, R.F., *Assyrian and Babylonian Literature: Selected Translations.* New York: D. Appleton, 1901.

Harton, G.M., 'An Interpretation of Daniel 11:36-45', *Grace Theological Journal* 4.2, (1983), 205-231.

Hasel, G.F., 'The First and Third Years of Belshazzar (Dan. 7:1; 8:1)', *AUSS* 15 (1977), 153–68.

Henze, M., *The Madness of King Nebuchadnezzar: The Ancient Near Eastern Origins and Early History of Interpretation of Daniel 4.* Leiden: Brill, 1999.

Hitzig, F., *Das Buch Daniel.* Leipzig: Weidman, 1850.

Hölbl, G., *A History of the Ptolemaic Empire.* Trans. T. Saavedra; Routledge, 2001.

Hooper, F.J.B., *Palmoni: An Essay on the Chronographical and Numerical Systems in Use Among the Ancient Jews.* London: Longman, Brown, Green & Longmans, 1851.

Horn, S.H., *Seventh-Day Adventist Bible Dictionary.* Washington: Review & Herald, 1960.

—. 'New Light on Nebuchadnezzar's Madness', *Ministry* (April 1978), 38-40.

Hunger, H. & S.A. Kaufman, *JAOS* 95 (1975).

Jamieson, R. & A.R. Fauset, *A Commentary, Critical and Explanatory, of the Old and New Testaments* (vol.1). Glasgow: William Collins, 1863.

Johnson, S.R., *Historical Fictions and Hellenistic Jewish Identity: Third Maccabees in Its Cultural Context.* Berkeley: University of California Press, 2004.

Johnston, S.I., *Religions of the Ancient World: A Guide.* Harvard University Press, 2004.

Jull, A.J.T., 'Radiocarbon Dating of the Scrolls and Linen Fragments from the Judean Desert', *Radiocarbon* 37:1 (1995), 11-19.

Keller, W., *The Bible as History.* London: Hodder and Stoughton, 1956.

Kitchen, K.A., 'The Aramaic of Daniel' in *Notes on Some Problems in the Book of Daniel.* London: Tyndale Press, 1965, 31-79.

—. *On the Reliability of the Old Testament* (Eerdmans, 2003).

Koch, K., *Das Buch Daniel.* Darmstadt: Wissenschaftliche Buchgesellschaft, 1980.

—. 'Dareios der Mede' in *The Word of the Lord Shall Go Forth.* C.L. Meyers & M. O'Connor eds.; Winona Lake: Eisenbrauns, 1983, 287-302.

—. 'Stages in the Canonization of the Book of Daniel' in *The Book of Daniel: Composition and Reception.* Eds. J.J. Collins & P.W. Flint; Leiden: Brill, 2001, 421-446.

Koldewey, R., *Excavations at Babylon.* A. Johns trans.; London 1914.

Kratz, R.G., 'The Visions of Daniel' in *The Book of Daniel: Composition and Reception.* J.J. Collins & P.W. Flint (eds.), 2001, 91-131.

Kutscher, E.Y., *Hebrew and Aramaic Studies.* Jerusalem: Magnes, 1977.
Laato, A., 'The Seventy Yearweeks in the Book of Daniel', *ZAW* 102:2 (1990), 212-225.
Lambert, W.G., *The Background of Jewish Apocalyptic.* London: Athlone, 1978.
Lang, G.H., *The Histories and Prophecies of Daniel.* London: Oliphants, 1942.
Leick, G., *A Dictionary of Ancient Near Eastern Mythology.* Routledge, 1991.
Lewy, H., 'Nitokris-Naqi'a', *JNES* 11 (1952), 264-286.
Lightfoot, J., *Works (vol.2): A Chronicle of the Times and the Order of the Texts of the Old Testament*, 1684.
Lucas, E.C., 'Daniel: Resolving the Enigma', *VT* 50:1 (Jan 2000), 66-80.
Malalty, T.Y., *The Book of Daniel* (trans. F. Moawad); http://www.truthnet.org/Daniel/Introduction/ [cited 01 Oct 08].
Mansfield, H.P. & G.E. Mansfield, *The Book of Daniel.* CE; Findon: Logos, 1992.
Marashi, M., *Persian Studies in North America.* Ibex, 1994.
Margalit, B., 'Interpreting the Story of Aqht: A Reply to H.H.P. Dressler *VT* 29 (1979), pp. 152-161', *VT* 30 (1980), 361-365.
Martin, W.J., 'The Hebrew of Daniel', in *Notes on Some Problems in the Book of Daniel.* London: Tyndale, 1965, 28-30.
Martínez, F.G., *The Dead Sea Scrolls Translated: The Qumran Texts in English.* Leiden: Brill, 1994.
Matheson, S., *Persia: An Archaeological Guide.* London: Faber and Faber, 1972.
Millard, A.R., 'Daniel 1-6 and History', *EQ* 49:2 (April-June 1977), 67-73.
—. 'Daniel and Belshazzar in History', *BARev* 11 (May-June 1985), 72-78.
—. *Discoveries from Bible Times.* Oxford: Lion, 1985; repr. 1997.
—. 'Daniel in Babylon: An Accurate Record?' in *Do Historical Matters Matter to Faith?: A Critical Appraisal of Modern and Postmodern Approaches to Scripture.* Eds. James K. Hoffmeier and Dennis R. Magary; Wheaton, IL: Crossway, 2012, 263-280.
Millard, A.R. & P. Bordreuil, 'A Statue from Syria with Assyrian and Aramaic Inscriptions', *BA* 45 (1982), 135-141.
Miller, G., 'Was Daniel written after the events he foretold?', http://christianthinktank.com/qwhendan3x.html [cited August 2014]
Miller, S.R., *The New American Commentary: Daniel.* NAC 18; Broadman & Holman, 1994.
Milik, J.T., *Ten Years of Discovery in the Wilderness of Judea.*
Missler, C., *The Book of Daniel: Supplemental Notes.* Koinonia House, 1994.
Mitchell, T.C. and R. Joyce, 'The Musicial Instruments in Nebuchadnezzar's Orchestra' in *Notes on Some Problems in the Book of Daniel.* London: Tyndale, 1965, 19-27.
Mitchell, T.C., 'Achaemenid History and the Book of Daniel' in *Mesopotamia and Iran in the Persian Period: Conquest and Imperialism 539-331 BC:*

Proceedings of a seminar in memory of Vladimir G. Lukonin. Ed. J. Curtis; London: British Museum, 1993, 68-78.

Montgomery, J.A., *The International Critical Commentary: A Critical and Exegetical Commentary on the Book of Daniel*. Edinburgh: T&T Clark, 1927.

Nesselrath, H.G., 'Herodot und Babylon: Der Hauport Mesopotamiens in den Augen eines Griechen' in *Babylon: Focus Mesopotamisher Geschichte, Wiege fruher Gelehrsamkeit, Mythos in der Moderne*. Ed. J. Renger; Saarbrucjen, 1999, 189-206.

Niskanen, P., *The Human and Divine in History: Herodotus and the Book of Daniel*. JSOTsupp 396; London: T&T Clark, 2004.

Oates, J., *Babylon*. London: Thames & Hudson, 1986.

Oppenheim, A.L., *Ancient Mesopotamia: Portrait of a Dead Civilization*. Chicago, 1964.

Owen, H., 'The Enigma of Darius the Mede: a Way to its Final Solution', *JTVI* 74 (1942), 72-99.

Parente, F., 'Onias III' Death and the Foundation of the Temple of Leontopolis' in *Josephus and the History of the Greco-Roman Period: Essays in Memory Morton Smith*. F. Parente & J. Sieves eds.; Leiden: Brill, 1994, 429-436.

Park, E.A. & S.H. Taylor (eds.), *Bibliotheca Sacra and Biblical Repository* (vol.17). Andover: Warren F. Draper, 1860.

Paul, S.M., 'A Traditional Blessing for the Long Life of the King', *JNES* 31 (1972) 351-355.

—. 'From Mari to Daniel: Instructions for the Acceptance of Servants into the Royal Court', *Eretz Israel* 24 (1993), 161-163.

—. 'The Mesopotamian Background of Daniel 1-6' in *The Book of Daniel: Composition and Reception*. Ed. J.J. Collins & P.W. Flint; Leiden: Brill, 2001, 285-297.

Peat, J., 'Cyrus 'King of Lands', Cambyses 'King of Babylon': The Disputed Co-Regency', *JCS* 41:2 (Autumn 1989), 199-216.

Porteous, N.W., *Daniel: A Commentary*. OTL; London: SCM, 1965.

Purvis, J.D. & E.M. Meyers, "Exile and Return: From the Babylonian Destruction to the Reconstruction of the Jewish State", *Ancient Israel,* 1999, 151-175.

Pusey, E.B., *Daniel the Prophet*. New York: Funk and Wagnalls, 1886.

Rawlinson, G., *The Seven Great Monarchies of the Ancient Eastern World* vol.2 ('Babylonia').

—. *The Seven Great Monarchies of the Ancient Eastern World*, vol.3 ("Media").

—. *History of Herodotus* (vol.II). London: John Murray, 1858.

—. *The Historical Evidences of the Truth of the Scriptural Records*. Boston: Gould & Lincoln, 1860.

Ripley, G. & C.A. Dana (eds.), *The New American Cyclopaedia: A Popular Dictionary of General Knowledge* (vol.12). New York: D. Appleton, 1861.

Robinson, J.A.T., *Redating the New Testament*. London: SCM, 1976.

Rowley, H.H., 'The Historicity of the Fifth Chapter of Daniel', *JTS* 32 (1931), 12-31.

—. *Darius the Mede and the Four World Empires in the Book of Daniel: A Historical Study of Contemporary Theories*. Cardiff: University of Wales Press, 1935; repr. 1964.

Saggs, H.W.F., *Babylonians*. London: British Museum, 1995.

San Nicolò, M., *Beiträge zu einer Prosoporagraphie neubabyloniscer Beamtender Zivil- und Tempelverwaltung*. Munich, 1941.

Saville, B.W., 'Darius the Mede and Darius Hystapes', *Journal of Sacred Literature and Biblical Record* 5:9 (April 1857) 175.

Schürer, E., *Geschichte des jüduschen Volkes im Zeitalter Jesu Christi*. Dritter Band, Vierte Auflage, 1909.

Scott, W.A., *Esther: The Hebrew-Persian Queen*. H.H. Bancroft, 1859.

Shea, W.H., 'An Unrecognized Vassal King of Babylon in the Early Achaemenid Period I', *AUSS* 9, (1971), 51-57.

—. 'An Unrecognized Vassal King III', *AUSS* 10 (1972), 100.

—. 'Daniel 3: Extra-Biblical Texts and the Convocation on the Plain of Dura', *AUSS* 20:1 (Spring 1982), 29-52.

—. 'Nabonidus, Belshazzar, and the Book of Daniel: An Update', *AUSS* 20:2 (Summer 1982), 133-149.

—. 'Darius the Mede: An Update', *AUSS* 20.3 (Autumn 1982), 229-247.

—. 'Bel(te)shazzar meets Belshazzar', *AUSS* 26:1 (1988), 67-81.

—. 'Darius the Mede in his Persian-Babylonian Setting', *AUSS* 29 (1991), 235-257.

—. 'Nabonidus Chronicle: New Readings and the Identity of Darius the Mede', *JATS* 7:1 (Spring 1996), 1-20.

—. 'The Search for Darius the Mede (Concluded), or, The Time of the Answer to Daniel's Prayer and the Date of the Death of Darius the Mede', *JATS* 12:1 (Spring 2001), 97-105.

Short, A.R., *Modern Discovery and the Bible*. London: Inter-Varsity Fellowship (1942, repr., 1954).

Smith, P., *A History of the World from the Earliest Records to the Present Time* (vol.1). New York: D. Appleton & Co., 1865.

Smith, S., *Babylonian Historical Texts* (1924).

Smith, W. (ed.), *A Dictionary of the Bible*. London: John Murray, 1863.

Smith-Christopher, D.L., 'Reassessing the Historical and Sociological Impact of the Babylonian Exile (597/587-539 BCE)' in *Exile: Old Testament, Jewish, and Christian Conceptions*. J.M. Scott ed.; Leiden: Brill, 1997, 7-36.

Sparks, H.F.D., 'On the Origin of 'Darius the Mede' at Daniel V.31', *JTS* 47 (1940), 41-46.

Stackhouse, T., *A History of the Holy Bible* (1836).

Stefanovic, Z., *The Aramaic of Daniel in the Light of Old Aramaic*. Sheffield: JSOT, 1992.

—. *Daniel: Wisdom to the Wise: Commentary on the Book of Daniel* (Pacific, 2007).

Steinmann, A., 'The Chicken and the Egg: A New Proposal for the Relationship between the 'Prayer of Nabonidus' and the 'Book of Daniel'', *Revue de Qumran* 20:4 (December 2002), 557-570.

Stern, M., 'The Death of Onias III', *Zion* 25 (1959-60), 1-16.

Stevenson, J.H., *Assyrian and Babylonian Contracts with Aramaic Notes.* America Book Company, 1902.

Stronach, D., 'Ecbatana (Hamadan)', *The Encyclopedia of Ancient History.* Wiley, 2012 [online].

Tabouis, G.R., *Nebuchadnezzar.* 1931; repr. Kessinger, 2003.

Tadmor, H., 'Rab-sārîs or Rab-shakeh in 2 Kings 18' in *The Word of the Lord Shall Go Forth: Essays in Honor of David Noel Freedman in Celebration of His Sixtieth Birthday.* Ed. C.L. Meyers & M. O'Connor; Eisenbrauns, 1983, 279-285.

Thiele, E.R., *The Mysterious Numbers of the Hebrew Kings.* Grand Rapids: Zondervan, 1983; new rev. ed., Grand Rapids: Kregel, 1994.

Thompson, H.A., 'British Museum Gossip', *The Testimony* 1:1 (Jan 1931), 20-21.

Tolini, G., 'Quelques elements concernant la prise de Babylone par Cyrus', ARTA 2005, 1-13.

Torrey, C.C., 'Medes and Persians', *JAOS* 66:1 (January-March 1946), 1-15.

Ulrich, E., 'Daniel Manuscripts from Qumran. Part 1: A Preliminary Edition of 4QDan[a]', *BASOR* 268 (1987), 17-37.

—. 'Daniel Manuscript from Qumran. Part 2: A Preliminary Editions of 4QDan[b] and 4QDan[c]', *BASOR* 274 (1989), 3-26.

—. 'The Text of Daniel in the Qumran Scrolls', in *The Book of Daniel: Composition and Reception.* Eds. J.J. Collins & P.W. Flint; Leiden: Brill, 2001, 573-585.

Unruh, U., *The Great Tree and Nebuchadnezzar's Insanity* [cited May 2008]. Online: http://dedication.www3.50megs.com/dan/daniel_4.html.

VanderKam, J.C., *From Joshua to Caiaphas: High Priests after the Exile.* Uitgeverij van Gorcum, 2004.

van der Toorn, K., 'Scholars at the Oriental Court: The Figure of Daniel against its Mesopotamian Background' in *The Book of Daniel: Composition and Reception.* Ed. J.J. Collins & P.W. Flint; Leiden: Brill, 2001, 37-55.

van der Woude, A.S., 'Prophetic Prediction, Political Prognostication, and Firm Belief Reflections on Daniel 11:40-12:3' in C.A. Evans, S. Talmon (eds.), *The Quest for Context and Meaning: Studies in Biblical Intertextuality in Honor of James A. Sander.* Leiden: Brill, 1997, 63-73.

Vasholz, R.I., 'Qumran and the Dating of Daniel', *JETS* 21 (1978), 315-321.

Vermes, G. (trans.), *The Complete Dead Sea Scrolls in English.* London: Penguin Books, 2004.

Wallace, D.B., 'To Bow or Not to Bow: An Essay on Daniel 3', 2005, http://www.bible.org/page.php?page_id=1579

Waltke, B.K., 'The Date of the Book of Daniel', *Bibliotheca Sacra* (Oct-Dec 1976), 319-329.

Ware, J.R., 'Ahasuerus and Xerxes', *The Classical Journal* 20:8 (May 1925), 489-490.

Watke, E. Jr., *A Study of the Book of Daniel.* Augusta: Revival in the Home Ministries, 1992.

Waterhouse, S.D., 'Why was Darius the Mede Expunged from History?' in *To Understand the Scriptures: Essays in Honor of William H. Shea.* D. Merling ed.; Berrien Springs: Andrews University Press, 1997, 173-189.

Wegner, W.E., 'The Book of Daniel and the Dead Sea Scrolls', *Quartalschrift Theological Quarterly* 455 (1958), 103-116.

Whiston, W. (trans.), *The Works of Josephus: Complete and Unabridged.* Peabody: Hendrickson, 2004.

Whitcomb, J.C., *Darius the Mede: A Study in Historical Identification.* Philadelphia: Presbyterian & Reformed, 1959.

Whittaker, H.A., *Visions in Daniel.* Wigan: Biblia, 1991.

—. *Exploring the Bible.* Wigan: Biblia, 1992.

Wilson, R.D., *The International Standard Bible Encyclopedia,* 1915

Wiseman, D.J., *Chronicles of Chaldean Kings (626-586 BC) in the British Museum.* London: British Museum, 1956.

—. *Notes on Some Problems in the Book of Daniel.* London: Tyndale, 1965.

—. *Nebuchadrezzar and Babylon: The Schweich Lectures.* Oxford University Press, 1985; repr., 2004.

Wolters, A., 'Belshazzar's Feast and the Cult of the Moon God Sin', *Bulletin of Biblical Research* 4 (1995), 199-206.

Wright, C.H.H., *Daniel and His Prophecies.* London: Williams & Norgate, 1906; repr., Kessinger.

Wright, E., *The Ancient World.* London: Hamlyn, 1979.

Wood, L.J., *A Survey of Israel's History.* D. O'Brien; Zondervan, 1986.

Wyns, P., *God is Judge: A Commentary on the Book of Daniel.* Biblaridion Media, 2011.

—. *The Agora Bible Comentary: Daniel* [Online: http://www.christadelphianbooks.org/agora/comm/27_dan/dan12.html]

—. *The Revelation of Jesus Christ* [Online: http://www.carelinks.net/books/wyns/12-1.htm]

Yamauchi, E.M., *Persia and the Bible.* Grand Rapids: Baker, 1990.

—. 'Greece and Babylon Revisited' in *To Understand the Scriptures: Essays in Honor of William H. Shea.* Ed. D. Merling; Berrien Springs: Institute of Archaeology, 1997.

Young, E.J., *A Commentary on Daniel.* Geneva Series; Eerdmans, 1949; repr., London: The Banner of Truth Trust, 1972.

Younger, K.L. Jr., 'Israelites in Exile', *BAR* 29:6 (Nov/Dec 2003), 36-45.

Zeitlin, S., "'The Tobias Family and the Hasmoneans': A Historical Study in the Political and Economic Life of the Jews of the Hellenistic Period', *Proceedings of the American Academy for Jewish Research* 4 (1932-33), 169-223.

Zimmermann, F., 'Some Verses in Daniel in the Light of a Translation Hypothesis', *JBL* 58.4 (December 1939), 349-354.

—. 'Hebrew Translation in Daniel', *JQR* 51.3, (January 1961), 198-208.

Anonymous, 'Correspondence', *JAOS* 5 (1855-56), 269.

—. 'Colonel Rawlinson's Assyrian Discoveries', *The Edinburgh Christian Magazine* 7 (November 1865), 253.

—. *Illustrations of Scriptural History from the Monuments of Egypt, Chaldee, Assyria and Babylonia.* London: Lothian & Co., 1866.

—. *Encyclopaedia Biblica.* London: Adam & Charles Black, 1899-1903.

—. *The Catholic Encyclopedia*, vol.10. New York: Robert Appleton, 1911.

—. 'Notes and News', *The Testimony* 1:11 (Nov 1931), 341.

—. *The International Standard Bible Encyclopedia.* Grand Rapids: Eerdmans, 1994.

—. *The Comprehensive Aramaic Lexicon* [Online: http://cal1.cn.huc.edu/]

—. http://forum.bib-arch.info/index.php?action=printpage;topic=67.0 [cited 01 Oct 08]

—. http://www.grovebaptist.freeserve.co.uk/800by600/dl039.htm [cited 01 Oct 08].

Indexes

Authors

Zimmermann, Frank   118
Zockler, O.   110

Names

Abed-Nego   *see Azariah*
Abraham   7
Adad-Guppi   45, 59, 62
Adam   133
Ahab   38
Ahasuerus   82, 85, 89, 90, 100
Alexander IV   107-109
Alexander the Great   107, 108, 113, 117, 126, 132
Amytis   89-90
Andronicus   105, 106
Antigenes   108
Antigonus   108-109
Antiochus Epiphanes   105, 112, 114, 115, 116, 117, 158
Antiochus I   113
Antiochus II   113
Antiochus III   114
Antipater   108
Arphaxad   134
Arridaeus (Philip III)   107-108
Artaxerxes I   32, 131, 151
Artaxerxes II   100, 131
Artaxerxes III   100, 131
Ashpenaz   33-34
Ashur-nadin-shumu   86
Assuruballit   13
Astyages   65, 83, 85, 87, 88, 89, 91, 125-126
Atraxerxes I   87, 100
Azariah   1, 12, 24-25, 27-28, 30, 36, 157

Belshazzar   1, 29, 52-64, 72, 75-77, 78, 80, 82, 83, 129, 150, 155, 156, 1 57
Belteshazzar   24, 29-30
Berenice   113, 114

Cambyses I   91

Cambyses II   86, 89-90, 92, 94, 96, 99, 131
Cassander   108, 109
Chileab   6
Constantine   116
Craterus   108
Croesus   65
Cyaxares I   85, 87, 90
Cyaxares II   83, 85, 87-88
Cyrus   1, 45, 56, 59, 62, 65, 66-77, 78-79, 82, 83, 86, 87, 88, 89, 90-91, 92, 96, 99, 100, 125-126, 132, 134

Darius Hystaspis   82, 83, 84, 92, 98, 99, 131
Darius II Nothus   32, 84, 100, 131
Darius III Codomanus   84, 100, 131
Darius the Mede   1, 56-57, 78-79, 82-97, 98-99, 100, 126, 129, 131, 134, 155
David   6
Deioces   85, 133
Demetrius   114
Dinah   133, 134

Eliakim   *see Jehoiakim*
Enoch   7, 8
Esau   7
Esther   133, 134
Eumenes   108
Evil-Merodach   27, 49-50, 58
Ezekiel   5-10, 157

Gabriel   100, 107
Gubaru   88, 96

Habakkuk   125, 126

Scripture
Old Testament

10:14   112
10:15   112
10:16-17   112
10:19   112
10:20-11:1   112
11:1   78, 82
11:2   99, 100, 101, 121
11:3   121
11:3-4   107
11:4   107
11:5   113
11:5-19   115, 116
11:5-20   111, 112
11:6   113
11:7   114, 121
11:10   114
11:17   114
11:20   121
11:21   114, 121
11:22   104, 115
11:28   115
11:30-35   116
11:33-35   115
11:36-39   115, 116
11:40-45   111, 116, 120, 158, 159
12:1   112
12:2   159
12:5   112
12:5-13   112, 121
12:8   112
12:8   112
12:13   1

Habakkuk
1:6   126

Apocrypha

Daniel
13:1   124
13:4   124
13:5-6   125
13:6   125
13:9   125
13:17   124
13:22-23   124
13:28   124, 125
13:31   124
13:45   124, 125
13:60   125
13:60-62   125
13:62   124
14:1   87, 125
14:2   125
14:22   126
14:34   125

Baruch
1:11   52, 58

Tobit
14:15   87

2Maccabees
1:10   104
4:33   105
4:34   105
4:38   105
15:12   106

New Testament

Matthew
24:30   4
26:64   4

Mark
13:14   159
13:26   4
14:62   4

Luke
21:27   4

Hebrews
11:33

ND - #0101 - 090625 - C0 - 229/152/11 - PB - 9781842279823 - Gloss Lamination